MOSCOW
ST. PETERSBURG
IN RUSSIA'S
SILVER AGE

JOHN E. BOWLT

MOSCOW AND ST. PETERSBURG IN RUSSIA'S SILVER AGE

JOHN E. BOWLT

1900–1920

Inside cover:
Natalia Goncharova. Set design for the
finale of *The Firebird*, 1926. Victoria
and Albert Museum, London.

Front cover:
Léon Bakst. Costume design for two
Béotiennes in *Narcisse*, 1911.
Lordprice Collection / Alamy Stock Photo

Back cover:
Nevskii Prospect, St. Petersburg, ca. 1910.
Library of Congress, Washington, D.C.

Page 1:
Boris Zvorykin. Cover of program for
the celebration of the Tercentenary of
the House of Romanov, St. Petersburg,
1913 (*see ill. 576*).

Page 2:
Aristarkh Lentulov. *St. Basil's Cathedral*
(detail), 1913 (*see ill. 593*).

Above:
Attributed to Miss (pseudonym of Natalia
Remizova). Poster for the Theater of
Miniatures, St. Petersburg (*see ill. 383*).

First published in the United Kingdom in 2008
by Thames & Hudson Ltd, 181A High Holborn,
London WC1V 7QX

www.thamesandhudson.com

Original edition © 2008 The Vendome Press

This paperback edition first published in 2020

British Library Cataloguing-in-Publication Data
A catalogue record for this book is available from the
British Library

ISBN: 978-0-500-29564-9

Printed and bound in China

CONTENTS

1. *Léon Bakst. Poster advertising* Dance Recital by Caryathis (Elise Jouhandeau), *ca. 1919. Hand-colored lithograph, 196 x 124 cm (77 1/4 x 48 3/4 in.). In this indulgence of the senses Bakst has pictured Elise Jouhandeau (nom de théâtre of Elise Toulemon, 1888–1979), a Parisian occasional dancer who bore the stage name Caryathis (a reference to the maidens who danced sacrificial rituals in the Temple of Artemis Caryathis in Ancient Greece). Drawing on his ample slavegirls and Béothiennes of Schéhérazade, Narcisse, and similar exotic ballets, Bakst intensifies their serpentine lines, heady colors, and erogenous zones to produce a poster that treads a fine line between breathtaking brilliance and vulgar satiety.*

ACKNOWLEDGMENTS

Many people and institutions have rendered invaluable assistance in the writing of this book, but my first thanks go to Nina Lobanov-Rostovsky, who, from the preliminary idea through publication, has been an unfailing champion of the project. In addition, I would like to acknowledge my debt to the following: Alexis Baatsch, Elena Barkhatova, Aurelia Barloff, Adele Di Ruocco, Alan Dodge, René Clémenti-Bilinsky, Valerian Dudakov. Elizabeth Durst, Tamara Esina, Shery Gury, Dmytro Horbachov, Lidiia Iovleva, Marina Kashuro, Mark Konecny, Nikita Lobanov-Rostovsky, Olga Matich, Irina Menchova, Oleg Minin, Nicoletta Misler, Evgeniia Petrova, Ivan Prilezhaev, Allison Pultz, Wendy Salmond, Dmitrii Sarabianov. Yuliia Solonovich, Elena Spitsyna, Denis Soloviev, Elena Terkel, Elizabeth Valkenier, Yuliia Volkhonovich, and David Wilson.

A sincere appreciation goes to my two editors at Vendome Press, Jackie Decter and Sarah Davis. Collaborating with them on the text, imagery, layout, and design has been a rewarding experience. Indeed, without their meticulous powers of observation, unfailing patience, and good humor, this book would hardly have been possible. Special thanks must also go to Christian Brandstätter for his inventive design, to Natalia Borisovskaia for her invaluable help with the selection and procurement of illustrative materials, and to Giao Luong for her photography expertise.

I would also like to thank the staff of the following institutions for their help with facilitating access to bibliographical and archival sources: the Albert and Elaine Borchard Foundation, Los Angeles; the Cultural Foundation, Moscow; the Fundación José Maria Castañé, Madrid; the Getty Center for the History of Art and the Humanities, Los Angeles; the Glinka Museum of Theatrical and Musical Art, St. Petersburg; the International Research and Exchanges Board, Washington, D.C.; the Institute of Modern Russian Culture, Los Angeles; the Museo Thyssen-Bornemisza, Madrid; the Museum of Ukrainian Art, Kiev; the National Endowment for the Humanities, Washington, D.C.; the Russian National Library, St. Petersburg; the Russian State Archive of Literature and Art, Moscow; the Russia Abroad Foundation, Moscow; the State Museum of Contemporary Art, Thessaloniki; the State Russian Museum, St. Petersburg; the State Tretiakov Gallery, Moscow; the University of Southern California, Los Angeles; and the Jane Voorhees Zimmerli Museum, New Brunswick.

TRANSLITERATION

The transliteration of Russian words modifies the Library of Congress system, whereby the soft and hard signs have either been omitted or rendered by an "i" (e.g., "Grigoriev"). This system is also used throughout the footnotes and the bibliographical data where references involve Russian-language sources. This book, presumably, will be read by people who appreciate the arts, but who may not know Russian, and, consequently, the more sophisticated academic transliteration systems have been avoided which, to the layman, may render a recognizable name (e.g., Chekhov) unrecognizable (e.g., Čexov). Many Russian artists and writers spent part of their lives in Europe or the USA and often their names received various, sometimes contradictory, transliterations from the original Russian into the language of their adopted home. For the sake of uniformity, names have been transliterated in accordance with the above system, except when a variant has long been established, e.g., Alexandre Benois (not Aleksandr Benua), Vaslav Nijinsky (not Vatslav Nizhinsky).

TIMES AND PLACES

In most cases, dates referring to events in Russia before January 1918 are in the Old Style. Consequently, if they are in the nineteenth century, they are twelve days behind the Western calendar, whereas if they are between 1900 and 1918 they are thirteen days behind.

The city of St. Petersburg was renamed Petrograd in 1914, Leningrad in 1924, and then St. Petersburg again in 1992. However, both the names Petrograd and Petersburg continued to be used in common parlance and in publications until 1924. As a general rule, Petrograd has been retained here as the official name of St. Petersburg for the period 1914–24.

Titles of works of art, books, catalogues, journals, and newspapers are italicized; titles of articles, manuscripts, and exhibitions are in quotation marks; names of societies and institutions are not.

The Christian name and surname of an individual are given in full when he or she is first mentioned in a given section or chapter. Generally speaking, subsequent references to the individual carry only the surname.

2. Moscow. View of the city from the Kremlin, ca. 1910.

INTRODUCTION

In the first decades of the twentieth century Russia's two great cities, Moscow and St. Petersburg, experienced a renaissance which affected many walks of artistic life, especially literature, painting, architecture, music, dance, and cinema. It was a dazzling period, but illumined perhaps more by the rays of the setting sun than by the cold light of dawn, and if witnesses recognized the creative upsurge of their time, they also tinged their enthusiasm with unease, foreboding, and a sense of reckoning [ill. 4]. In any event, that the Russian visual, literary, and performing arts were entering a moment of unprecedented flowering and would achieve creative brilliance was evident to poets and painters in particular, prompting them to refer to their time as a "Silver Age."[1] In applying this sobriquet to an era which lasted little more than twenty years (from the late 1890s until the late 1910s), the representatives of the Silver Age were comparing their Parnassian heights to Russia's literary flowering of the 1810s–30s, which, with the dazzling poetry and prose of Alexander Pushkin, Mikhail Lermontov, and Nikolai Gogol, had constituted the Golden Age of Russian literature. But the originality and prescience of this

Opposite:
3. Kazimir Malevich. Female Torso, 1928–32. Oil on wood, 73 x 52.5 cm (28 3/4 x 20 5/8 in.). State Russian Museum, St. Petersburg.

Below:
4. Nikolai Kalmakov. Death, 1913. Oil and bronze paint on canvas, 68 x 100 cm (26 3/4 x 39 3/8 in.). Regional Picture Gallery, Vologda. Before the October Revolution and the nationalization of private collections, the original provenance of this picture was the St. Petersburg home of Elena and Vladimir Nabokov, parents of the celebrated writer Vladimir.

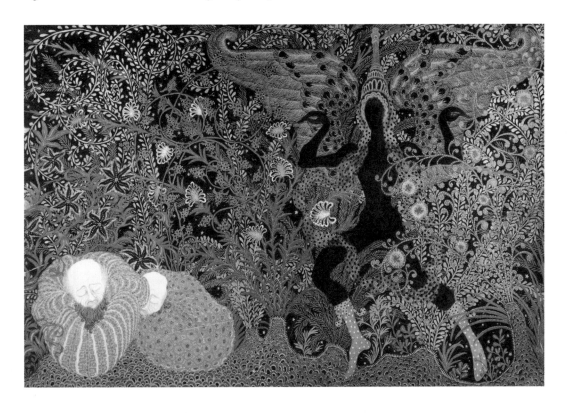

5. *Mikhail Vrubel.* Self-portrait, *1904–05.*
Charcoal and sanguine on paper, 35.5 x 29.5 cm
(14 x 11.5 in.). State Tretiakov Gallery,
Moscow.

second precious age also distinguished the disciplines of Russian science and technology, not least aviation and medicine. As the musician and painter Mikhail Matiushin asserted in 1913, "even objects will be resurrected in the new and amazing world of the future."[2]

What is so special about the *Russian* Silver Age as opposed to the early Modernist movements in France, Italy, or America?[3] In assessing its status and achievement, perhaps we should remind ourselves of certain platitudes which, because they are platitudes, tend to be underrated in serious discussion of the subject. One is the rapid, if still partial, modernization of Russian society toward the end of the nineteenth century; another is the insistent "capitalization" of the Russian economy with its new individual fortunes and patronage of the arts; yet another is Russia's traditional openness to other national cultures, especially French, German, and Italian, and her easy, but distinctive, adaptation to Western Modernism; and still another might be the traditional Russian tendency to envision rather than to implement and to give preference to idea rather than to deed, to absence rather than to presence. Prominent expressions of this condition are Mikhail Vrubel's masterpiece *Demon Cast Down* (1902) [ill. 6], which he repainted continually, but never completed, Aleksandr Scriabin's unfinished opera *Misterium*, and Kazimir Malevich's intended utopian applications of Suprematism to architecture, spaceships, and even human beings [ill. 3].

But perhaps the most pressing domestic condition here is the

territorial enormity of Russia, which, incalculable and formless like the long, still winter, became a tabula rasa for unprecedented investigations into contrary idioms of expression such as cryptic language, silence, abstract painting, and dissonant music. All this is to say that the Russian Modernists' quest for innovation may have derived as much from territorial and meteorological elements (the vast and deserted landscape defying rational imposition and division) as from imported doctrines. Aleksei Stepanov's picture *Wolves* (1912) [ill. 7], with its appeal to the animalistic sounds and customs of the wilderness, illustrates this condition perfectly. Presumably, this same organic consistency colored the fin de siècle of the Ukraine, Georgia, and Armenia, territories which remain outside the purview of this study, but which are equally fascinating in the richness and distinctiveness of their cultures.[4]

Whether or not it is these particular conditions which impart specificity to Russian Modernism, there was something unique and unrepeatable about the Russian Silver Age. It acknowledged the new art and science of the West, but tailored them to local exigencies so as to produce an effervescent cocktail; it convoked the separate disciplines into dazzling syntheses such as the Ballets Russes and illustrated,

Below:

6. *Mikhail Vrubel.* Demon Cast Down, *1902. Oil on canvas, 139 x 387 cm (54 3/4 x 152 3/8 in.). State Tretiakov Gallery, Moscow. Contemporaries identified the Nietzschean demon in this and analgous pictures (see ills. 170 and 221) as Vrubel's self-portrait. Tormented by mental disease, Vrubel grappled desperately with the concepts of good and evil, looking to the Romantic poet Mikhail Lermontov, in particular, for resolution and inspiration.*

Above:

7. *Aleksei Stepanov.* Wolves, *1912. Oil on canvas, 42 x 68 cm (16 1/2 x 26 3/4 in.). Isaak Brodsky Museum, St. Petersburg.*

Overleaf:

8. *Léon Bakst.* Supper, *1902. Oil on canvas, 150 x 100 cm (59 x 39 3/8 in.). State Russian Museum, St. Petersburg. Paradoxically, the sitter for what Vasilii Rozanov called a "stylish decadent . . . with the enigmatic smile of La Gioconda" was, in fact, Anna Karlovna (née Kind), the prim and proper wife of Alexandre Benois. Somov painted a milder portrait of the young lady in 1896 (also in the collection of the State Russian Museum, St. Petersburg).*

deluxe editions of Decadent verse; it expanded the rubric of fine arts to subsume a new range of aesthetic endeavors, including haute couture, free dance, and interior design [ills. 1, 8–10]; it encouraged artists to turn their lives into works of art or *zhiznetvorchestvo* (literally: "life creativity") and aligned, constantly, the artistic word, image, and sound with the greater destiny of Mother Russia.

Many creative individuals associated with Russia's cultural rebirth have long assumed international prominence, among them Anna Akhmatova, Léon Bakst, Alexandre Benois, Marc Chagall, Fedor Chaliapin, Anton Chekhov, Sergei Diaghilev, Carl Fabergé, Vasilii Kandinsky, Vladimir Maiakovsky, Kazimir Malevich, Vaslav Nijinsky, Boris Pasternak, Fedor Shekhtel, and Igor Stravinsky [ills. 12–16, 18, 19, 21, 24, 26, 27, 29, 37, 39, 40, and see 561], to mention but a few; and the cultural empires and initiatives which they served—such as the Ballets Russes, the Moscow Art Theater, and the Symbolist press—have become milestones in the history of twentieth-century arts and letters. Their achievements coincided with extraordinary

Above right:
9. An evening dress designed by Nadezhda Lamanova, Moscow, 1910. State Hermitage, St. Petersburg.

Below:
10. Interior of a fashion store in St. Petersburg, ca. 1910.

Left:
11. *Nikolai Gumilev at home, St. Petersburg, ca. 1910. Akhmatova and Gumilev were married in 1910.*

Below:
12. *Iosif Braz.* Portrait of the Writer Anton Chekhov, *1898. Oil on canvas, 100 x 80 cm (39 3/8 x 31 1/2 in.). State Tretiakov Gallery, Moscow.*

Opposite:
13. *Olga Della-Vos-Kardovskaia.* Portrait of Anna Akhmatova, *1914. Oil on canvas, 85 x 82 cm (33 1/2 x 32 1/4 in.). State Tretiakov Gallery, Moscow.*

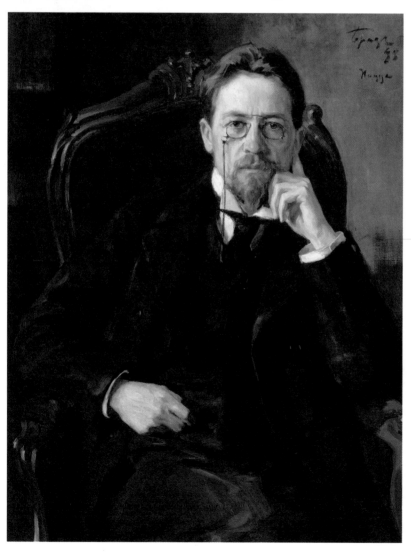

Above:

14. *Fedor Chaliapin with a group of artists visiting Ilia Repin's estate, "Penaty," in Kuokkala on the Gulf of Finland, 1914. Penaty, close to St. Petersburg, was not only Repin's primary studio and retreat, but also a cultural center where artists and writers would congregate to discuss life and art and to partake of Repin's vegetarian meals. Repin is seated second from the left; his wife, Natalia Nordman-Severova, is standing second from the right.*

Left:

15. *Fedor Chaliapin posing for Ilia Repin at Penaty. Chaliapin, Russia's greatest basso, was at the height of his fame when Repin painted this portrait. Chaliapin's exceptional physique, majestic bearing, and vivid personality attracted many other painters, including Boris Grigoriev, Konstantin Korovin, and, of course, Aleksandr Golovin (see ill. 153). Eventually, Repin's portrait, which is now in a collection in Czechoslovakia, was overpainted with another—female—portrait, though the dog remained intact.*

16. *Léon Bakst.* Portrait of Alexandre
Benois, *1898. Watercolor and pastel on paper
on cardboard. 63.5 x 100.3 cm
(25 x 39 ¹/₂ in.). State Russian Museum,
St. Petersburg. In a moment of retreat from the
hectic preprations for the first issues of the* World
of Art *magazine, the studious Benois is pictured
in his apartment on the Moika in St. Petersburg.
By this time Benois had already amassed an
impressive collection of books, engravings, and
paintings, including what seems to be a
portrait of Empress Elizaveta Petrovna by
Louis Caravaque.*

Above:
17. *Marc Chagall.* Above the Town,
*1914–18. Oil on canvas, 141 x 198 cm
(55 ¹/₂ x 78 in.). State Tretiakov Gallery,
Moscow.*

Right:
18. *Marc Chagall in Paris, 1925. By the time
this photograph was taken, Chagall was a
celebrated painter, known for his lyrical
renderings of Jewish life with floating maidens,
peremptory roosters, and playful cows. But
although Chagalll drew upon the stetl and his
Vitebsk background for inspiration, tinging it
occasionally with the forms of Cubism and the
colors of l'école de Paris, he also owed
something to the Style Moderne, studying under
Léon Bakst at the Zvantsevia School in St.
Petersburg before moving to Paris in 1910.*

Left:

19. Vasilii Kandinsky, Munich, 1911. Above Kandinsky's desk hangs a 19th-century lubok *(hand-colored broadsheet) of a* sirin, *the mythical bird of paradise—with female face—whose song was thought to predict misfortune. The central presence of the* lubok *here indicates Kandinsky's strong and lasting interest in Russian folk art, which played a formative role in his search for new kinds of pictorial expression.*

Below:

20. Vasilii Kandinsky. Improvisation No. 10, *1910. Oil on canvas, 120 x 140 cm (47 $\frac{1}{4}$ x 55 in.). Beyeler collection, Basel.*

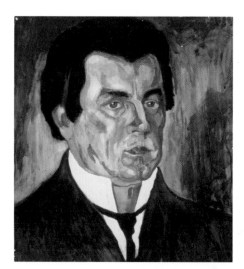

Left:
21. *Kazimir Malevich*, Self-portrait, *1910–11. Gouache, watercolor, Indian ink, and varnish on paper, 46.2 x 41.3 cm (18 x 16 ¹/₄ in.). State Russian Museum, St. Petersburg.*

Below:
22. *Kazimir Malevich.* Woman in Childbirth, *1908. Oil and pencil on board, 24.7 x 25.6 cm (9 ³/₄ x 10 in). State Museum of Contemporary Art, Thessaloniki. Heeding the call of the Eternal Feminine and under the influence of the Blue Rose artists, Malevich crowds the background of this mysterious picture with tiny images of fetuses. In fact, Malevich had hoped to contribute to the "Blue Rose" exhibition the year before and to appear alongside painters such as Pavel Kuznetsov and Sergei Sudeikin with their evocations of motherhood and infancy (see ills. 392, 393), but his submission was rejected.*

Above:
23. Ivan Kliun. Portrait of the Artist's Wife, 1910. Watercolor,
charcoal, and pencil on paper, 34.2 x 29.1 cm (13 ¹/₂ x 11 ¹/₂ in.).
State Museum of Contemporary Art, Thessaloniki. Heavily indebted to
Synbolism, Kliun, the future Suprematist, painted this moving portrait
of his wife when she was gravely ill with tuberculosis.

Above:
25. *Léon Bakst. Costume design for the Golden Slave in* Schéhérazade, *1910.*

Below:
26. *Léon Bakst. Self-portrait, 1906. Charcoal, sanguine, and crayons on paper on cardboard, 75.8 x 51.8 cm (29 7/8 x 20 3/8 in.). State Tretiakov Gallery, Moscow.*

Above:
24. *Vaslav Nijinsky as the Golden Slave in* Schéhérazade, *1910.*

Opposite:
27. *Léon Bakst.* Portrait of Sergei Diaghilev and His Nanny, *1906. Oil on canvas, 161 x 116 cm (63 3/8 x 45 5/8 in.). State Russian Museum, St. Petersburg.*

Above left:
28. Karl Schmidt, architect. Residence,
workshops, and store of Carl Fabergé
on Bolshaia Morskaia Street in
St. Petersburg.

Above right:
29. Carl Fabergé in his St. Petersburg
office, ca. 1910.

Left:
30. Henrik (Heinrich) Wigström
(workmaster). Timepiece, St. Petersburg:
Fabergé Workshops, ca. 1900. Vari-color
gold and enamel, height 21 cm (8 1/4 in.).

Opposite top left:
31. The Biologist Ilia Mechnikov, Nobel
Prize Winner for 1908.

Opposite top right:
32. Ilia Repin. Portrait of the
Neurologist Vladimir Bekhterev,
1913. Oil on canvas, 107 x 78 cm
(42 x 30 3/4 in.), State Russian
Museum, St. Petersburg.

Opposite center:
33. Helen Huntington Hooker,
photographer. The physiologist Ivan
Pavlov, 1928–29.

Opposite bottom:
34. Rocket scientist Konstantin
Tsiolkovsky, ca. 1910. Tsiolkovsky poses
in his house-cum-laboratory in Kaluga,
surrounded by his models for airships and
by the tools and instruments of his own
invention.

progress in the Russian sciences—the neurologist Vladimir Bekhterev, the biologist Ilia Mechnikov, the psychologist Ivan Pavlov, and the rocket scientist Konstantin Tsiolkovsky are now household names [ills. 31–34].[5] Obviously, the ideas or repertoires of ideas which these individuals and their enterprises advocated were also an organic part of the Silver Age and no appreciation of that "hysterical, spiritually tormented time"[6] can be complete without due reference to the philosophy of Symbolism, the aesthetics of the Style Moderne (the Russian term for Art Nouveau), and particular practices and concepts, whether structural engineering or the apocalypse.

The philosophical and aesthetic motor of the Russian Silver Age was, indeed, Symbolism, and its body of ideas—the denial of the world of appearances, the search for a more pristine artistic form, the transcending of established social and moral codes, the emphasis on the inner world—left a profound and permanent imprint upon the literary, visual, and performing arts. But the temporal boundaries of Symbolism and the Silver Age are fluid, for some of the basic concepts can be recognized in preceding movements, not least in German and Russian Romanticism, and what may be regarded as the guiding principle of the Russian fin de siècle, i.e., "A thought uttered is a lie," had been formulated by the lyrical poet Fedor

Tiutchev half a century before.[7] Some might argue also that the Symbolist notion of the external world as irrational had also been presented half a century ago in Gogol's absurd stories and Pavel Fedotov's haunting elicitations of a dark presence beyond the pictorial frame [ill. 35], and that the abstracted imagery of Symbolist painting found a much earlier parallel in the diaphanous watercolors of Aleksandr Ivanov [ill. 36].

Objective appreciation of the Russian Silver Age is compromised by its dense composition, for, in questioning the values of nineteenth-century Positivism and Realism, its representatives still took advantage of scientific discovery in the search for a higher truth; and while dwelling upon the legacies of the antique and the classical, they still questioned the new primitivism espoused so eagerly by the radicals of the 1910s. Indeed, the relationship of the Russian Silver Age to what, generally, is now packaged and promoted as the "avant-garde" is especially complex. While avant-garde artists such as Ivan Kliun [ill. 23] and Malevich [ill. 22] certainly drew upon the attitudes and world views of early Modernism, it would be rash to identify the avant-garde in general as simply another component of the Silver Age.[8]

In any case, this book focuses not on the art of the avant-garde, but rather on the phenomena, characteristics, and tendencies which preceded Cubo-Futurism, Suprematism, and Constructivism and which defined the Silver Age as a recognizable and viable entity (belief in the representational function of art, in its spiritual or occult dimension, in the aesthetic freedom of the artist, and in the call for a synthesis of the arts and allied notions).[9] Of course, some of these ideas can also be associated with the prominent avant-gardists such as Malevich, but by and large it was the emphasis on a religious or, at least, private content which defined the creativity of the Silver Age—and the impulse to remove or transcend that content which defined the avant-garde, Kandinsky, of course, being a major exception to the rule [ill. 20]. Naturally, references to the major exploits of the avant-garde such as the experimental opera *Victory over the Sun* and abstract painting do occur in this book, especially when they are immediately relevant to the topic under discussion (see the chapter "Aesthetes and Barbarians," in particular). Inasmuch as the visual arts, above all, defined, distinguished, and propelled the Russian Silver Age, painting and design receive pride of place.

Below:
38. Aleksandr Scriabin at his grand piano, Moscow, ca. 1910. A composer and pianist of mercurial temperament, Scriabin developed an elaborate philosophical basis for his music, drawing liberally upon Theosophical, Buddhist, and Wholist philosophies (see ill. 145).

Above:

39. Leonid Pasternak. Portrait of Boris Pasternak, *1916. Sanguine and Italian pencil on paper, 16.6 x 10.8 cm (6 ¹/₂ x 4 ¹/₄ in.).*

Right:

40. Fedor Shekhtel, Moscow, 1910s. In architecture Shekhtel was Russia's foremost practitioner of Art Novueau and responsible for some of the most elaborate Moscow villas built in that style.

Below:

41. Andrei Belyi, ca. 1910.

Born at the twilight of the Imperial Order, the Russian Silver Age coincided with major social and political dislocations signaled by the Russo-Japanese War, the First Revolution (1905), World War I, and the October Revolution, a tragic cycle which informed and enriched Russia's Modernism, distinguishing it from counterparts in Belgium, France, Great Britain, Italy, and America. Not surprisingly, artists and intellectuals responded to these events, investigating concepts of violence, denial, shock, and utopian vision. Some, such as the poet Aleksandr Blok [see ill. 337], the composer Scriabin [ill. 38], and the painter Vrubel [see ill. 5], sacrificed their strength on the altar of aesthetic dreams; others, such as the dancer Nijinsky and the architect Shekhtel, were driven by the urge to create bold, new artistic systems; yet others, such as the poet Maiakovsky and the designer Rodchenko, offered their talents to the service of political doctrine.

The Russian Silver Age did not "stop" with World War I or the Bolshevik Revolution of October 1917, even if it had spent much of its momentum by the mid-1910s and even if the ideological tenets of the new, Soviet Russia soon countered and compromised private vision and spiritual quest. During the 1920s the erotic, the occult, and the necrological continued as principal themes in Russian art, literature, and dance; the Orthodox brotherhood Makovets continued to emphasize the spiritual, subjective purpose of creativity, and even state institutions, including the Russian (State) Academy of Artistic Sciences, maintained a special interest in the topics and formulae of the Silver Age such as Decadence, synesthesia, the Gesamtkunstwerk, and the interaction of the natural sciences, occult beliefs, and the arts. Moreover, a few steadfast artists and writers continued to embark on their flights of fancy during the Soviet period, including Mikhail Nesterov [ill. 43], Andrei Belyi [ill. 41], Mikhail Kuzmin [see ill. 402], Boris Pasternak, and Viktor Zamirailo [ill. 42]. But by and large, they were finishing an established trajec-

tory rather than initiating bold and untested ideas. With the imposition of Socialist Realism in 1934, the values and accomplishments of the Silver Age were lost from view or, at least, camouflaged by the external demands of the Socialist state.

It is important to remember, however, that the Russian Silver Age continued to flourish, albeit with a lesser brilliance, within the Russian diaspora of the 1920s and 1930s—which is not surprising,

Above:
42. Viktor Zamirailo. Witch, *1924. Watercolor on paper, 32.5 x 34 cm (12 3/4 x 13 3/8 in.).*

Below:
43. Mikhail Nesterov. Passion Week, *1933. Oil on canvas, 95 x 111 cm (37.5 x 43 3/4 in.). Archaeological Cabinet of the Theological Academy, Sergiev Posad.*

given the fact that primary contributors to the Russian Silver Age such as Léon Bakst, Konstantin Balmont, Alexandre Benois, Marc Chagall, Viacheslav Ivanov, Vasilii Kandinsky, Konstantin Somov, and Igor Stravinsky spent their remaining years in Berlin, Paris, New York, Rome, and other Western cities. Some, such as the painters Boris Bilinsky [ill. 44] and Simon Lissim and the writers Nina Berberova and Vladimir Nabokov, secured their reputations only in emigration, perpetuating the values of a Silver Age by then tarnished and distant, but still exquisite and suggestive.

During its banquet years (1900–20) the Russian Silver Age witnessed at least two generations of writers and artists who trod the fatal path of self-immolation, who turned their very lives into artifacts, and who squandered their mental energies as they sought to register the higher harmony of the Muses. In grappling with such daunting concepts as Good and Evil, God and Satan, cognition and knowledge, the fourth dimension and Materialist reality, and in exploring new linguistic and visual combinations to express these things, artists of the fin de siècle produced works of lasting genius—but also ephemeral failures. Here were stars, perhaps brilliant for a moment, but often fast falling, some in control of the grammar of their medium, others indifferent to technique, but all guided by the cosmic herald whose tracks now appeared, now disappeared, in the shifting sands of time and space [ill. 45].

A century later we may look back to the Russian Silver Age with a degree of sobriety—and also with a certain indiscriminateness of taste whereby, for better or for worse, high and low, the original and the banal, the leader and the epigone tend to merge and lose the original contours of their distinctiveness. Recent scholarship—for example, the publications of Irina Muravieva, Avril Pyman, Alla Rusakova, and Dmitrii Sarabianov,[10] and the monographic exhibition "Russian Symbolism" at the State Russian Museum, St. Petersburg, in 1996,[11] and "L'Art Russe dans la seconde moitié du XIXe siècle: en quête d'identité" at the Musée d'Orsay, Paris, 2005—have done much to broaden the standard definitions, adding unfamiliar names and works to the public repertoire, forging richer international connections, and offering new conclusions regarding the aesthetic and philosophical assets of Symbolist painting, sculpture, and design. In particular, a number of artists of indubitable talent, long neglected, such as Boris Anisfeld, Vasilii Denisov, Mstislav Farmakovsky, Nikolai Kalmakov, Vsevolod Maksimovich, Vasilii Masiutin, Vasilii Vladimirov, and Zamirailo, have been recognized and awarded their rightful place in the pantheon of twentieth-century Russian culture.

The ten chapters which follow address these and many other issues and, in placing the subject within a broad comparative context, focus attention on one of the most vibrant episodes in recent Russian history. Advancing by concepts and topics rather than by a strict sequence of events, an individual exploit, or a particular enterprise, this book recounts the story of a cultural phenomenon distinguished as much by conflict and diversity as by unity of purpose.

45. Konstantin Bogaevsky. Reminiscence of Mantegna, *1910. Oil on canvas. 111 x 173 cm (43³/₄ x 68 in.). State Tretiakov Gallery, Moscow.*

A DOUBLE-HEADED EAGLE
RUSSIA, LAND OF PARADOX

RUSSIA

What kind of place was Imperial Russia at the beginning of the twentieth century? What were her vital statistics, identifying features, ideas, and ideals? Here was a land mass stretching 2,905 miles (4,675 kilometers) north to south and 6,669 miles (10,732 kilometers) west to east, with a latitude from the Arctic wastes to the mountain ranges in the south and longitude from Europe to the Pacific Ocean. In 1900 the population of Russia was over 150 million, 10 percent of whom lived in cities, 1.5 million living in St. Petersburg. By 1913, however, the population had increased to over 174 million, with the two metropolitan populations almost doubling in size, while Russia's railroads had expanded from a mere 15½ miles (25 kilometers) in 1840 to over 236,000 miles (380,000 kilometers)—demographic and technological developments which help to explain the major economic, social, and cultural changes which St. Petersburg and Moscow, especially, witnessed during the Silver Age [ills. 46–48]. On the other hand, even as late as 1913 land was still owned largely by the gentry,

Opposite:
46. *View of the street at the St. Nicholas Tower entrance to the Kremlin, ca. 1910.*

Above:
47. *Daziaro's art and art supply store on Kuznetskii Most, one of Moscow's major shopping districts, ca. 1900.*

Below:
48. *Nevskii Prospect, St. Petersburg, ca. 1910.*

and in St. Petersburg alone there were 25,000 homeless[1] [ill. 49]. If, in 1913, Russians reportedly consumed over 39,000,000 pounds (18 million kilos) of potatoes and could have read 26,629 books published in Russian, and if Moscow alone boasted 263 bookstores,[2] poverty, disease, and undernourishment were rampant and only half the total population was literate.[3] True, recent decades had seen urgent reforms or, at least, efforts to introduce palpable change, such as the emancipation of the serfs in 1861 (two years before the emancipation of the slaves in the United States), the assassination of Alexander II by anarchists in 1881, and the completion of the Trans-Siberian Railroad in 1904 [ills. 50–53].

Above:
49. A soup kitchen for the unemployed in St. Petersburg, ca. 1910. The meal, eaten from communal bowls, seems to be kasha, the traditional Russian buckwheat porridge.

Below:
50. Peasants on the Trans-Siberian Railroad, ca. 1910.

On the other hand, Russia of the early twentieth century was still a predominantly rural and agricultural power and, at least outwardly, maintained a patriarchal, hierarchical order with the Tsar of all the Russias at the apex of the social pyramid [ills. 54–57] and the peasants at the base [ill. 58]. Russian noblemen still lived most of the year in France or Italy and the Orthodox Church continued to mark the calendar with numerous feasts and saints' days. Hawkers and vendors plied their trades as they had done for centuries, markets and bazaars abounded, and coachmen still egged on their horses [ills. 59–63].

Above left:
51. *Construction of the Trans-Siberian Railroad. Inauguration of the bridge over the River Enisei, 1904.*

Above right:
52. *A train on the Trans-Siberian Railroad, ca. 1900.*

Below:
53. *Sergei Mikhailovich Prokudin-Gorsky, photographer. A switch operator on the Trans-Siberian Railroad, ca. 1910.*

Above:

54. The Imperial Family. Left to right: Olga, Maria, Tsar Nicholas, Tsarina Alexandra, Anastasia, Tsarevich Alexei, and Tatiana. Photograph taken at Livadiia Palace in the Crimea, 1914.

Below left:

55. Tsar Nicholas II with daughters Olga, Maria, Tatiana, and Anastasia on the royal yacht, Standart, June 22, 1912. From the photograph albums of Ana Vyrubova.

Below right:

56. Tsar Nicholas II at Spala, near Warsaw, stands beside his shoot of the day, 1912. From the photograph albums of Ana Vyrubova.

Opposite:

57. Ilia Repin. Portrait of Tsar Nicholas II, 1895. Oil on canvas. 210 x 107 cm (82 5/8 x 42 in.). State Russian Museum, St. Petersburg.

Opposite:
58. A peasant in sheepskins next to a samovar.

Above left:
59. Hawker of items of haberdashery.

Above right:
60. Hawker of fruits and vegetables.

Right:
61. Coachman outside a Moscow mansion.

Above:
62. *Traders and their wares at the Tatar market, St. Petersburg, ca. 1900.*

Right:
63. *Musicians at a market, St. Petersburg, ca. 1910.*

Opposite:
64. *Fedor Shekhtel. The Riabushinsky Bank on Birzhevaia Square, Moscow, 1904. The upper storey, designed by Ivan Kuznetsov, was added in 1908.*

Overleaf:
65. *Photochrome view of the Kremlin from the Moscow River.*

Left:
66. The south entrance to the Winter Palace, ca. 1900. The photograph highlights the Atlantes sculpted by Aleksandr Terebenev in 1848 for Tsar Nicholas I.

Below:
67. Celebration of the Tercentenary of the House of the Romanovs, 1913. The Tsar and his court enter the Moscow Kremlin.

Opposite top:
68. The Winter Palace, St. Petersburg, ca. 1900–1910.

Opposite bottom:
69. Ceremonial prayers on Senate Square during the Bicentenary celebrations of St. Petersburg, 1903.

Right:
70. Costume ball at the Winter Palace,
St. Petersburg, celebrating the Bicentenary of
St. Petersburg, 1903.

Below:
71. Gavriil Baranovsky and Marian
Peretiatkovich, architects. Ceiling of the Eliseev
Bros. gourmet food store, Moscow, 1901.

Opposite top:
72. Gavriil Baranovsky and Marian
Peretiatkovich, architects. Interior of the Eliseev
Bros. gourmet food store, Moscow, 1900s.

Opposite bottom:
73. Semeon Minash, architect. Vitebsk Railroad
Station, St. Petersburg. Interior, 1902–04.

Even if landlocked, Moscow was gaining increasing momentum as the new financial and cultural axis [ill. 64],[4] while St. Petersburg, on the Gulf of Finland, was still the governmental capital. The winds of change may have been ruffling the waters of historical time, but to a casual observer during those banquet years, the pillars of the Russian establishment—Tsar, ministries, and Orthodox Church—must have seemed ever secure and permanent (just as their Soviet counterparts seemed in the 1980s), and the rigid majesty of the Winter Palace [ills. 66, 68] or the medieval fortitude of the Moscow Kremlin [ill. 65] seemed to symbolize the strength and constancy of the Imperial regime. This illusory grandeur was no more evident than in the magnificent celebrations of St. Petersburg's Bicentenary in 1903 (Peter the Great founded the city in 1703) [ills. 69, 70] and the Tercentenary of the Romanov dynasty in 1913 [ill. 67].

ALL QUIET ON THE EASTERN FRONT?

On closer inspection, however, a visitor returning to St. Petersburg and Moscow after a long absence would have been struck by the many sudden changes occurring in the material environment, not least by the construction boom and the proliferation of houses, stores, and offices, both pompous and modest, in the style of Art Nouveau [ills. 71–75]. Our visitor would have seen the hackney horses scurrying in alarm at the speed and noise of the Renault and Packard motorcars and of the first electric streetcar in 1907 (and of the first taxicab in Moscow) [ills. 78–80, 82]; our visitor might have been just as disturbed by the scantily clad and barefoot Isadora Duncan dancing her *danses plastiques* at the Hall of the Nobles in St. Petersburg in December 1904 [ills. 76, 77]; and, together with the passersby on Nevsky Prospect, would have been riveted by the first solo flights above the city in 1909–10 [ill. 81].

Opposite top:
74. Mathilde (Matilda) Feliksovna Kshessinskaia (Kshesinska, 1872–1971) in her St. Petersburg villa, ca. 1910. Kshessinskaia was the Prima Ballerina Assoluta at the Mariinsky Theater and at one time the favorite of the future Tsar Nicholas II.

Opposite bottom:
75. Aleksandr Gogen, architect. Mathilde Kshessinskaia's residence, St. Petersburg, 1904–06.

Top:
76. Isadora Duncan and the Isadorables, ca. 1910.

Bottom:
77. Isadora Duncan, 1904.

Above left:
78. Advertisement for Packard cars, the "most expensive and finest in the world," 1910s.

Above right:
79. Cars in front of the Winter Palace, 1910s.

Moscow held even more surprises—not only the first, experimental shafts for the Metro,[5] but also the vigor, brazenness, and brashness of the new intelligentsia with their "loud, Moscow accent, peculiar words, manner of clicking the heels as they walked along, Tatar cheekbones and eyes, moustaches twirled upward, shocking neckties and colored vests and jackets."[6] The boldness of this new folk extended to the exotic titles and functions of their major cultural enterprises such as the "Blue Rose" exhibition of Symbolist art in

Opposite bottom:
80. *Elizaveta Pautynskaia, wife of cement baron Stanislav Pautynsky, next to her car in Moscow, early 1910s. During Moscow's construction boom, Pautynsky made his fortune from the manufacture and selling of building materials, including Portland cement, bricks, and marble.*

Above:
81. *Flight of a biplane over Kolomiagi Aerodrome, St. Petersburg, 1910.*

Right:
82. *Streetcar at the Alexandrovskii Garden Stop on the day of inauguration of streetcar service in St. Petersburg, September 16, 1907.*

Right:
83. Nikolai Sapunov. Cover of the catalog for the "Blue Rose" exhibition, Moscow, 1907.

Below:
84. "Blue Rose" exhibition, Moscow, 1907.

1907 [ills. 83, 84], the provocative literary and artistic reviews *Vesy* (Scales, 1904–09) and *Zolotoe runo* (Golden fleece, 1906–09) [ill. 86], and the shocking Futurist manifestoes such as *Poshchechina obshchestvennomu vkusu* (Slap in the face of public taste) of 1912. The tension between the old and the new must have seemed especially strong in late 1910—with the announcement of the death of Lev Tolstoi at the Ostapovo Railroad Station in November [ill. 85] and the opening of the avant-garde exhibition called the "Jack of Diamonds" in Moscow the following month, at which Natalia Goncharova, Kandinsky, Mikhail Larionov, Malevich, and many other radicals showed their newest pictorial experiments. 1910 also witnessed Mikhail Kuzmin's publication of the Acmeist manifesto, "On Beautiful Clarity: Notes about Prose," ushering in a new literary movement which, if neither ultraconservative nor ultraradical, was still a bright manifestation of Russia's cultural plurality during the Silver Age [ill. 87].

Strange paradoxes manifested themselves: abrasive in their modernity, phonographic and cinematographic technology had preserved Tolstoi's voice on 78rpm records[7] and his movements on a nine-minute celluloid film.[8] These miracles of engineering could now revive the venerable past; at the same time, as the visitor recognized immediately, the brave, new painting of the Jack of Diamonds members, informed by French Cubism, relied just as heavily on the ancient traditions of indigenous folklore, including the Orthodox

Above:
85. *Funeral of Lev Tolstoi, Yasnaia Poliana, 1910.*

Below:
86. *Evgenii Lancéray (after a design by Mikhail Vrubel). Cover of the journal* Zolotoe runo *(Golden fleece), Moscow, 1908, no. 2.*

icon, the store signboard, peasant embroidery—and graffiti [ill. 88]. The poetess Elizaveta Kuzmina-Karavaeva listed some of these contrasts as she remembered the year 1910:

> In that period everything was mixed up: apathy, despondency, decadence—and the expectation of new catastrophes. We lived in the midst of a huge country as if on a desert island. Literacy was foreign to Russia and yet within our milieu was concentrated the whole of global culture. We quoted the Greeks by heart, were keen on the French Symbolists, considered Scandinavian literature our own, knew philosophy and theology, poetry and the history of the entire world, and in this sense we were citizens of the universe and the bearers of the great cultural museum of mankind. This was the Rome of decadence . . . we were the revolution before the revolution.9

Above:
87. Nikolai Feofilaktov. Autumn. Illustration for Mikhail Kuzmin's Kuranty liubvi *(Chimes of love), Moscow: Skorpion, 1910, between pp. 16 and 17.*

Right:
88. Mikhail Larionov. Soldier Relaxing, *1911. Oil on canvas. 119 x 122 cm (46 7/8 x 48 in.). State Tretiakov Gallery, Moscow. In the spirit of Neo-Primitivism, Larionov borrows the crude distortions of the* lubok *(broadsheet) as well as salacious language and gestures from graffiti in order to stress the immediacy and simplicty of this scene.*

Even to the casual observer, it was clear that the social and cultural fabric of Russia was changing. The scars of the General Strike of January 7, 1905, and of the ensuing revolution (which Lenin described as the dress rehearsal for 1917) were still visible [ills. 89, 90], reminding the world that Russia was an autocratic power, uninformed by parliamentarian democracy and subordinate to the laws of

a dictatorial arbitrariness of which Nicholas II seemed to be painfully uncaring. As the celebrated portrait painter Valentin Serov wrote to his mentor and friend Ilia Repin in the wake of the civic violence: the "restrained, majestic, and unarmed crowd advancing toward the cavalry attacks and the aimed gunfire was a terrible spectacle. . . . What was the meaning of that slaughter? Whose decision had it been? No one, nothing, can erase that stain."[10] But on the other hand, perhaps the 1905 Revolution illustrated Russia's iconoclastic tendency to smash and destroy just for the sake of smashing and destroying, and what the art historian Baron Nikolai Vrangel wrote a little later is sad confirmation of this dubious national quality: "[for years

Above:
89. Valentin Serov. "Brave soldiers . . . ,"
1905. Tempera and charcoal on cardboard,
47.5 x 71.5 cm (18 3/4 x 28 in.). State Russian
Museum, St. Petersburg.

Below:
90. First Russian Revolution, 1905. Barricades
on Moscow streets.

Russians] have been destroying everything they could and simply from a love of destruction germane to Russians, something which is part of their nature. Even icons—sacred relics and the marvelous, inspired, and ecstatic faces of God and His saints—have been annihilated by the Russians. . . . Whatever had survived by some strange fortuity perished in the ruination of the [first] revolution."[11]

There were also the searing memories of Russia's ignominious defeat in the Russo-Japanese War of 1904–05 with its exposure

of military corruption and mismanagement [ills. 91–94] and the awareness of an ever widening gap between the conservative and progressive forces of the Russian administration, wherein rigidity and passivity (Petr Stolypin, Minister of the Interior and then Prime Minister) [ill. 95] prevailed over flexibility and lucidity (Count Sergei Witte, Minister of Finance and then Prime Minister) [ills. 96, 97]. Symptoms of this moment of reaction—what the writer Maxim Gorky once described as the "most disgraceful and shameful decade in the history of the Russian intelligentsia"[12]—were easily recognizable, not least Bloody Sunday on January 9, 1905, when troops fired on a crowd of demonstrators; the massacre of striking workers at the Lena goldfields in April 1912 [ill. 98]; and the pernicious and destructive influence of the monk Grigorii Rasputin on the Imperial family and, consequently, on Russian military and foreign policy during World War I [ills. 99–101]. Even the establishment of an outwardly more liberal system of government, the deliberations of the State Council, and the opening of the first Duma in January 1906 [ills. 102, 103] did not bring democracy to Russia: the tragic effect of this tension between ingrained tradition and the urgent demand for change was

Top:
95. *Arrival of Tsar Nicholas II in Kiev on August 29, 1911. Among those receiving him is Petr Stolypin, the Minister of the Interior and Prime Minister.*

Center:
96. *Sergei Witte (backseat left) and Baron Roman Rozen (backseat right) returning from church at the Russo-Japanese Peace Conference, Portsmouth, New Hampshire, 1905.*

Bottom:
97. *Russo-Japanese peace conference. Count Sergei Witte (seated left) and Baron Roman Rozen (seated right) in front of a group of Russian staff members (Secretary Ivan Korostovets, Georgii Planson, Ivan Shipov, and Prince Nikolai Kudashev, among others) at the Wentworth Hotel, Portsmouth, New Hampshire, August 5, 1905.*

Opposite top:
98. *Workers at one of the Lena goldmines, ca. 1910.*

Opposite bottom left:
99. *Grigorii Rasputin at tea with admirers, ca. 1910. Standing fifth from the left is Anna Vyrubova, a close friend of Tsarina Alexandra. Vyrubova is credited with introducing Rasputin to the Romanovs.*

Opposite bottom right:
100. *Grigorii Rasputin, 1910s.*

illustrated perhaps no more graphically than in a rash of bombings and assassinations, culminating in the detonation of Stolypin's dacha on August 12, 1906, killing twenty-seven guests but not Stolypin himself (who was, however, assassinated in September 1911).

Viewed with hindsight, these social and political displacements seemed to signal dramatic change and propel Russia inexorably toward the Bolshevik coup of October 1917 and the Soviet transformation. Germany's declaration of war on Russia on August 1, 1914, the assassination of Rasputin in December 1916, the general strike and dissolution of the last Duma and the revolution in February 1917, the tsar's abdication and Prince Georgii Lvov's establishment of the Provisonal Government in March, the coalition formed by Alexander Kerensky in July, and the storming of the Winter Palace in October [ills. 104–109]—all these episodes seem, in retrospect, to have been following an inevitable course preordained by the force of history. On the one hand, the visitor to St. Petersburg and Moscow of the early 1910s might have sensed the magnitude of the impending rupture from the often brutal ways in which art, literature, and music

Opposite top:
101. *Anna Vyrubova holding hands with Tsarina Alexandra at Vyrubova's house not far from the Alexander Palace at Tsarskoe Selo. The Tsarina met Rasputin regularly at Vyrubova's house, so that his visits would not be listed in the official Court Register, 1913. From the photograph albums of Anna Vyrubova.*

Left:
102. *Ilia Repin.* Ceremonial Session of the State Council on 7 May, 1901, *1903. Oil on canvas, 400 x 877 cm (157 ½ x 345 ¼ in.). State Russian Museum, St. Petersburg.*

Above:
103. *Public prayer in the Winter Palace on the occasion of the opening of the State Duma, 1906.*

Above:

*104. Demonstration during the February
Revolution (on March 1, 1917) near the Tauride
Palace in Petrograd.*

Above:

*105. Alexander Kerensky, Minister and Chairman of the
Provisional Government, exhorting a regiment, 1917.*

were being treated and conventional "beauty" being soiled, especially at the hands of the avant-garde [ill. 110].

On the other hand, the more things changed, the more they stayed the same, and it would be wrong to assume that Russian society as a whole was more "enlightened" or more "liberal" on the eve of World War I than it had been in the nineteenth century. In fact, what occurred was an increasing polarization of right and left—which, for example, the Beiliss Trial illustrated so clearly [ill. 111].

The Beiliss affair took place in September–October 1913, in Kiev. Mendel Beiliss, a Jew, was charged with the ritualistic murder of a little boy, Yushchinsky, on the property of his employer, Jonah Zaitsev. Actually, the murder had been committed by thieves and Beiliss was unconnected to the crime. But although the authorities knew this, the trial of Beiliss proceeded mainly under pressure from the Black Hundreds, an extremely conservative, monarchist organization, and

Opposite bottom:
106. Demonstration on Palace Square in Petrograd, May Day, 1917.

Above:
107. Sharpshooters near the Smolnyi Palace, Petrograd, in October, 1917.

other anti-Semitic groups. Eventually, public outcry, protests from members of the intelligentsia both at home and abroad (Blok, Gorky, Anatole France, and many others voiced their indignation), and the obvious falsity of the charges brought the trial to an end and Beiliss was acquitted. Many people, rightist and leftist, were implicated in the trial, including Vladimir Purishkevich (an anti-Semite and member of the Duma) and Vasilii Shulgin (an anti-Semite and editor of the Kiev daily *Kievlianin*, who, nevertheless, condemned the trial).

The Black Hundreds, the Union of the Russian People, the Nationalists, the Secret Police, the archconservative politicians, and activists such as Vladimir Gringmut and Purishkevich constituted a watchful defense mechanism for an institution which inwardly may have been very weak, but which outwardly was still very impressive and, if it advanced more by inert traction than by fresh sources of energy, still governed the vast empire, played badminton, and organized magnificent costume balls—not that the cultural bohemia, with its all-night parties, café culture, and licentious lifestyle was especially different in this respect.

Opposite:
108. Tsar Nicholas II and the Tsarevich Alexei shoveling snow at Tsarskoe Selo, spring, 1918.

Above:
109. Grand Duchess Tatiana transporting sod with the aid of a soldier at Tsarskoe Selo.

Below left:
110. "Grimaces in Art. In Connection with the Project for a Theater of the Futurists." Photograph of Natalia Goncharova, her face painted, 1913, captioned "Initial makeup for an actress of the Futurist theater."

Below right:
111. Anonymous artist. Sketch made at the trial of Mendel Beiliss, Kiev, 1913.

AZURE HEIGHTS, SAPPHIRE DEPTHS
PHILOSOPHICAL CONCEPTS
OF THE RUSSIAN SILVER AGE

"A CHAIN OF MY DOUBLES DENYING EACH OTHER"[1]

The culture of the Russian Silver Age evoked a climactic and ominous mood, for its poetry and painting spoke of femmes fatales and fleshly indulgence, purple twilights and mythical beasts [ills. 112, 114, 115]. Perhaps even more than the Western European Symbolists, the poets, painters, and philosophers of the Russian Silver Age made every effort to escape the present by looking back to an Arcadian landscape of pristine myth and fable or forward to a utopian synthesis of art, religion, and organic life [ill. 113]. In any case, for Russia's children of the fin de siècle, Symbolism was far more than a mere aesthetic tendency; rather, it represented an entire world view and a way of life which engendered intense dreams, religious explorations, decorative rhetoric, and various kinds of metaphysical creativity, including table tapping and abstract painting. Belyi's novel *St. Petersburg* (1913), Blok's poem "Neznakomka" (The Stranger, 1906), Vrubel's images of prophets, saints, and demons, and Scriabin's galvanizing music all express the nervous tension and febrile energy of the Russian Silver Age.

The Russian Symbolists, like the Surrealists later, seemed to be moving in the direction of the "collective individuality,"[2] for, as champions of individualism, this "subjective generation"[3] was aspiring to transcend the impersonal conventions of sociopolitical reality and of false, mimetic reproduction so as to reach the spiritual plane of existence. Consequently, in examining the work of art, they posed

Opposite:
112. Miss (pseudonym of Natalia Remizova, sister of Nicholas Remisoff). Illustration from her collection Kupidony prokazy, Les aventures galantes *(Cupid's pranks. Les aventures galantes). St. Petersburg: Kornfeld, 1913, unpaginated. This particular design illustrates the poem by Petr Potemkin "Come with me, It is sinful to be alone."*

Above:
113. Konstantin Bogaevsky. Ships, *1912. Oil on canvas, 133 x 155 cm (52 3/8 x 61 in.). State Russian Museum, St. Petersburg.*

Below:
114. Nikolai Kalmakov. Two Women with a Deer, *1925. Oil on cardboard, 46 x 58 cm (18 x 22 7/8 in.).*

a leading question: To what extent is the picture, the poem, the musical composition based on the internal demands of the artist? Perhaps that is why Benois felt that a "good" drawing does not necessarily have to be "accurate"—the expression of the "I" in artistic form was of much greater import than formal precision.[4] Similarly, only when inebriated and, therefore, confused, could Blok perceive a higher world:

> And transfixed by a strange closeness,
> I look beyond the dark veil
> And see an enchanted shore
> And an enchanted distance.[5]

The power of the artistic personality and the private world was also crucial to the program of the group known as the World of Art (discussed in the chapter "World of Art") and was perhaps responsible for its eclectic preferences for John Ruskin and Dimitrii Merezhkovsky, Maurice Denis and Friedrich Nietzsche, Aubrey Beardsley and Vasilii Rozanov, etc. Although the doctrine of individualism might also be pernicious, as Benois pointed out in 1906,[6] it was, allegedly, a primary force separating the twentieth century from the nineteenth, because the Realists' allegiance to external conditions had nullified the subjective world only to produce a "formless

Above:
115. Léon Bakst. Cover depicting an "Inferior Divinity" for the score of Nicholas Tcherepnin's ballet Narcisse, *Moscow: Yurgenson, 1911.*

Below:
116. Nicholas Roerich. Battle in the Heavens, 1912. Tempera on cardboard, 66 x 95 cm (26 x 37 ³/₈ in.). State Russian Museum, St. Petersburg.

hydra."[7] Reference to this individualistic conception of art occurs again and again on the pages of *Mir iskusstva* (World of Art) magazine [see ills. 316–320], from Stanislaw Przybyszewski ("The artist is neither a servant nor a guide, does not belong to the people or to the world, does not serve any idea or any society")[8] to Diaghilev himself ("The great strength of art lies precisely in the fact that it is self-sufficient, self-purposeful, and, above all, free").[9]

The Symbolists' emphasis on the private experience and on the work of art as a reflection of the inner world was allied with their desire to produce works of literature, art, and music which would not only be aesthetically unique but also carry elements of national character. If the Symbolists were quite aware of modern European culture, their attitudes toward it were colored by the impulse to distinguish Russian poetry from the French or Russian painting from the German. The result was not always successful or commendable, but the quest for national identity informed much of the Symbolist philosophy and constituted a major reason why the painters, in particular, looked to the Russian Middle Ages and to Russian Orthodoxy as sources for inspiration. The art of Mikhail Nesterov, Viktor Vasnetsov, and Vrubel, for example, with its references to Slavic myth and the Russian Church, was seen by some observers to be the incarnation of an archaic and pure condition and of an elemental cohesion lacking in the imperfect fabric of contemporary society. For others, especially Nicholas Roerich [ill. 116], the triumph of Russian culture would come about through a new appreciation of ancient myth and legend. For still others, it was the hieratic tradition of the Orthodox Church which would guarantee the spiritual reawakening. Such conditions were present in Vasnetsov's evocations of pagan and Orthodox hagiography—which might explain the extensive discussion and illustrations of his work in the first issues of both *World of Art* magazine and Vladimir Stasov's rival *Iskusstvo i khudozhestvennaia promyshlennost* (Art and industrial art) [ills. 117, 118]. The same ambience informed the Neo-Nationalist designs which Maliutin and his colleagues created for the Abramtsevo and Talashkino workshops and the parallel fashion at both the Stroganov and Stieglitz schools of applied art.

A LITURGY OF THE SENSES

This Orthodox or ecclesiastical dimension of the Russian Silver Age in general and of Symbolist philosophy in particular constituted a special feature of Russian Modernism, separating it from its European counterparts. The philosopher Nikolai Berdiaev alluded to Russia's quest for a special identity via religious engagement in his description of Russia's "Cultural Renaissance" as a "flowering of poetry and intensification of aesthetic sensibility, of religious excitement and seeking, of interest in mysticism and occultism."[10] Indeed, it is important to remember that not only were some of the most original thinkers of the Russian Silver Age priests, such as Fathers Sergei Bulgakov and Pavel Florensky[11] [ill. 119], but many of the poets and painters, from Blok to Malevich, were upholders of the Orthodox faith, drawn to its rites and relics such as choral singing and the icon.

In no small degree and on many levels, Russian Orthodoxy made a direct and vital contribution to the culture of the Russian Silver Age and the avant-garde, from mystical evocation (cf. Blok's poem "I enter darkened temples")[12] and aesthetic innovation (Vladimir Tatlin's combination of methods from the Russian icon and the painting of Paul Cézanne) to formal transposition (Aleksei Kruchenykh's adaptation of the Lord's Prayer to his transrational poem "Heights")[13] and emblematic transmutation (the Bolsheviks' adaptation of the ecclesiastical procession to the political rally) [ills. 120, 121]. After all, with its ancient rituals, call to the spirit, and belief in life after death, Russian Orthodoxy, obviously, already offered a light and lightness perhaps comparable to the rarefied ether respired by the pilot high in the sky. Of course, there are many examples of the reverse, i.e., of Orthodox interference and compromise of artistic license, such as the obliteration of Pavel Kuznetsov's, Kuzma Petrov-Vodkin's, and Petr Utkin's "heretical" murals in the Kazan Church in Saratov in 1902,[14] prohibition of

Oscar Wilde's *Salomé* at Vera Komissarzhevskaia's theater in 1908[15] [see ill. 484], and censorship of David Burliuk and Pavel Filonov's drawings for the miscellany *Rykaiushchii Parnas* (Roaring Parnassus) as being pornographic in 1914.[16]

In 1910 there were 480 practicing Orthodox churches in greater St. Petersburg alone, not perhaps the legendary "forty forty" (1,600) of Moscow, but still symptomatic of the strong and abiding support among the public at large. In fact, it would be misleading to assume that the culture of the Russian Silver Age—dissident, provocative, and even iconoclastic—was necessarily at loggerheads with Orthodoxy. After all, a number of the Russian artists, moderate and radical, began their careers as icon painters (e.g., Filipp Maliavin) or attended theological seminaries (e.g., Boris Kustodiev, Aristarkh Lentulov, and Vasnetsov).

In any case, many of the first-generation Modernists were associated with the Neo-Nationalist movement in the 1880s and 1890s at Abramtsevo, near Moscow,[17] where Savva and Elizaveta Mamontov prompted visitors to appreciate the traditions of wood carving, embroidery, ceramics, and icon painting [ills. 122–124]. One result of their endeavor was the collective construction of the Abramtsevo church in Novgorodian style in 1883 with icons painted by

Vasilii Polenov, Repin, and Vasnetsov [ills. 125, 126]. Just a few kilometers from the Orthodox center at Sergiev Posad (Zagorsk), Abramtsevo was a place of aesthetic and spiritual sanctuary for many young artists and writers, including Nesterov, Vrubel, and Konstantin Yuon [ill. 127], who were sympathetic to the Orthodox renaissance of Russia's fin de siècle and who made a special contribution to the revival of Zagorsk as a religious and intellectual center under the auspices of Florensky just after the October Revolution.[18]

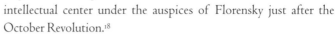

Above left:
122. Elena Polenova. Cupboard produced at the Abramtsevo Woodwork Studio, 1885. State Russian Museum, St. Petersburg.

Above right:
123. Mikhail Vrubel. Combination stove and bed, 1890. Majolica. Abramtsevo Museum and Reserve.

Curiously enough, in spite of the first atheist campaigns of the Bolshevik regime, the Orthodox component of the Silver Age still flourished in the form of societies and journals such as the Moscow group known as Makovets. Deriving their name from that of the hill where St. Sergii had resided, the Makovets group continued to

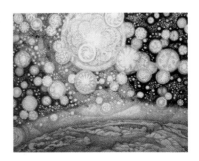

impart an Orthodox or, at least, religious function to art and even to defend the church service as a precious synthesis of word, image, gesture, and smell (incense) which was to be preserved as an artistic, if not as an ecclesiastical, expression.[19] Leading members of Makovets included Florensky, the painter Nikolai Chernyshev, and the graphic artist Vasilii Chekrygin, whose febrile interpretations of the Apocalypse may be telling us more about the Communist Anti-Christ than about Revelation [ill. 128].

The association of professional studio artists with the Russian Orthodox Church has a rich legacy, especially within the context of nineteenth-century academic painting, and St. Isaac's Cathedral in St. Petersburg and the Cathedral of the Savior in Moscow, with their decorations by such distinguished artists as Fedor Bruni and Genrikh Semiradsky, bear witness to this. The tradition persisted and

Opposite bottom:
124. Guests at Abramtsevo seated around Savva Mamontov, including the painter Viktor Vasnetsov and the sculptor Mark Antokolsky, 1890s.

Top left:
125. Iconostasis of the Church at Abramtsevo, 1882. The plan for the Abramtsevo church was devised by Apollinarii and Viktor Vasnetsov, Mikhail Nesterov, Vasilii Polenov, and Ilia Repin, while Viktor Vasnetsov carried primary responsibility for the iconostasis and the frescoes.

Bottom left:
126. Viktor Vasnetsov, Vasilii Polenov, Ilia Repin, and other designers and painters. Church at Abramtsevo, 1881–82.

Above:
127. Konstantin Yuon. Birth of the Nocturnal Luminaries from the cycle Creation of the World, 1908–09, Indian ink on paper, 51 x 66.9 cm (20 x 26 3/8 in.).

Below:
128. Vasilii Chekrygin. The Beginning of the Resurrection. From the series The Resurrection of the Dead, 1919–21. Charcoal on paper, 29 x 29 cm (11 1/2 x 11 1/2 in.).

Above left:

129. Viktor Vasnetsov. Descent of Christ, 1896–1904. Sketch for mosaic in the Church of St Georgii in Gus-Khrustalnyi near Vladimir. Charcoal, gouache, and gold on paper, 77.6 x 56.3 cm (30 1/4 x 22 1/8 in.).

Above right:

130. Fedor Shekhtel. Private chapel in Stepan Riabushinsky's residence on Malaia Nikitskaia Street in Moscow, 1900–03.

Below left:

131. Kuzma Petrov-Vodkin. Holy Virgin with Child, 1903–04. Majolica panel on the front of the Vreden Institute of Traumatology and Orthopedy, St. Petersburg. 600 x 350 cm (236 1/4 x 137 3/4 in.).

expanded at the end of the nineteenth century through 1917, when artists loosely associated with the Symbolist movement and the Style Moderne also produced holy images for sacred and civic buildings. We think, for example, of Vasnetsov's and Vrubel's designs for St. Vladimir's Cathedral in Kiev, including Vrubel's *Angel with Censer* (1887), or Vasnetsov's *Descent of Christ* (1896–1904) for the Church of

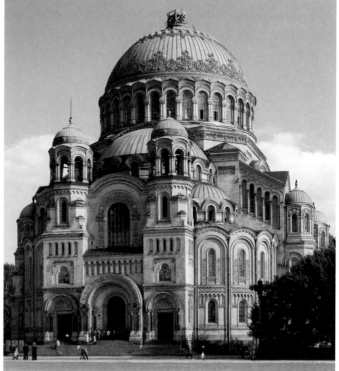

Left:
133. *Mikhail Nesterov.* Holy Virgin of the
Sign. *Mural for the apse in Aleksei Shchusev's
Church of the Intercession of the Holy Virgin at
the Convent of Martha and Mary, Moscow,
1908–12.*

Above:
134. *Mikhail Nesterov.* Christ Visiting
Martha and Mary. *Mural on the north wall of
the Church of the Intercession of the Holy Virgin
at the Convent of Martha and Mary, Moscow,
1911–14.*

Below:
135. *Nicholas Roerich.* Queen of Heaven.
*Fresco for the interior of the Church at
Talashkino, near Smolensk, 1912. Destroyed (see
ill. 283). Roerich is seated on the table. Standing
in the center is his son, Georgii; seated on the floor
to the right is his second son, Sviatoslav.*

Opposite bottom right:
132. *Vasilii Kosiakov, architect. Naval
Cathedral in Kronstadt, 1903–13.*

St. Georgii near Vladimir [ill. 129], as well as Fedor Shekhtel's chapel
and iconostasis for Stepan Riabushinsky's villa in Moscow [ill. 130].
Petrov-Vodkin also fulfilled commissions for icons and frescoes,
perhaps the most notable being the *Holy Virgin with Child* external
panel for the Vreden Institute of Traumatology and Orthopedy in
St. Petersburg (designed by Roman Meltser in 1902–05) [ill. 131] and
the *Annunciation* for the Naval Cathedral in Kronstadt [ill. 132]. Nesterov painted similar frescoes, including the Virgin Mary for the
Martha and Mary Convent in Moscow in 1911–14 [ills. 133, 134], and
during the same period Roerich designed his curious frescoes for the
church at Talashkino, Princess Mariia Tenisheva's estate near
Smolensk, including the Madonna, which reminded the more quizzical
visitors of "Tibetan and Thai religious paintings"[20] [ill. 135].

Even if they accepted commissions for the painting of long-
established subjects and, to a considerable extent, were bound by the
codes of ecclesiastical tradition, artists such as Petrov-Vodkin and
Vrubel were disturbing the "atrophy of artistic taste"[21] endemic to
later nineteenth-century Russian society, and it is a credit to the tolerance of the Orthodox Church that the Holy Synod did not always

reject their interpretations (a comparative study of Russian Orthodox commissions and the position of the Anglican Church vis-à-vis
the Pre-Raphaelites would make a fascinating case study). Aleksei
Shchusev, perhaps best remembered as the architect of Lenin's mau-
soleum in 1924, achieved his initial reputation as a prolific and original designer of religious edifices, including such masterpieces of the
Style Moderne as the cloister in Obruch and the Martha and Maria
Cloister in Moscow (both 1908–12) [ills. 136, 137]. In some cases,
Shchusev also designed the interior details and appointments such as
the murals for the refectory of the Trinity Cathedral at the Pochaev
Monastery [ills. 138, 139] and the iconostasis for the corporate chapel
at the Maltsev Glass Factory in Gus-Khrustalnyi.

Still, when a premeditated iconoclasm was, allegedly, perpetrated
by an artist, the Holy Synod was quick to act. Such was the case with
Goncharova's one-woman exhibition at the Society of Free Aesthetics in Moscow in 1910 when, with her iconic paraphrases, she was
accused of traversing the "boundary of decency."[22] Similarly, the
Moscow censor, on the insistence of the Synod, removed Goncharova's

Opposite top:
136. Aleksei Shchusev. Church of the Intercession of the Holy Virgin at the Convent of Martha and Mary, Moscow, 1908–12.

Opposite bottom:
137. Aleksei Shchusev and Mikhail Nesterov in the Convent of Martha and Mary, ca. 1910.

Above:
138. Aleksei Shchusev. Mural in the Refectory of the Trinity Cathedral at the Pochaev Monastery, 1910–12.

Left:
139. Aleksei Shchusev. Trinity Cathedral at the Pochaev Monastery, 1910–12.

140. Natalia Goncharova. Evangelist in Blue, Evangelist in Red, Evangelist in Grey, *and* Evangelist in Green, *1910. Oil on canvas, 204 x 58 cm (80 3/8 x 22 7/8 in.). State Russian Museum, St. Petersburg.

suite called *The Evangelists* [ill. 140] from the "Donkey's Tail" exhibition in 1912, on the grounds that the religious subject was incompatible with such an irreverent exhibition title.

Apart from Orthodox Christianity, there were many oblique systems which stimulated metaphysical flight and release of the spirit, including theosophy and anthroposophy, of which Belyi, Kandinsky, Nikolai Kulbin, Boris Lossky, Matiushin, Petrov-Vodkin, Roerich, Lev Sabaneev, Scriabin, Maksimilian Voloshin, and many other luminaries of the Silver Age were enthusiasts, if not adepts[23] [ill. 143]. Oriental medicine, Buddhism, yoga, Indian esoteric philosophy, vegetarianism, eurythmic dancing, sectarian ritual, and sorcery [ill. 141], especially in St. Petersburg,[24] also had their converts. Even Natalia Nordman, Repin's morganatic wife [ill. 142], was a vegetarian and barefoot dancer, while Kulbin defined the higher goal of art as "nirvana"[25] and Belyi studied the Skoptsy (an eighteenth-century sect that practiced voluntary castration) before writing his novel *The Silver Dove* [ill. 144].[26] True, Blok, for one, had little patience for these occult fads with their lectures, sermons, and

Above:
143. Nikolai Kulbin. Seascape, *1916–17. Oil on canvas, 97 x 62 cm (38 x 24 3/8 in.). State Russian Museum, St. Petersburg.*

Below left:
144. Petr Utkin. Unused design for the dust jacket of Andrei Belyi's novel Serebrianyi golub *(The Silver Dove), 1910. Watercolor and ink on paper.*

Below right:
145. Aleksandr Scriabin. Untitled drawing (design for the opera Misterium*), ca. 1914. Drawing from Scriabin's notebook (see ill. 38).*

ecstatic performances, regarding them as "pernicious . . . like cells of social reaction."[27]

A central problem accompanying objective exploration of theosophy and parallel movements in Russia is not one of documentation. Rather, the difficulty lies in their "universality" in the sense that, as the fusion of various spiritual outlooks (Christian, Rosicrucian, Buddhist), the occult systems often resemble one another. Primary claims—that the world is a totality consisting of a hierarchy of consciousnesses (mineral, vegetable, animal, and human) aspiring toward the higher plane; that to see is not to know; that we are primitive vehicles of perception at the threshold of a cosmic revelation, hardly cognizant of ulterior dimensions; or that the blending of matter and spirit can be achieved through a "theurgic performance"—express idealist and existential concepts also immanent to the Symbolist world view, especially of Belyi and Viacheslav Ivanov. Clearly, the theosophists' aspiration toward religious and physical synthesis reinforced Kandinsky's call for a monumental art wherein form and content would be mutually inclusive or Scriabin's dream to produce the rhapsodic *Misterium*, with mass choirs and full orchestration, high in the Himalayas[28] [ill. 145]. The result would have been a transcendent liturgy of the senses.

SPHERES OF MUSIC

The spirit of music commanded a special place in the Symbolist debate, thanks to the strong musical element in Russian and German Romanticism and the particular resonance which Goethe and Schopenhauer enjoyed in Russia. Of no less importance here is the fact that in terms of composition, performance, and appreciation, music assumed a new momentum during the Silver Age—both as an

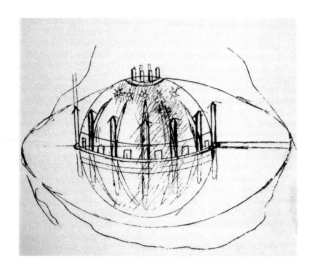

aesthetic exercise (e.g., Vladimir Rebikov's piano pieces) and as an applied synthesis (e.g., the Ballets Russes). Most of the artists and writers of the Silver Age studied music. Kandinsky, for example, played the violin; Kuzmin was a talented composer; Nijinsky played duets with Ravel; and Diaghilev took singing lessons. In fact, Diaghilev used to entertain the World of Art group, singing Rubinstein, Schubert, and Wagner in a fine baritone or playing piano duets. At one time, like his friend Somov, he intended to make music his career, taking lessons in musical theory from Nikolai Sokolov at the St. Petersburg Conservatory and even composing pieces for an opera entitled *Boris Godunov*. Nikolai Rimsky-Korsakov was also teaching there at that time, and Diaghilev asked Rimsky-Korsakov to examine some of his compositions [ill. 146]. Unexpectedly for the self-assured Diaghilev, Rimsky-Korsakov criticized them harshly. The result of this confrontation, so it is rumored, was that Diaghilev left the composer remarking that history would show which of the two men was greater. Perhaps it would not be unreasonable to view Diaghilev's doctoring of Rimsky-Korsakov's

146. Valentin Serov. Portrait of the Composer Nikolai Rimsky-Korsakov, *1898. Oil on canvas, 94 x 111 (37 x 43 ³/₄ in.). State Tretiakov Gallery, Moscow.*

Above:

147. *Alberto Camille Kavos, architect. The Mariinsky Theater, St. Petersburg (finished in 1859). The building was commissioned by Tsar Alexander II after a fire had destroyed the previous theater.*

Below:

148. *Enrico Cecchetti and Anna Pavlova, St. Petersburg, ca. 1906. Allegedly, the portrait on the wall is of Isadora Duncan in a Greek tunic.*

Schéhérazade for the Paris production of 1910 and, consequently, his sharp polemics with the composer's widow, less as the manifestation of a fine musical sensibility than as his final moment of victory over Rimsky-Korsakov. Diaghilev's knowledge and appreciation of music, both ancient and modern, was particularly evident in the early days of his career.

In opera Diaghilev and Benois had very definite opinions. Paying homage to a vogue of their time, they praised Wagner and the operatic drama, publishing appreciations of *Tristan und Isolde*, *Die Walkyrie*, and *Die Götterdämmerung* in the *World of Art* magazine,[29] and a translation of Nietzsche's statements on Wagner at Bayreuth.[30] "I'm fed up with Beethoven," wrote Benois in 1896. "What is he in comparison with Bach!! Or Wagner!!!"[31] As for the ballet, neither Diaghilev nor Benois evinced a particular enthusiasm in the early days and their attitude toward the Imperial ballet was, to say the least, restrained, as Diaghilev made clear in his 1902 review "In the Theater. 1. The Ballets of Delibes," referring to the "clumsy" Petipa and the "tedious" corps de ballet at the Mariinsky[32] [ill. 147]. The critic and philosopher Vasilii Rozanov, in his appreciation of the Siamese ballet, which visited St. Petersburg in 1900, even implied that the Western classical ballet as a whole was moribund, since "our heads may be ablaze, but our body hardly lives."[33]

Essentially, the writers and artists of the Russian Silver Age saw little of merit in productions of the state-controlled ballet, and Diaghilev's abrupt disengagement from his temporary position as artistic director of the Imperial theaters in 1901 and his general intolerance of the cumbersome state bureaucracy impelled him toward the establishment of his own troupe in 1909. Nevertheless, it would be wrong to assume that all was unwell in the Imperial theaters in the late nineteenth and early twentieth centuries. After all, most of Diaghilev's key dancers received their training within the Imperial ballet system and a number of his balletic interpretations had their premieres (albeit in tamer versions) on the Imperial stage. For example, *Egyptian Nights*, which became *Cléopâtre* in 1909 in Paris, was first produced by Michel Fokine at the Mariinsky in 1908, as was *Le Pavillon d'Armide* in 1907. Furthermore, Enrico Cecchetti [ill. 148], who coached many of Diaghilev's dancers, was ballet master at the Mariinsky and ballet teacher at the Theater Institute in St. Petersburg from 1892 to 1902. Of course, it would have been impossible for the Imperial ballet to have staged the avant-garde productions that Diaghilev realized in Paris, such as *Schéhérazade* in 1910 and *Jeux* in 1913, yet, as far as dancing and choreographic technique were concerned, Diaghilev and his colleagues not only did not undermine or destroy the Imperial tradition, but rather maintained and enhanced it.

Above:
149. A montage of portraits showing teachers at the St. Petersburg Conservatory, Russia's oldest music academy. Nikolai Rimsky-Korsakov is pictured in profile in the center (bearded and wearing glasses), 1890s.

Below:
150. Students at the St. Petersburg Conservatory, 1912.

The upsurge of interest in music during the Russian Silver Age was catered to, and stimulated further by, a growing number of special organizations, agencies, and enterprises which formed the administrative infrastructure vital to professional musical life. True, the St. Petersburg and Moscow conservatories [ills. 149, 150] continued to host domestic and foreign concerts and recitals (e.g., by the violinists Leopold Auer and Eugène Ysaye, among others), the theaters went on presenting grandiose ballets and operas (e.g., Prince Igor at the Mariinsky in 1909), and the Imperial household maintained its philharmonic orchestras. Yet private initiative began to play an ever-increasing role in the propagation of newer or more

experimental music. In 1901, for example, Alfred Nurok and Walter Nouvel, both members of the World of Art, initiated the Evenings of Contemporary Music in St. Petersburg, which sponsored regular performances of works by modern Russian and European composers until 1911. The Stray Dog cabaret in St. Petersburg did the same with its Musical Mondays. There were numerous private soirées, aristocratic and mercantile, and musicians and composers such as Mischa Elman, Jascha Heifetz, Serge Rachmaninoff, Sergei Prokofiev, Dmitrii Shostakovich, Scriabin, and Stravinsky owed much to this fertile ambience.

The well-stocked music stores of the Yulii Tsimmerman (Zimmerman) Corporation in Moscow, St. Petersburg, and other major

cities sold Russian and foreign sheet music, musical instruments, and the latest lines of phonographs and Gramophones [ill. 151]. Indeed, the rapid growth of the recording industry spurred both the importation of cylnders and 78rpm records carrying Enrico Caruso, Chaliapin, Ignacy Jan Paderewski, Adelina Patti, Camille Saint-Saens, and many other star performers, and the establishment of a vernacular record industry which, with brass bands, gypsy romances, and Russian folk songs, tended to cater to a less discretionary taste. The Amur (Cupid) Gramophone Company in Riga, an affiliation of Victrola and His Master's Voice, produced splendid recordings of stars such as Chaliapin, Ivan Ershov, Antonina Nezhdanova, and Leonid Sobinov. Often their labels were color-coded—pink, for example, indicating a celebrated basso such as Chaliapin—and served as status symbols for the aspiring Russian household. Even today these preelectric recordings astound by their purity and depth of sound and still convey something of the magic of Russia's Golden Age of opera.

During the Russian Silver Age, opera, perhaps even more than instrumental music, witnessed a renaissance in performance and appreciation. Keenly aware of this, Diaghilev ensured that opera was well represented at the Five Concerts of Russian Music which he organized for the "Salon d'automne" in Paris in 1907, also inviting Scriabin as concert pianist. The following year Diaghilev presented Chaliapin to Paris in *Boris Godunov* [ills. 152, 153] and later on he promoted Stravinsky's *Le Rossignol* and *Mavra*, the brave new harmonies of which echoed in the operas of a new generation of Russian composers, above all, Prokofiev (*Love for Three Oranges*, 1919) and Shostakovich (*Lady Macbeth of the Mtsensk District*, 1932).

Above:
152. Fedor Chaliapin in the title role of Modest Musorgsky's opera Boris Godunov, *1913.*

Left:
153. Aleksandr Golovin. Portrait of Fedor Chaliapin as Boris Godunov, *1912. Gouache, pastel, chalk, gold paint, and silver foil on canvas, 211.5 x 139.5 cm (83 ¹/₄ x 55 in.). State Russian Museum, St. Petersburg (see ill. 15).*

Right:
154. Nicholas Roerich. Battle of Kerzhenets. *Sketch of entr'acte curtain for Nikolai Rimsky-Korsakov's opera* The Legend of the Invisible City of Kitezh and the Maiden Fevronia, *1911. Tempera on cardboard. 52 x 70.5 cm (20.5 x 27 3/4 in.). State Russian Museum, St. Petersburg.*

Opposite top:
155. Nicholas Roerich. Costume design for a polovets *in* The Polovtsian Dances, *1909. The Polovtsian Dances, extracted from Aleksandr Borodin's opera* Prince Igor *as choral dances with choreography by Michel Fokine and sets and costumes by Nicholas Roerich, was part of Sergei Diaghilev's program for the first Saison Russe in Paris.*

Opposite bottom:
156. Nicholas Roerich. The Polovets Camp. *Set design for the second act of* Prince Igor, *1909. Pastel, charcoal, gouache on paper on cardboard. 52 x 70.5 cm (20.5 x 27 3/4 in.). State Tretiakov Gallery, Moscow.*

Drawing on the impressive legacy of the Mighty Five (the group of nationalist composers who revitalized Russian music by looking to indigenous sources), especially Modest Mussorgsky with his *Boris Godunov* (1874) and *Khovanshchina* (1886), Russian opera of the late nineteenth century took ready account of indigenous traditions. The tendency paralleled similar concerns in the visual and literary arts, coinciding with the Neo-Nationalist activities of Mamontov's retreat at Abramtsevo and Princess Tenisheva's at Talashkino, and it appealed to the patriotic spirit of the vociferous and xenophobic music critic Vladimir Stasov. Examples of this incorporation of the "Russian" sentiment into professional compositions are legion: Rimsky-Korsakov drew upon Russian folklore in *Pskovitianka* (The Maid of Pskov), *Snegurochka* (The Snow Maiden), *Sadko, Coq d'or* (Golden cockerel), and *The Tale of the Invisible City of Kitezh and the Maid Fevronia* [ill. 154]; Peter Tchaikovsky was not far behind with his renderings of Pushkin's *Eugene Onegin* and *Pikovaia dama* (Queen of spades), while Borodin won immediate recognition with *Prince Igor* (which Diaghilev extracted and produced as *The Polovtsian Dances* in Paris in 1909) [ills. 155, 156]. Sergei Zimin was also an unfailing champion of their cause, producing *Snegurochka, Coq d'or,* and other Russian pieces at his private opera company in Moscow, founded in 1904.

Mamontov's and Zimin's opera troupes and Diaghilev's Ballets Russes were symptomatic of the richness of musical life during the Russian Silver Age. But if these enterprises were oriented toward the classics or at least toward "serious" music, there were many composers and performers who were testing musical boundaries and exploring novelty of tone, scale, and harmony. The undisputed pioneer in this area was, of course, Stravinsky [see ill. 37], whose *Le Sacre du printemps*

(The Rite of Spring, 1913) [see ills. 344, 563–565] still amazes by its dissonance and syncopation. Others who were also questioning musical convention and propriety included Kulbin, Arthur Lourié, Matiushin, Prokofiev, and Nikolai Roslavets (the "Russian Schoenberg"). Constituting a musical avant-garde, they broke the mold of the nineteenth-century Romantic legacy to experiment with the whole-tone scale, enharmonics, melisma, and other mechanisms of "modern" music.[34] Viewed from this perspective, the grandiose and mellifluous compositions of Scriabin, such as *Poem of Ecstasy*, for all the aspiration to synthesize sound and color, are closer to Chopin and Liszt than to Stravinsky—or, for that matter, to Mussorgsky.

Kulbin and Roslavets, in particular, felt that music should codify and apply new conceptions of melody and harmony based on the principles of "free" music, which was to use "quarter-tones, eighths, and tones of even smaller denominations in addition to normal tones and semi-tones."[35] The result, according to Kulbin, would be "discord" (which excited mankind) instead of concord (which signified death).[36] Like Malevich, Roslavets and Lourié were convinced that by 1913, Russian art, in its originality, had surpassed French Cubism and Italian Futurism, and they offered their tonal systems—

the "music of interference, higher chromatics, and chromo-acoustics"[37]—as the rightful heir to Luigi Russolo's art of noise. In turn, they were laying the foundation for the even "noisier" music of the Soviet composer Aleksandr Mosolov with the factory sirens and machines of the orchestral episode called *Iron Foundry* from his ballet *Steel* (1926–27). The young Shostakaovich and especially Prokofiev with the machine music of *Le Pas d'acier* were not far behind.

Introduced to Diaghilev in 1914, Prokofiev made his reputation as a composer for the Ballets Russes with *Chout* (Buffoon, produced in 1921), *Le Pas d'acier* (1927), and *Le Fils prodigue* (Prodigal Son, 1929) in particular [ill. 160]. Here were radical compositions which attracted radical stage designers (Larionov, Georgii Yakulov, and Georges Rouault, respectively) and radical choreographers (Mikhail Larionov/Thadée Slavinsky, Leonid Massine, and George Balanchine, respectively) who, from the first, appreciated the structural novelty of Prokofiev's music. If *Chout* evoked the ancient traditions of peasant Russia, including folk melodies [ills. 157–159], *Le Pas d'acier* was a strong gesture to the industrial and proletarian culture of the new Russia [ills. 161, 162]. Responding to the October

Revolution, the Constructivist aesthetic, and the "labor gymnastics" formulated by Aleksei Gastev at the Moscow Institute of Labor, *Le Pas d'acier* was received and derided by some Western audiences as an instrument of Communist propaganda.[38]

Reference to Prokofiev and the Ballets Russes confirms not only that Diaghilev himself possessed a sophisticated understanding of music, old and new, but also that the company and its global performances provided the public with a very important exposition of modern music, Russian and Western. As Arsène Alexandre wrote in his early appreciation of Bakst: "There are regions where words seem never to have lived—regions, in truth, where they could not live. These are the realms of sound, the kingdoms of Melody and Harmony."[39] Suffice it to recall that Debussy and Stravinsky, Ravel and Prokofiev, Jules Massenet and Nikolai Cherepnin, Paul Dukas and Aleksandr Glazunov, and Erik Satie and Nicolas Nabokov were among the many modern composers whom Diaghilev commissioned for his Ballets Russes and that, as a result, a great number of people were first introduced to modern music through the Ballets Russes.

MUSIC OF THE SPHERES

The musical sphere of the Silver Age is of particular relevance to an appreciation of Russian Modernism, not only because it recalls the names of many pioneering composers, instrumentalists, singers, and dancers, but also because it connects with a special abstract, philosophical perception which the Symbolists cultivated. Belyi, for example, contended that the more an art form aspired toward music, the more closely it approached the ultimate revelation, whereas the more

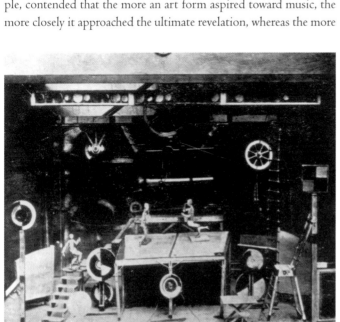

spatial or material it was (e.g., architecture), the more static and distant it became. Belyi went on to elaborate a metaphysical system far removed from the ordinary tonal interpretation, defining the essence of reality as music: "Movement is the basic feature of reality. Only music goes to the heart of images, i.e., movement. Every artistic form has as its starting point reality and as its finishing point—music. . . . In music images are absent."[40] For Belyi and Ivanov, poetry—after music—was the second most vital art form because of its prerequisites of rhythm and sound, while, for them, painting contained the "empirical" elements of color and perspective.

What Belyi and Ivanov chose to ignore, however, was that music, like painting, was also based to a large extent on perspective, i.e., the need to arrange orchestral instruments at a certain predetermined distance in order to hear a certain sequence of sounds—and that painting, in turn, had its own equivalent of rhythm, namely, line. What Belyi had in mind, presumably, was the more abstract, more experimental, and more "visceral" music of Nikolai Medtner, Scriabin, and Stravinsky rather than the more narrative or thematic music of, say, Serge Rachmaninoff [ill. 163] and Tchaikovsky [ill. 164], even though the most active conduits of music during the Silver Age, i.e., the Ballets Russes, presented an enormous variety of music, including Baroque and Romantic, as well as Modernist, composers.

Presumably, it was the ability of music to avoid simplistic narrative, to expose the intrinsic devices of the medium, and to stimulate the other senses with particular acuity which attracted the attention of the Symbolists. As Ivanov observed, what was important was not the force of the sound, but the power of its resonance.[41] In part, this would help to explain the general fascination with the music of colors, i.e., with the capacity of such composers as Rimsky-Korsakov and Scriabin to "hear" colors and to explore the condition of synesthesia. It was a concept, in reverse, which guided many of the early explorations of abstract art in Russia, for the new painting, as Berdiaev observed, was "passing from physical bodies to the ether."[42] One result of this procedure was, as Kandinsky implied, acceleration toward abstraction, a development which Belyi predicted when he mentioned in 1907 that a possible, albeit undesirable, path of art was in the direction of "objectlessness [where] the method of creation becomes an *object in itself.*"[43] Incidentally, this appears to be the first usage of the term *bespredmetnost* (non-objectivity) in Russian aesthetic discourse.

If, for Belyi and Ivanov, rhythm was the mobile and cohesive factor in music and poetry, then line was seen to play a similar role in painting. This is evident, for example, in the work of Bakst, Benois, and Somov [ills. 165, 166], where the entire composition may

be constructed so as to transmit a sensation of rhythmic dynamism, especially through the "reflections" of verticals, horizontals, and diagonals in various planes and through the rapid perspective achieved by a sequence of horizontals. Both in poetry and in painting, therefore, the emphasis on rhythm may be interpreted as an attempt to transcend and rupture the boundaries of the form and content, to interconnect aesthetic units, and, thereby, to create an organic and synthetic whole.

THROUGH A GLASS, DARKLY

The common denominator—thematic, philosophical, and aesthetic—of any religious quest and of the Russian Silver Age in particular, is, surely, the constant aspiration to move from the mundane to the celestial, from *realia* to *realiora*, from darkness to light. While recognizing the dimensions and perimeters of the world of appearances, the Symbolists strove to apprehend a superior structure beyond the outward flesh of things. Perhaps this impetus to move from *ici-bas* to *l'azur* was expressed no more urgently than in their attitude toward the mirror and the kind of light, natural or artificial, in which it was bathed. This simple, everyday object assumed a powerful symbolic resonance among both poets and painters of the Silver Age and, in some sense, can be viewed as a central leitmotif of their creativity [ill. 168].

The Symbolists questioned the solidity of material reality and, in their search for an ulterior harmony, approached the mirror not as a virtual reflection of the concrete world, but rather—with its distortions, haunting shadows, and sudden luminescence—as an interlocutor with the other shore. Here was a spiritual medium which, with careful adjustment and transposition, could connect with secret doctrines and mystical powers. Not surprisingly, therefore, the self-portrait, often created by means of a mirror, became a favorite genre during the Russian Silver Age. The mirror can serve

many functions, although that of the autobiographical extension and the admiration of the self is perhaps the most celebrated, and the Symbolists, not least the St. Petersburg painter Zinaida Serebriakova, used the looking glass precisely for this effect, as in her *At Toilette* of 1909 [ill. 167].

The self-portrait, like the diary, the confession, and the autobiography, appealed to the egocentricity of the Russian Silver Age, and many celebrities resorted to the mirror to render both physical and psychological likeness. Here was the siren's voice, the Lorelei, which the Symbolists identified with the irresistible impulse to find the alter ego—the reverse image which looks out of the mirror back to the model, simultaneously confirming the existence of the model and threatening with a second, contrary projection.

Vrubel painted and drew many self-portraits and most of the interpretations of his principal pictorial motif—the demon—can easily be identified as self-portraits, too, or, at least, portraits of the soul [ill. 170]. That Vrubel used the mirror *en face* is clear, for example, in *Self-Portrait with Shell* [ill. 169], where he presents himself seated at a three-quarter turn, the head slightly inclined away from the mirror, as if literally taken aback in disbelief or recoiling in order to

168. *Valentin Serov.* Portrait of Genrietta Girshman, *1907. Tempera on canvas, 140 x 140 cm (55 x 55 in.). State Tretiakov Gallery, Moscow.*

return to the mirror with redoubled curiosity. The setting is an interior of objects and furniture unrelieved by exit or secondary action. Inasmuch as Vrubel is, of course, looking at himself in the mirror (and not, therefore, at us), the picture emerges as a dialogue between two egos, one real, the other virtual, the staring eyes as windows to the artist's soul and the raised eyebrows as expressions of question and unease. The time is evening or night (hence the candle on the left and the oil lamp on the right) and the bric-a-brac constitutes the physical and metaphysical environment which haunted Vrubel's artistic imagination: the ceramic swan vase atop the wardrobe served as the model for *The Swan Princess* (1900) [ill. 172], the abalone shell in the lower left corner inspired *The Pearl* (1904), and the chaise longue and fireplace in the background reappeared in After the Concert (1905), with Vrubel's wife, the opera singer Zabela-Vrubel, replacing the candle in the self-portrait [ill. 171].

Above:

169. Mikhail Vrubel. Self-Portrait with Shell, *1905. Watercolor, charcoal, and gouache on paper, 58.2 x 53 cm (23 x 20 7/8 in.). State Russian Museum, St. Petersburg.*

The crepuscular mood of Russia's fin de siècle is reflected no more powerfully than in Chagall's *Mirror* of 1915 [ill. 173], one of the most trenchant works of his Russian years. In this enigmatic close-

Opposite bottom:
170. Mikhail Vrubel. Demon Seated, 1890. Oil on canvas, 115 x 212.5 cm (45 1/4 x 83 5/8 in.). State Tretiakov Gallery.

Left:
171. Mikhail Vrubel. After the Concert, 1905. Unfinished. Pastel and charcoal on canvas, 168.5 x 191.5 cm (66 3/8 x 75 3/8 in.). State Tretiakov Gallery, Moscow. The sitter is Nadezhda Ivanovna Zabela-Vrubel, the artist's wife, who is wearing a dress designed by him.

Below:
172. Mikhail Vrubel. The Swan Princess, 1900. Oil on canvas, 142.5 x 93.5 cm (56 x 36 7/8 in.). State Tretiakov Gallery.

up we see a gigantic mirror in a florid frame reflecting an oil lamp against a purple background, perhaps a hyperbolic reflection of the tiny oil lamp that we have just seen in the Vrubel self-portrait, and that had been such a central part of everyday life in the nineteenth century. The looming lamp, larger than life, is almost spent, and the concentric circles of its wan flame illuminate some remote, cosmic limbo. But the mirror scarcely mirrors "reality," because the purple spread, reminiscent of a funerary shroud, is not the reflection of the bright yellow tablecloth, the Thonet chair, or the tiny crouching figure so incommensurate with the vastness of the glass and the lamp.

Mirror is a picture where many moods and visions intersect: it tells us of the weight and majesty of a central domestic object, of semantic perspective dictating size by significance rather than by spatial progression, of defamiliarization of the familiar, of the transvaluation of values whereby the inanimate becomes more powerful than the animate (in this picture the Lilliput seems to be cringing in awe of the mirror), and above all, of the falsity of the

173. *Marc Chagall. The Mirror, 1915. Oil on cardboard, 100 x 81 cm (39 3/8 x 31 7/8 in.) State Russian Museum, St. Petersburg.*

mirror image—for the mirror has now become an anti-mirror. Chagall's *Mirror*, with its huge but receding oil lamp on a violet background, might be read also as an allegory of homage and mourning for an object whose long earthly and temporal function has now been usurped by other sources of power, i.e., electric illumination. *Mirror*, therefore, reflects a kind of unctuous lying in state as oil lamps yield to electric ones and as the smoke and shadows of the puttering wick yield to the brightness and uniformity of the electric filament.

But at least Chagall's mirror reflects *something*, in this case, an oil lamp, and, however topsy-turvy the relationship between here and there, the viewer can still peer into the mirror and gratify a visual curiosity. Not so with Goncharova's magnificent *Looking Glass* of 1912 [ill. 174], where the ominous and towering mirror on the chest of drawers offers a pale reflection of a desolate floor and wall. Here is a mirror almost without imagery or, rather, what should be the virtual, mirror image now appears as a denial and liquidation of the material world and a reduction almost to zero. In this Cubist enterprise we are left with a syncopated interplay of linear distortions in a glass surface, the kind of powerful absence that we sense on the edge of a precipice, at a musical rest, or in the primeval expanse of the desert. At this point we enter an essential world of pure forms, sensual, tactile, and removed from the human everyday. So imperious and complacent is the *The Looking Glass* that it seems to be walking away from us and, thereby, displacing the drawers, the leaning cupboard opposite, and the bizarre green phenomenon on the right.

Fascinated by the mirror, Chagall and Goncharova were not alone among the Modernists. That Malevich entitled one of his main theoretical essays "The Suprematist Mirror" (1923) also indicates a special attitude toward the concept of the mirror. For Malevich, the mirror and its aesthetic extension or metaphor—the easel painting—was not a duplicating machine, but a supreme reflection of an absolute and real world, ruled by intangible and invisible conditions such as essence, ether, and spirit. The *White on White* paintings symbolize that world, where the true reflection of our full material presence is empty, immaterial absence, for they are also about light, a light that is everlasting and, ultimately, Biblical [ill. 175]. Here is a supreme light that is neither natural (solar) nor artificial (generated), one that is unusual in the later Russian avant-garde, when artists, unabashed, tended to praise the technological, the industrial, and hence the electrical—rather than the metaphysical—notion of light. The metaphysical dimension of Malevich's conception of a Suprematist light reinforces his strong philosophical obligation to the Symbolist legacy.

Above:
174. *Natalia Goncharova.* The Looking Glass, *1912. Oil on canvas, 115 x 92 cm (45 ¹/₄ x 36 ¹/₄ in.)*

Left:
175. *Kazimir Malevich.* Suprematist Composition: White on White, *1918. Oil on canvas, 79.4 x 79.4 cm (31 ¹/₄ x 31 ¹/₄ in.). The Museum of Modern Art, New York.*

THE SHOCK OF THE NEW
Technology, Science, Engineering

GAINING MOMENTUM

"She wanted to get up and lean back, but something enormous, something inexorable pushed her in the head and dragged her along by the back."[1]

Such was the tragic and ignominious suicide of Anna Karenina, the heroine of the famous novel, as she threw herself under the passing train [ill. 177]. Paterfamilias and assertive moralist, Tolstoi [ills. 178, 180] inflicted this violent death upon an adulteress who had ventured to transgress the Christian commandments. On one level, of course, Anna was being punished for her contestation of polite civic values and for her vaunting of such prodigal behavior. But on the other, the inexorable crush of the engine's wheel upon the weak flesh of a Russian socialite marked the abrupt invasion of a new and diabolical force upon tradition and convention—a machine age which, in the closing decades of Tsarist Russia, would transform the Russian nation into what Blok would call the "New America"[2] [ill. 176].

The consequent and fundamental dichotomy between the vestiges of a patriarchal social order and the semaphores of a new modus vivendi, between country and town, stasis and action, aristocracy and democracy, released an energy and dynamism which, in turn, guided many of the explorations and discoveries of the Russian Silver Age. Tolstoi's friend and sympathizer, the painter Repin, expressed the shock of the new just as urgently in his celebrated picture of an

Opposite:
176. Mstislav Dobuzhinsky. The Kiss, *1916. Sanguine and pencil on cardboard, 109 x 76 cm (43 x 30 in.).*

Above:
177. Anna Karenina about to commit suicide. Production still from the film Anna Karenina *directed by Vladimir Gardin in 1914.*

Below:
178. Lev Tolstoi and Ilia Repin, ca. 1900.

179. *Ilia Repin.* They Did Not Expect
Him, *1884. Oil on canvas, 160.5 x 167.5 cm
(63 ¹/₈ x 66 in.), State Tretiakov Gallery,
Moscow.*

anarchist who, after the Imperial amnesty, has returned unexpectedly
to the bosom of his bourgeois family, i.e., *They Did Not Expect Him*
(1884) [ill. 179]. Like the train in *Anna Karenina*, the invader now
crosses the threshold of decent deportment as he advances relent-
lessly toward the mother and the capacious easy chair, symbols of
bourgeois order, complacency, and arrival. In his Symbolist manifesto of 1892, "On the Reasons for the Decline and on New Trends
in Contemporary Russian Literature," the writer Dmitrii
Merezhkovsky [ill. 181] spoke of the younger generation's "presentiment of a divine idealism" and of "indignation at the soulless, Positivist method," as if he were describing the same kind of social and
cultural conflict captured in Repin's picture.[3]

It is tempting to follow the course of Tolstoi's fateful train
through the vagaries of the fin de siècle and to associate its locomotive

movement with the aesthetic achievements of the Russian Silver Age, the avant-garde, and even the agitational culture of the early Soviet republic. After all, Savva Mamontov, owner of the art colony Abramtsevo [ill. 182] and a central force in Russia's decorative revival of the late nineteenth century, made his fortune (and misfortune) by investing in Russia's railroads; it was the film by Auguste and Louis Lumière of a train arriving at the station (*L'Arrivée d'un train en gare de la Ciotat*) which so alarmed visitors to the Nizhnii-Novgoord Fair of 1896 (the country's first exposure to the cinema at this showcase of the new, technological Russia) [ill. 183]; it was a speeding train which informed many of the key works of the avant-garde, from Goncharova's *Aeroplane above a Train* (1913) to Kliun's *Landscape Rushing Past* (1914) and from Malevich's *Simultaneous Death of a Man in an Aeroplane and on the Railroad* (1913) to Liubov Popova's *Traveling Woman* (two versions, both 1915) [ills. 184–187]; it was the notorious sealed train which brought Lenin back to Russia in 1917, heralding the dawn of the Communist state; and finally, it was Vsevolod Ivanov's story "Armored Train No. 14-69" of 1922 which prefigured the code of Socialist Realism, rejecting the fragile dreams and visceral experiences of the Russian Silver Age. Perhaps, as Diaghilev observed sardonically, it was simply the "difference in track gauge or a certain sluggishness about our goods trains" which molded the evolution of modern Russian art.4

Of course, to recount the history of the Russian Silver Age in terms merely of railroads and locomotives would be partial, to say the least. Rather, the purpose of this momentary detour is to

Left:
180. Ilia Repin. Lev Tolstoi Barefoot, *1901. Oil on canvas, 207 x 73 cm (81.5 x 28 3/4 in.). State Russian Museum, St. Petersburg.*

Above:
181. Dmitrii Merezhkovsky, ca. 1900.

Below:
182. Artists (from left to right) Ilia Repin, Vasilii Surikov, Konstantin Korovin, Valentin Serov, and Mark Antokolsky visiting Savva Mamontov (playing the piano) at his Moscow house. In the background is Antokolsky's sculpture Christ before the People's Court, *1890s.*

Above:
183. Production still from the film L'Arrivée d'un train en gare de la Ciotat directed by Auguste and Louis Lumière in 1895.

Below:
184. Natalia Goncharova. Airplane above a Train (Landscape with Train), 1913. Oil on canvas, 55.7 x 83.8 cm (22 x 33 in.). National Museum of Fine Arts of Tatarstan, Kazan.

underline the importance of technological invention and the positive sciences to the process of Russia's cultural rebirth.[5] The attainments of, say, Blok, Kandinsky, and Stravinsky, for example, tend to be appreciated and studied outside of this mechanical environment, although it was this environment which nurtured or, at least, accommodated many innovations of the Silver Age. True, the artists and writers themselves were often reluctant to accept the signs of "progress." For example, the paintings and designs of the World of Art members such as Bakst, Benois, and Somov disregard the new high-rise buildings, mass transport systems, and household gadgets— a major exception being Mstislav Dobuzhinsky, whose cityscapes, sinister in their propensities [ill. 188; see also 176], express unease and alarm at the advance of the new civilization, cruel and inhuman.

At best, the artists and writers of the Silver Age were suspicious of what Benois called "Americanism,"[6] because, like nineteenth-century Materialism, it still dealt with outer appearance and not with inner essence. If, for example, the phonograph [ills. 189, 190] now rendered the music of Beethoven and Wagner and the voice of Tolstoi instantly accessible, the Symbolists regarded such immediacy as mendacious, arguing that the effect was outward only and still did not transmit the music of the spheres (even if Blok did see fit to record his own declamations). Perhaps the same paradox is intrinsic to Nikolai Gumilev's poem "The Streetcar Which Went Astray"

Above:

185. *Kazimir Malevich.* Simultaneous
Death of a Man in an Airplane and on
the Railroad, *1913. Illustration for Aleksei
Kruchenykh's book* Vzorval (Explodity), *St.
Petersburg: Svet, 1913. Lithograph, watercolor,
11.7 x 17.5 cm (4 5/8 x 6 7/8 in.),
Kupferstichkabinett, Basel.*

Right:

186. *Liubov Popova.* Traveling Woman,
*1915. Oil on canvas, 158.5 x 123 cm (62 3/8 x
48 3/8 in.), State Museum of Contemporary
Art, Thessaloniki.*

Right:
187. *Ivan Kliun.* Landscape Rushing Past,
*1914. Wood, oil, metal, porcelain, and rope,
74 x 58 cm (29 1/8 x 22 7/8 in.).
State Tretiakov Gallery, Moscow.*

Below:
188. *Mstislav Dobuzhinsky.* St. Petersburg,
*1914. Oil on canvas, 75.5 x 52.2 cm
(29 3/4 x 20.5 in.). State Russian Museum,
St. Petersburg.*

Opposite top left:
189. *"Everything for Music." Advertisement for
the Adler Corporation, Rostov-on-Don, ca.
1908. Color lithograph, 51 x 75 cm (20 x 29.5
in.). Russian National Library, St. Petersburg.*

(1921), where the streetcar refuses to curb its waywardness in spite of
its electric motor (the first motorized streetcar appeared on Nevskii
Prospect in September, 1907) [ill. 191].

INDUSTRIAL PROGRESS

Still, even the most subjective and withdrawn of the Modernist
poets and painters were fascinated by the streamlined and powerful
beauty of the machine and of the new structural engineering, by its
outlandish forms and formal functionality. The thick, illustrated
trade catalogues of machinery and machine tools, issued by international corporations with representatives in St. Petersburg, Moscow,
and other Russian cities—such as Bloch's office furniture, supplies,
and motors or Schütte's tools and instruments [ill. 192]—offer a
plethora of mechanical novelties which must have impressed the
average reader: here are elevators, cantilevered ceilings, plate-glass
surfaces, heating systems, pumps, lamps, cranes, and other industrial
paraphernalia—objects of detached harmony and illumination, irre-
spective of their ultimate destination on a factory floor, in a public

sewer, or inside a carburetor. In his story "The New Dacha" (1899), Chekhov discerned this new beauty as a haunting and powerful counterpoint to Mother Nature [ill. 193]:

> A huge bridge had been built. You could see its lattice frame from the village high up on the steep bank. In misty weather, on serene winter days, when its slender iron beams and all the surrounding forest were covered in hoarfrost, it made for a vivid, even fantastic, picture.[7]

Above:
190. The folk singer Mitrofan Piatnitsky recording Russian songs via a phonograph, 1910.

Below:
191. Motorized streetcar in Moscow on the Kremlin Embankment, ca. 1910.

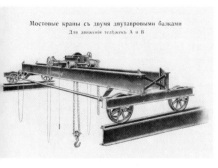

Above:

192. *Illustration from the Schütte Corporation (Alfred Shiutte) trade catalog for Russian consumers advertising tools and instruments, St. Petersburg, 1914, p. 446. The advertisement is for a bridge crane.*

Right:

193. *The Alexander Bridge (named after Tsar Alexander III) over the Volga River in Saratov, ca. 1900.*

By the late nineteenth century Russia had entered a stage of unprecedented economic acceleration. Capitalism was thriving, cities were expanding rapidly, transit systems were growing at an alarming pace. This advancement from an agrarian to a more urban nation occurred almost within a generation and there are many references to the astonishment, bewilderment, or admiration felt by the witnesses of this process. Wonders of the machine age manifested themselves in St. Petersburg, Moscow, and the provinces in swift succession—the movie house, electric power station, automobile, airplane, motorcycle, telephone, reinforced-concrete building with plate-glass windows, and so on [ills. 194–201]. The reading public supplemented their translations of Jules Verne and H. G. Wells with exuberant accounts in magazines such as *Zhurnal prikliuchenii* (Journal of adventures] and *Vokrug sveta* (Around the world), which often carried essays about the city of the future, interplanetary travel, and, in general, the marvels of engineering [ill. 203].

The basic notion that the function of a man-made object such as a railroad bridge should determine its structure and that this should

not be disguised by ornament [ill. 202] (a tenet which becomes especially pressing during the period of Constructvism) had been evident in Russian architectural practice since at least the 1830s–40s with the formation of the so-called Rationalist School. In spite of the Victorian passion for decorating objects, the idea that the "mechanical construction constitutes the single basis for beauty in architecture"[8] gathered increasing support as the nineteenth century advanced. True, Russia could boast no equivalent to the Eiffel Tower or the

Above:
194. Roman Klein, architect. The Coliseum Movie House on Chistoprudnyi Boulevard in Moscow, 1912–16.

Below:
195. Roman Klein, architect. Interior of The Coliseum Movie House on Chistoprudnyi Boulevard in Moscow, 1912–16.

Crystal Palace, but she did have some remarkable suspension and lattice bridges crossing her great rivers, and the Machine Hall at the "All-Russian Industrial and Art Exhibition" in Nizhnii-Novgorod in 1896 demonstrated her ability to catch up and overtake. Not that all parties at the Nizhnii-Novgorod fair were open and progressive—after all, Vrubel's folkloric panels *Princess Reverie* and *Mikula Seliani-novich* were promptly rejected by the selection committee.[9]

Important disseminators of functionalist ideas in the late nineteenth century were the St. Petersburg Society of

Above:
196. *Electric power station of the Electric Lighting Corporation at Obvodnoi Canal in St. Petersburg, 1886.*

Right:
197. *Advertisement for oil, grease, and gasoline from The Nobel Bros. Corporation, St. Petersburg. 68.5 x 59 cm (27 x 23 ¹/₄ in.). Russian National Library, St. Petersburg. Some members of the Nobel family, by origin Swedish, lived and worked in St. Petersburg. Alfred and Emmanuel Nobel, in particular, were known for their initiatives in the mining and oil and gas industries. Alfred invented dynamite, while in the early 1900s Emmanuel opened the first diesel engine plant in St. Petersburg and powered his fleet of oil tankers with these engines. After Alfred's death in 1896, his estate disbursed the funds for the Nobel Prizes, the first of which was awarded in 1901.*

Opposite top:
198. *Chocolat "Aviatique." Candy wrapper carrying design of an airship, Krakhmalnikov Bros. Sweetmeat Manufactory, Odessa, ca. 1910.*

Left:
199. *Participant in the second Moscow–St. Petersburg–Moscow motorcycle rally, early 1900s.*

Below left:
200. *A lady talking on the telephone, first decade of the 1900s.*

Below right:
201. *Konstantin Roshfor and Vladimir Lipsky, architects. The Esders and Scheffals Corporation on the Moika Embankment, St. Petersburg, 1907.*

Architects and the Institute of Civil Engineers in St. Petersburg, which disapproved of the overly decorative style being promoted by the Neo-Nationalist or Neo-Russian artists at Abramtsevo and Talashkino. Writing in the professional journal *Zodchii* (Architect) in the early 1880s, Nikolai Sultanov, a professor at the Institute, emphasized the need to ensure that a building "fulfill its utilitarian purpose"[10] and dispense with the "marble hand-woven towels and brick embroideries"[11] which architects were applying to facades. Actually, just two decades later Russian cities were already in possession of splendid examples of "utilitarian architecture" which relied on the functional harmony of purpose and design, although the public did not always associate them with "artistic beauty"—and these were the water towers and reservoirs, natural-gas tanks, lighthouses, and other iron and glass structures which Russia's capitalist boom was encouraging and for which a single engineer, Vladimir Shukhov, must take primary responsibility [ills. 204–206].

Above all, Shukhov is remembered for the Moscow Radio Tower (1924), which inspired the Constructivists such as the designers Rodchenko and Tatlin and the filmmaker Lev Kuleshev, but as chief engineer in Aleksandr Bari's construction office in Moscow he was the

Opposite top:
202. *Lev Proskuriakov, designer. Metal truss bridge on stone piers for the Trans-Siberian Railroad over the Kama River near Perm, ca. 1910. Photograph by Sergei Prokudin-Gorsky.*

Opposite bottom:
203. *"Drama on a Locomotive." Cover of the journal* Vokrug sveta *(Around the world), Moscow, 1893, no. 1.*

Right:
204. *Vladimir Shukhov, engineer. Lookout Tower at the "All-Russian Industrial and Art Exhibition" in Nizhnii-Novgorod, 1896.*

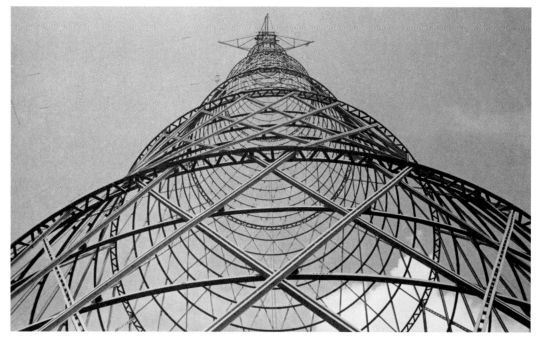

Top:
205. *Vladimir Shukhov, engineer. Double-curvature, diagonally framed shell of a metallurgical workshop in Vyksa near Nizhnii-Novgorod during construction, 1897.*

Center:
206. *Aleksandr Rodchenko, photographer. Vladimir Shukhov's Radio Tower, Moscow, 1929.*

Bottom:
207. *Vladimir Shukhov, engineer. Platform area at the Briansk (now Kiev) Railroad Station in Moscow, 1911–17. The station was designed by Ivan Rerberg and Viacheslav Oltarzhevsky.*

designer of many other buildings which changed the skyline of Russia's cities well before the October Revolution. One of his most important undertakings was the construction of the seventy-five-foot "little Eiffel Tower" in open, lattice iron with a viewing facility for the 1896 Nizhnii-Novgorod Fair; he also designed the iron pillars and suspended roof for the Factory and Plant Pavilion there; and his iron supports for the roof of the Briansk (Kiev) Railroad Station in Moscow (1911–17) still impress by their graceful majesty [ill. 207].

AND THERE WAS LIGHT

The conflict between the physical item of modern convenience and the metaphysical aspirations of the Silver Age is encapsulated in the "reverse illumination" experienced by the novelist and philosopher Merezhkovsky. Convinced of the power of mind over matter, Merezhkovsky announced at one of his soirées that it was enough to proclaim "Let there be light!" and the night would turn to day—at which point the room was cast into total darkness owing to an electrical fault.[12] Mystical or

208. Valentin Dubovskoi, designer. Electric elevator in an apartment house on Znamenskii Lane, Moscow, 1900s.

not, Merezhkovsky's counterenlightenment brings us to a concept and phenomenon central to the development of the poets and painters—and engineers—of the Silver Age, i.e., their attitudes toward light, natural and artificial, and toward the instruments which induced those conditions.

Among the many technological innovations that came to Russia just before and after 1900, electricity or, rather, the application of electric light to public and private spaces, was foremost [ills. 208, 209]. By 1905 the ideal Russian home, restaurant, or bank was graced by electric chandeliers, electric bracket lamps, electric table lamps, electric elevators, and electric doorbells, while movie houses with their flickering silver screens were known as electric palaces. Electric light illuminated not only St. Petersburg and Moscow, but also more distant cities such as Kiev, where in 1908 the radical David Burliuk made sure that his "Link" exhibition was lit up by electricity. In her paintings called *Electric Machine* (also known as *Dynamo Machine*, 1912) and *Electric Lamp* (1913) [ill. 210], Goncharova also seems to be eulogizing this specimen of technical wizardry.

Reference to Russian magazines "for family reading" such as Niva (Field) and *Solntse Rossii* (Sun of Russia) around 1910 demonstrates just how popular the subject of electricity was and how, through didactic explications of physical phenomena such as incandescence, radioactivity, and the X-ray (invented by Wilhelm Conrad Röntgen in Munich in the 1890s and propagated in Russia by his disciple Abram Ioffe), the average Russian reader, not least the artist Larionov, would have learned of electricity's basic functions and applications [ill. 211]. What X-ray photography, for example, meant for both science and art students in the early twentieth century was of momentous importance: one could actually see the world beyond appearances. For the rationally minded, here was undeniable proof of natural, indefeasible connections between outer and inner constructions; for the irrational, X-ray photographs were proof of the existence of the "real" reality beyond the facade of physical objects. No sooner was the X-ray discovered than the concept entered the worlds of both cheap entertainment and high society [ill. 212].

Above:
209. *Karl Gippius, architect. Stairway in the house of Aleksei Bakhrushin, Moscow, 1895–96. Bakhrushin's superb collection of theater art became the basis of what is now the Bakhrushin State Central Theater Museum, Moscow, still located in Bakhrushin's house.*

Right:
210. *Natalia Goncharova. Electric Lamp, 1913, oil on canvas, 105 x 81.3 cm (41 3/8 x 32 in.). Musée National d'Art Moderne, Centre Georges Pompidou, Paris, France.*

Opposite top:
211. *Wilhelm Conrad Röntgen. X-ray of Siamese twins, 1896.*

Opposite bottom:
212. *Satirical illustration from* Life *magazine, 1896, New York, with the caption: "That delicious moment when you find you are to take into dinner the girl who yesterday refused you. For those of our readers who like to get at the inside facts of a case we publish these companion pictures. They are intended to show the possibilities of the art of the future when developed by advanced photography. We have selected a well-known drawing from* Life *as better illustrating our point."*

In this respect, the celebrated "Dada" opera or buffoonery called *Victory over the Sun* of 1913 can also be perceived as a gesture to the electric obsession, as well as a response to Italian Futurism, particularly to Filippo Marinetti's *Uccidiamo il chiaro di luna!* (Let us kill the moonlight!) Here was a transrational synthesis with prologue by Khlebnikov, libretto by Kruchenykh, sets and costumes by Malevich, and music by Matiushin, in which a group of robotic strongmen set off to capture the sun and throw it into a sack, eager to replace its solar light with an artificial one. Sponsored by the group of avant-gardists known as the Union of Youth, *Victory over the Sun* explored new systems of language, visual representation, and musical composition which, in turn, were intended to coincide with new perceptions of space and with the new electric light (see chapter "The Year 1913").

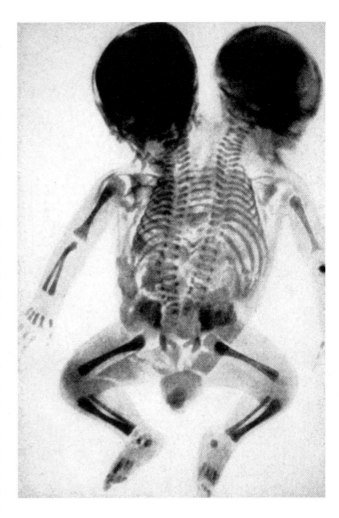

In his 1923 interpretation of the same opera for a marionette performance El Lissitzky, Malevich's student, alluded to this confrontation between the old solar energy and the new electric one: "The sun as the expression of the world's age-old energy is torn down from the sky by modern man; the power of his technological supremacy creates for itself a new source of energy."[13] Obviously, the new source of energy was electricity—which is explicit in the title which Lissitzky gave to his portfolio of designs, i.e., *Die Plastische Gestaltung der Elektro-mechanischen Schau "Sieg über die Sonne"* (Plastic Formation for the Electro-mechanical Spectacle "Victory over the Sun") [ill. 213].

Parallel to the 1913 production of *Victory over the Sun*, Malevich imbued his paintings, such as *Englishman in Moscow* (1914) [ill. 214], with similar concepts, often applying the word "eclipse" to the canvas, as if bidding farewell to the material world and to the sun that illumined it. *Englishman in Moscow*, for example, juxtaposes the words "eclipse partial" at the top right with the piercing yellow rays of an electric source at the top left—which Malevich recycles in the triangular yellow ray of his Suprematist *Dissolution of Sensation* of 1917. Perhaps, therefore, Malevich's abstract compositions in black and

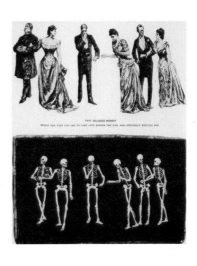

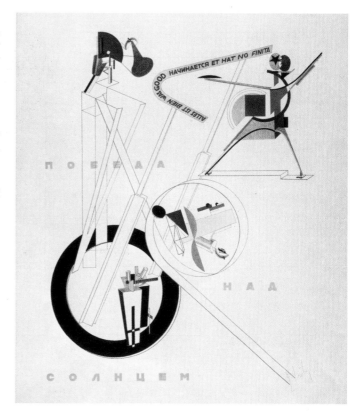

white, such as the Black Square and Black Circle [ills. 215, 216], might be read as metaphors for the positive and negative forces, the two electrical filaments identified as black (positive) and white (negative) which create the electric spark.

The diffusion of electric light left a profound and permanent imprint on the way Russian artists viewed the world and interpreted perspective, proportion, chiaroscuro, and color in their paintings. As Maiakovsky affirmed in 1914, "We see the electric street lamp more often than the old Romantic moon,"[14] and many of the avant-gardists were drawn to the energy and intensity of the electric bulb, rendering its vibrations, flashes, rays, and oscillations. In her cityscapes of the early 1910s, for example, Alexandra Exter emphasized the streetlights of Florence and Venice [ill. 217], turning these ancient cities into American metropolises. Lentulov, too, not without the influence of Sonia Delaunay and her Simultanism in Paris, expressed the fascination with electric illumination in his pictures such as the spectacular Self-Portrait (Le Grand peintre) of 1915 [ills. 218, 220].

Right:
215. *Kazimir Malevich.* Black Square,
*1915. Oil on canvas, 79.5 x 79.5 cm
(31 ¹/₄ x 31 ¹/₄ in.). State Tretiakov Gallery,
Moscow.*

Below:
216. *Kazimir Malevich.* Black Circle, *early
1920s. Oil on canvas, 105 x 105 cm
(41 ³/₈ x 41 ³/₈ in.). State Russian Museum,
St. Petersburg.*

Above:
217. *Alexandra Exter.* Florence,
*1914–15. Oil on canvas, 88 x 71 cm
(34 5/8 x 28 in.). State Russian
Museum, St. Petersburg.*

Right:
218. *Sonia Delaunay.* Electric
Prisms, *1914. Oil on canvas,
238 x 250.9 cm (93 3/4 x 98 3/4 in.),
Musée National d'Art Moderne, Centre
Georges Pompidou, Paris.*

Left:

219. *Mikhail Larionov.* Portrait of Igor
Stravinsky, *1916. Oil on canvas, 60 x 50 cm
(23 5/8 x 19 5/8 in.).*

Below:

220. *Aristarkh Lentulov.* Self-portrait
(Le grand peintre), *1915. Oil and applications
of color paper on canvas, 142 x 104.5 cm
(56 x 41 1/8 in.). State Tretiakov Gallery,
Moscow.*

Last but not least, Larionov evinced a particular interest in electric light, especially in the
interaction of light on glass surfaces—which is
evident from his painting called *Glass* of 1913, in
which tumblers and a carafe serve as instruments
of prismatic refraction, emitting rays that criss-
cross in space to form a complex of filaments,
crystalline in their rigorous geometric arrange-
ments. Larionov developed the theme in his Ray-
ist paintings [ill. 219]—prompted, no doubt, by
the repeated articulations and force lines of Italian Futurism, even though relevant works such as
Giacomo Balla's *Street Light* (1909–11) were not in
Russian collections at that time.

FLIGHT

In his 1906 poetical dedication to Mikhail Vrubel, Valerii Briusov wrote:

> *From life so false, so known,*
> *Your dream draws you*
> *Into the expanse of celestial azure*
> *Or into the depths of sapphire waters.*[15]

This heavenly aspiration may not be the primary association which Vrubel's charcoal portrait of Briusov brings to mind (one of Vrubel's very last works before the onset of blindness) [ill. 222]. But flight or escape to other worlds was the common denominator of his work and the cycle of his autobiographical demons is the story of an astral, existential voyage, the demon now at rest, now in flight, now prostrate [ill. 221].

Of course, Russian flight of the fin de siècle not only was metaphysical but also paralleled the rapid technological development of the aviation industry in general, of flying machines, and of the infrastructure which catered to the new technology, including Nikolai Zhukovsky's Aerodynamic Institute in Kuchino near Moscow (established in 1904) [ill. 223]. The gigantic hot-air balloon which riveted the attention of visitors to the Nizhnii-Novgorod Fair [ill. 225] was one of many spectacular public promotions of flying machines within the next decades. Although most airplanes flown in Russia at that time were European—at least until Igor Sikorsky, working in the aviation department of the Russian-Baltic Aeroplane Factory in

Left:
221. *Mikhail Vrubel.* Demon in Flight, *1899.*
Unfinished oil on canvas, 138.5 x 430.5 cm
(54 ½ x 169 ½ in.). State Russian Museum,
St. Petersburg.

Opposite bottom:
222. *Mikhail Vrubel.* Portrait of the Poet
Valerii Briusov, *1906. Charcoal, sanguine, and*
chalk on paper, 104.2 x 69.5 cm
(41 x 27 ³⁄₈ in.). State Tretiakov Gallery,
Moscow.

Below:
223. *Wind tunnel in the Aerodynamic Institute*
at Kuchino near Moscow, ca. 1910.

Top left:
224. Airplane designer Igor Sikorsky, early 1910s.

Top right:
225. Hot-air balloon in the Aeronautic Training Park at the "All-Russian Industrial and Art Exhibition" in Nizhnii-Novgorod, 1896.

Center:
226. Igor Sikorsky preparing for takeoff, early 1910s.

Bottom:
227. Tsar Nicholas II and Igor Sikorsky with a group of aviators next to the Russian Knight airplane, 1913.

Opposite top:
228. Poster advertising Artur Anatr's Airplane and Hydroplane Factory, Odessa, ca. 1912. 53 x 71 cm (20 7/8 x 28 in.). Russian National Library, St. Petersburg.

Opposite bottom:
229. Airplane crash, ca. 1910.

St. Petersburg, produced his heroic *Russian Knight*, *Grand*, and *Ilia Muromets* vehicles in 1913 [ills. 224, 226, 227]—Russians designed and flew airplanes, constructed wind tunnels and aerodromes [ill. 228], organized air competitions and displays, and even convinced the conservative military establishment to adopt the airplane as an engine of war.

The airplane, in particular, played a formative role in literature and the visual arts, too, connecting immediately with a long "aerial" tradition in Russian culture. For the Symbolist poets and painters, bent upon the celestial journey, the airplane was also a diabolical instrument which brought death and destruction [ill. 229], as Blok indicated in his remarkable poem "The Aviator" of 1911:

Why did you take to the sky so bold
For your first time and your last?
So that the fashionable and venal socialite
Would raise the violets of her eyes to you?[16]

Above:
230. Rocket engineer and airplane designer Konstantin Tsiolkovsky, 1910s.

Right:
231. The poet Vasilii Kamensky as a pilot, 1911.

Below:
232. Leonid Pasternak. Three Philosophers (Nikolai Fedorov, Vladimir Soloviev, Lev Tolstoi), 1903. Italian pencil on paper, 73 x 58.4 cm (28 3/4 x 23 in.). State Museum of Lev Tolstoi, Moscow.

We might contrast Blok's admonitory position to that of the succeeding generation, i.e., the Cubo-Futurists led by David Burliuk and Maiakovsky, who, in their raucous manifesto of 1912, exhorted their public to throw tradition "overboard from the Steamship of modernity," the recent tragedy of the *Titanic* notwithstanding.[17]

That physical and metaphysical flight were, to the Russian mind, tightly interconnected is demonstrated no more clearly than in the close alliance between the scientific formulation of interplanetary space travel and idealist philosophy. The father of the Soviet space program, rocket engineer and aircraft designer Konstantin Tsiolkovsky, for example, who in his Kaluga workshop first conceived of a "space elevator" or multistage rocket in the late 1890s [ill. 230], came to his bold vision not only through rigorous aeronautical deduction but also through an almost fanatical religious belief in the afterlife: supporting the eschatological ideas of the philosopher

233. *Kazimir Malevich.*
Aviator, 1914. Oil on canvas,
125 x 65 cm
(49 ¹/₄ x 25 ⁵/₈ in.). State
Russian Museum, St. Petersburg.

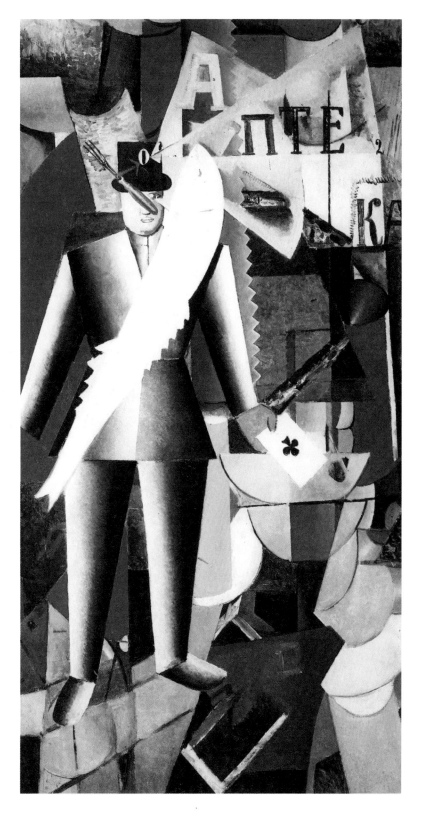

234. *Poster for the "International Exhibition of the Latest Inventions," St. Petersburg, 1909.*

Nikolai Fedorov (chief librarian at the Rumiantsev Museum in Moscow)[18] [ill. 232], Tsiolkovsky proposed that human resurrection was not only possible but also inevitable, and that this resurrection would be comprehensive and collective. In practical terms, the "Common Cause" would necessitate the mass transportation and redistribution of millions of returnees, whose astronomical number could not be accommodated by the surface of the Earth—hence the need to conquer and colonize extraterrestrial sites and hence the need for multistage rockets.

Less bizarre examples of the marriage between aeronautics and the humanities abound in the Russian Silver Age: the poet Vasilii Kamensky was also a professional pilot [ill. 231]; Malevich painted and drew compositions related to flight, e.g., the Cubist *Aviator* of 1914 [ill. 233] and the Suprematist *Airplane Flying* of 1915; while in the

1920s Petr Miturich and Tatlin, of course, designed vehicles resembling monstrous birds and hang gliders [ill. 235]. Also indicative of this close relationship between technological calculation and artistic fantasy is the poster for the 1909 "International Exhibition of the Latest Inventions" in St. Petersburg [ill. 234], touting a folksy airplane looking more like a Neo-Nationalist firebird than a functional flying machine. The Soviet Union reinforced and amplified Russia's aeronautical tradition to become one of the most advanced partners in the space race of the later twentieth century.

If in 1910 most Russians could only dream of flying in an airplane and had still not even experienced an automobile ride, used a flush toilet, or spoken by telephone in spite of marked progress in the distribution of such conveniences (by 1910 St. Petersburg had 31,099 telephone subscribers),[19] their access to metaphysical transport—to the occult journey and the astral plane—was immediate and widespread. Obviously, as in other countries, the new marvels of technology were welcomed in Russia for their convenience and efficiency, for their commercial advantage, or simply as status symbols. But the peculiar fascination with certain objects and phenomena during the Russian Silver Age might indicate deeper, more esoteric concerns which informed the aesthetic and philosophical culture of that time: electricity was accepted as a metaphor for divine light, the airplane denied the terrestrial pull, the automobile confused perspective and direction, the Gramophone communicated the voices of the dead, and the telephone overcame enormous distances. On this level, the machine, for all its hard, material presence, maintained a curious relationship with the Symbolists' wish to transcend local time and place, to enter higher dimensions, and hence to "see the light."

235. *Vladimir Tatlin's flying machine,* Letatlin, *on display at the Museum of Fine Arts (later the State Pushkin Museum of Fine Arts), Moscow, in 1932.*

THE STYLE MODERNE
RUSSIAN REFRACTIONS OF ART NOUVEAU

However erratic the predilections of the World of Art, however different the artistic modes and aesthetic standpoints of Bakst, Benois, Somov, and their colleagues, they were all aware of, if not influenced by, the vogue for Art Nouveau in France, Jugendstil in Austria and Germany, Stile Liberty in Italy, or, as the trend was known in Russia, the "Style Moderne."[1] In a wider perspective, with its organic motifs, botanical flourishes, and graphic references to the animal and vegetable world, the Style Moderne captured and symbolized the very ethos of the flowering of the Silver Age. Like a persistent liana, the Style Moderne invaded the objects of the material environment from public buildings to private homes, from ashtrays to antimacassars, from set designs to bond certificates [ills. 237–240]. As Valerian Dudakov has remarked, the Style Moderne consisted of opposites: "the grotesque and the lyrical, irony and drama, aesthetic isolation of the self and democracy."[2]

A striking example of the richness of the Style Moderne at least in architecture was Shekhtel's design for the Derozhinskaia-Zimina villa in Moscow in 1901 (now the seat of the Australian Embassy) [ills. 241–243]. Incorporating the principal elements of Art Nouveau

Opposite:
236. The teremok *(chamber) at Talashkino, ca. 1900 (photograph from the 1990s).*

Below:
237. Vladimir Egorov. Design for "The Palace of Fairies. The Cat" in Maurice Maeterlinck's play The Blue Bird *produced by Konstantin Stanislavsky at the Moscow Art Theater in 1908.*

Opposite top left:
238. *Share for 250 rubles issued by the Russian Telegraph Agency, St. Petersburg, 1910s.*

Opposite top right:
239. *Operations Hall of the Siberian Trade Bank on Nevskii Prospect, St. Petersburg, 1910s.*

Opposite bottom:
240. *Interior of the house of violinist Natalia Dulova, Moscow, ca. 1916.*

and planned according to an efficient and rational scheme, the villa was light and spacious, with large rooms and high ceilings. The accoutrements (furniture, fabrics, electric lamps, exterior ironwork), also designed by Shekhtel, integrated seamlessly with the architecture itself—the artist (to paraphrase the critic and ceramicist Petr Vaulin) had himself become part of the industrial organism.[3] The pure, undecorated surfaces of the walls, ceilings, and floor point toward Shekhtel's "proto-Constructivist" buildings such as the offices for the newspaper *Utro Rossii* (1907) with their emphasis on simplicity and efficiency, and that he was deeply concerned with the integration of inside and outside is demonstrated by his application

Above left:
241. *Fedor Shekhtel. The residence of Aleksandra Derozhinskaia-Zimina in Podkolokolnyi Lane, Moscow, 1901–02 (now the seat of the Australian Embassy).*

Above right:
242. *Fedor Shekhtel. Fireplace in the Derozhinskaia-Zimina residence, 1901–02.*

Left:
243. *Fedor Shekhtel. Interior of the Derozhinskaia-Zimina residence, 1901–02.*

Opposite top:
244. Alexandre Benois and Evgenii Lancéray, designers. Dining room for the Contemporary Art enterprise, St. Petersburg.

Opposite bottom left:
245. Ivan Fomin, designer. Sideboard for the Contemporary Art enterprise, St. Petersburg.

Opposite bottom right:
246. Ivan Fomin, designer. Fireplace in sandstone and tile with frieze designed by Vladimir Egorov for the Contemporary Art enterprise, St. Petersburg.

Right:
247. Konstantin Korovin, designer. Tea room designed for the Contemporary Art enterprise, St. Petersburg.

of the same abstract pattern to the upholstery of the chairs in the study as to the iron fence surrounding the house. The Derozhinskaia-Zimina residence was a shining example of Shekhtel's basic philosophy of architectural design:

> *Every particular premise or aggregate thereof should correspond to the purpose of the building; moreover, its interior content should be expressed and imprinted— in a very obvious manner—on both the exterior and interior appearance of the edifice.*[4]

CONTEMPORARY ART

If Shekhtel's villas for the Moscow plutocracy could be regarded as visual manifestos—and the crystallization—of his understanding of the Style Moderne, it was a collective business venture, rather than a single individual, that tried to impose the style upon a more reluctant public in St. Petersburg. This was the so-called Contemporary Art enterprise, a showroom and boutique modeled in part on the Maison Bing in Paris, which specialized in interior design [ills. 244–248]. The principal organizers and financiers were Prince

248. *Alexandre Benois and Evgenii Lancéray, designers. Dining room for the Contemporary Art enterprise, St. Petersburg. Benois's panneau* Daphnis et Chloë *can be recognized in the background.*

Sergei Shcherbatov and Baron Vladimir fon Mekk (von Meck), both close to the World of Art and contributors to its exhibitions. Like their colleagues, Shcherbatov and von Meck were tired of what Vrubel described as the "faded, colorless, philistine rooms" of St. Petersburg homes[5] and endeavored to formulate new principles of furnishing and interior design, to which end they commissioned artists to design chairs, jewelry, embroidery, etc., exhibited the results, and hoped to sell them.

In the summer of 1902 Shcherbatov and von Meck bought large premises on the Bolshaia Morskaia in St. Petersburg and, with the artistic and technical assistance of Igor Grabar and Sergei Sobin, completely restructured the inside. Many World of Art artists took part in this procedure. According to Grabar,[6] Benois and Evgenii Lancéray designed the living and dining rooms, Bakst the boudoir, Konstantin Korovin decorated the tea room with a motif of "green rye and daisies," Grabar himself designed the main entrance and the Dutch stoves, and Aleksandr Golovin transformed one room into a *terem* (highly stylized peasant room) with wood carving supervised by the young Sergei Chekhonin. In addition, plaster decorations were carried out by Artemii Ober and Aleksandr Matveev, and furniture in the Style Moderne was designed by Bakst, Ivan Fomin, and Lancéray. Carpets and fabrics were installed in the boudoir under the supervision of Natalia Davydova and Mariia Yakunchikova, and ceramic details were borrowed from Abramtsevo. According to an early advertisement, Somov was also scheduled to help with the interior design.

Needless to say, the enterprise received eager support from the World of Art group, and its magazine, *Mir iskusstva*, dedicated a special illustrated section, showing the layout of the showrooms. Diaghilev did, however, have some reservations about the undertaking, as he explained in his article "Contemporary Art":

> I really don't think there's much need for us to turn into a society of wagons-lits, but I do think that, in order to attain the goals which "Contemporary Art" has set itself, it should come nearer to life and comprehend present-day demands; only then will it become an "enterprise" and not a fantasy.[7]

Perhaps Diaghilev was right, because, unfortunately, when the permanent exhibition opened on January 26, 1903, the public and press reacted negatively. One reason for this was that the organizers, as a critic wrote, had not given adequate consideration to what the public wanted and had simply aspired to "parade their practical inapplicability."[8] This may have been true of Golovin's *terem*, but hardly of the elegant, simple boudoir designed by Bakst, or the chairs, table, and dresser by Fomin.

During its existence of only eighteen months or so, Contemporary Art presented a number of small art exhibitions. Somov, for example, had his first one-man show there; Roerich also arranged a small exhibition; and there was even an exhibition of Japanese engravings, which Bakst helped to organize. The permanent exhibition represented a number of foreign artists, including Bonnard, Denis, Lalique, Félix Vallotton, and Vuillard. Shcherbatov and von Meck also published a number of books, including the first monograph on Somov (1903) and the handsome *Staryi Peterburg 1703–1850* (Old St. Petersburg 1703–1850, 1903). Indeed, the particular attention which Contemporary Art gave to the design of art-historical literature, one of its lasting assets, can be discerned in a number of subsequent fine editions such as Vasilii Vereshchagin's several appreciations of Russian art, architecture, and book design [ill. 249].

But in spite of such artistic diversity and such grand ambitions, Contemporary Art attracted few visitors and "only one chair was sold,"[9] a failure which was attributed to various elements: Grabar's excessive outlay on the interior design, the alleged dishonesty of the accountant, the

249. *Sergei Chekhonin. Cover for Vasilii Vereshchagin,* Pamiati proshlogo *(In Memory of the past), St. Petersburg: Sirius, 1914. Vasilii Vereshchagin was a prominent art historian and bibliophile, not to be confused with the battle painter of the same name.*

inordinately high prices of the wares, von Meck's own financial collapse, and the fact that the venture had been founded on commercial patronage. Shcherbatov responded to these suppositions long after the shop had closed down, arguing that the demise of his brainchild had been due not to financial mismanagement but to the indifference of the Russian public for whom "'it's not worth it'" is the watchword and slogan of life."[10]

Shcherbatov's statement should be qualified at least in part because the St. Petersburg aristocracy and bourgeoisie were not wholly indifferent to the new applied art, as the World of Art exhibitions were indicating. In any case, other private business enterprises dealing in products for interior design managed to remain solvent—for example, Vaulin's Artistic Ceramic Manufactory in Kikerino near St. Petersburg and the Murava Ceramic Workshops in Moscow.

MARKETING MODERN

It would be misleading, however, to assume that the Style Moderne, now identified almost automatically with Russia's cultural renaissance, was promoted by all the progeny of the fin de siècle. For some artists and critics, not least Benois, the Style Moderne was capricious and contradictory. As Grigorii Sternin observes: "On the one hand, [it] aspired to decorate and design the everyday life of the individual and, on the other, called upon 'other worlds.'"[11] Blok even identified the Style Moderne with philistine taste and lack of stylistic integrity, arguing that it denoted "dilettantism, frivolity, hooliganism, absence of respect for self, for art, and for the public, i.e., it is whatever makes for an atmosphere of triteness and vulgarity."[12]

But inasmuch as the Style Moderne appealed to the nouveaux riches, to the new bourgeoisie, and even to the Church, Blok was fighting a losing battle—which a casual stroll through the streets and courtyards of St. Petersburg and Moscow confirms to this day.[13] As the demographic, industrial, and architectural boom continued in Russian cities, so the new mansion, apartment complex, factory, department store, church, and commercial center adopted and adapted the structural and decorative principles of the Style Moderne. To many this process was a galloping disease infecting walls, wrought-iron fences, roofs, doors, windows, balconies, fixtures, and gadgets [ills. 250–256]. The painter and architectural historian Georgii Lukomsky was appalled at the eclectic contagion of the Style Moderne—mixed with the historicism of the popular Style Russe (a flamboyant and highly imaginative style often copying pre-Petrine ornament)—which, he alleged, was destroying the harmony and grace of Russia's traditional architecture, especially that of St. Petersburg, now being "beautified" with "garish molding, hipped

Top left:
250. *Lev Kekushev, architect. Bay window in the residence of Petr Mindovsky on Povarskaia Street in Moscow (now the seat of the New Zealand Embassy), 1909.*

Top right:
251. *Semeon Minash, architect. Window in apartment house on Shirokaia Street, St. Petersburg, 1910.*

Center left:
252. *Aleksandr Zelenko, architect. Front door of the Kurlin residence in Samara, 1897–1900.*

Center right:
253. *Sergei Vashkov, architect. Detail of a window in a rental property belonging to the Church of the Holy Trinity (also called the Church on the Mud) on Chistoprudnyi Boulevard, Moscow, 1908–09.*

Bottom left:
254. *Mikhail Kviatkovsky, architect. Window in the Novokreshchenova residence in Samara, 1900s.*

Bottom right:
255. *Aleksandr Galetsky, architect. Exterior decoration on the Beliaev residence in Moscow, 1903–04.*

Right:
256. *Fedor Shekhtel, architect. Electrolier in the residence of Zinaida Morozova on the Spridonovska, Moscow, 1893-98.*

Below left:
257. *Aleksandr Khrenov, architect. Stained-glass window in rental property on Znamenksaia Street (now Vosstanie Street), St. Petersburg, 1902–03.*

Below right:
258. *Anonymous designer. Stained-glass window in the apartment house belonging to the Russia Insurance Corporation on Bolshaia Morskaia Street in St. Petersburg. 1905–07.*

roofs, cupolas, and statues . . . the Style Russe, the pseudo-Renaissance, Ottoman, Mauritanian styles (and any other style which comes to mind)"[14] [ill. 259].

By 1902 the Style Moderne was common currency in Russia, but, viewed within the European chronology, it arrived late, for Walter Crane, Charles Rennie Mackintosh, Arthur Heygate Mackmurdo, and Charles Ricketts had begun developing the style at least two decades before. In any case, by the mid-1890s the major English magazines promoting the new style had commenced publication (*The Studio* in 1893, *The Yellow Book* in 1894, and *The Savoy* in 1896) and by the 1880s Samuel Bing's shop, L'Art Nouveau, was thriving in Paris, while Jugendstil came to dominate Munich the following decade (*Pan* began publication in 1895, *Die Jugend* in 1896). On the other hand, in the 1900s Antoni Gaudí was working on his most radical Art Nouveau buildings, including the Church of the Sagrada Familia and the Casa Milà, while Henri Van de Velde was still gaining recognition as an Art Nouveau designer in Belgium

Left:
259. *Konstantin Rosenshtein and Andrei Belogrud, architects. House at the intersection of Bolshoi Prospect and Kamennoostrovskii Prospect (now Lev Tolstoi Square) in St. Petersburg. 1913–17.*

Below:
260. *Konstantin Golovkin and Valentin Tepfer, architects. The Golovkin summer residence in Samara, 1908–15.*

and Germany as late as 1914. Consequently, the fact that Art Nouveau developed and flourished in Russia only after 1900 is not especially reprehensible, for by 1902 its main exponents in St. Petersburg and Moscow (Bakst, Golovin, Kalmakov, Lev Kekushev, Shekhtel, and Vrubel) were creating pulsating symbioses that carried all the requisite images of swans, peacocks, thistles, and weeping willows [ill. 258].

Above:
261. *Fedor Shekhtel, architect. Stained-glass window in Stepan Riabushinsky's residence in Moscow, 1900–03.*

Below left:
262. *Hermann Obrist. Cyclamen (Whip-lash), 1895. Wall hanging in fabric. Stadtmuseum, Munich.*

Below right:
263. *Fedor Shekhtel, architect. Stepan Riabushinsky's residence on Malaia Nikitskaia Street in Moscow, 1900–03.*

If Art Nouveau was born in Western Europe, it came to rest in Russia, for St. Petersburg, Moscow, and the provincial towns were among the final destinations of its stylistic development and, as often happens with the peripheral importation of a cosmopolitan style, the Style Moderne exceeded prior limitations, becoming, on this fertile, if untried soil, even more "Art Nouveau" than it had been in Brussels, Paris, or Munich [ill. 260]. To argue, however, that the expression of Art Nouveau in Russia was peculiarly "Russian" is a fruitless task. Obviously, it developed in Russia and other countries of Eastern Europe, especially Hungary and Poland, thanks to a favorable combination of conditions, not least the presence of a sophisticated cultural community in touch with international artistic movements. Yet in the case of Russia, some of the key ideas and, of course, personalities which inspired the development in the West were missing: Russia had no Pre-Raphaelite school, no William Blake or John Flaxman, no Celtic or Gothic era to revive, and while William Morris and John Ruskin were discussing the detrimental effect of the machine on the human spirit, the great agrarian empire of Russia was still at the very threshold of an industrial revolution.

Belyi once remarked that "rhythm is the force of life, meter its denial,"[15] an intellectual division which helps to illuminate many of the cultural manifestations of his time, including the Style Moderne. At the time of writing Belyi had in mind the dialectical oppositions of rhythm and meter in poetry and, by implication, was praising the new poetry of the Symbolists such as Blok and Paul Verlaine for its centrifugal disengagement from meter and bold engagement with rhythm. But his assertion also relates to the Style Moderne, which skims the surface of things rather than fills their space, treating more

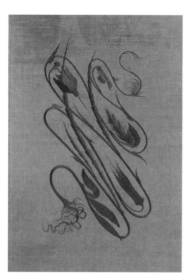

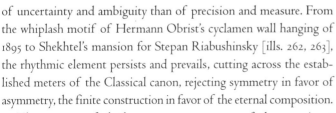

of uncertainty and ambiguity than of precision and measure. From
the whiplash motif of Hermann Obrist's cyclamen wall hanging of
1895 to Shekhtel's mansion for Stepan Riabushinsky [ills. 262, 263],
the rhythmic element persists and prevails, cutting across the established meters of the Classical canon, rejecting symmetry in favor of
asymmetry, the finite construction in favor of the eternal composition.

The concept of rhythm encompasses many of the prominent
images associated with the Russian Silver Age—the rhythm of the
underwater kingdom in the Riabushinsky villa inhabited by salamanders
amid swirling waves (a paraphrase of Victor Horta's Tassel residence
in Brussels of 1892–93) [ills. 264–266] and the swaying movements of
Isadora Duncan's Moscow dances in 1905 captured perhaps in the
organic flourish of a stained-glass window in the Riabushinsky villa
[ill. 261], Scriabin's and Stravinsky's bold disharmonies, and the
equine waves of Vrubel's *Thirty-Three Bogatyrs* of 1904 (as scintillating
as Walter Crane's *Horses of Neptune*) [ills. 267, 268]. But if often dramatic and disturbing, the Style Moderne surrendered itself to a luxury of ornament which often overwhelmed the ultimate purpose and
application of the object: Golovin's Gaudiesque chamber for the

Contemporary Art enterprise bears clear witness to the "uselessness" of the rhythmical flourishes of Art Nouveau.

A surface art, the Style Moderne indulged its decorative excesses in "redundant" areas such as the façade, the *panneau* (wall painting), the *vitrage* (stained-glass window) [ill. 257], which were often alien to structural utility or commercial destination and sometimes even interfered with the basic function of a building. Shekhtel's flowers on the facades and waterweed on the submarine ceiling of the Riabushinsky villa, Vaulin's sunflowers spreading over the surface of an apartment building, the spiders and butterflies that grace balconies and gates [see ill. 241], the flora and fauna that ornament facades and doorframes, even the Korovin and Vrubel themes on William Walcot's Metropole Hotel in Moscow [ills. 269, 270]—these applications have little, if anything, to do with the ultimate purpose of the building in question. In this respect, the Style Moderne

Right:
269. *Mikhail Vrubel. Majolica decoration on the facade of the Metropole Hotel in Moscow, 1896–1906.*

Below:
270. *William Walcot, architect. Metropole Hotel in Moscow, 1898–1906.*

was at odds with the European and Russian decorative revival of the 1860s–80s, which tended to justify and explain ornament in rational, ethnographical terms—as is clear from Owen Jones's *Grammar of Ornament* (1856) with its emphasis on Eastern ornament, Christopher Dresser's *Unity in Variety* (1859), or Vladimir Stasov's *Slavianskii i vostochnyi ornament* (Slavic and eastern ornament, 1887) [ill. 275].

Like some vast stretch of water, the facade, the *panneau*, and the theatrical backdrop offered untested spaces for artistic investigation, extending the rhythm from exterior to interior. Borisov-Musatov's pools and fountains [ill. 271] reverberate through the curves and undulations of foliage, lace, and female forms, while Kuznetsov's and Petr Utkin's designs for Yakov Zhukovsky's estate at Kuchuk-Koi in the Crimea [ills. 272, 273] often resemble ganglia of sea plants swaying in the currents of unpredictable tides, gazed upon by unknown ichthyological species. Like water, the mirror, the smalt tile, the enamel, the chandelier, lacquered furniture, and accessories in precious metals, the *vitrage* was yet another shimmering surface. *Vitrages* were used to divide rooms, replace outside walls, grace mantelpieces, advertise wares, and attract customers to store windows. Incorporating the standard motifs of exotic plants such as the tulips on the staircase for Lev Kekushev's Mindovsky residence in Moscow (1903–04) or a mythological scene such as Vrubel's Arthurian motif for Morozova's villa, the vitrage could assume vast or miniature proportions, occupying entire landings in rental blocks or serving as a partition between service areas [ill. 274].

DOMESTIC OR FOREIGN

The facades and frescoes of Russian buildings often extended the rhythm of their composition into the internal space via murals, screens, iconostases, *panneaux*, and tapestries. The main house at Talashkino, designed by Maliutin, and its church (1903), designed

by Princess Tenisheva, with its exterior and interior decoration supervised by Roerich [ill. 276–280, 282, 283, see also 236], constitute a compelling example of this total integration, but they are not an isolated case. The interior space of numerous Art Nouveau churches constructed in Russia between about 1900 and 1914 remains one of the richest and most rewarding avenues of research in the history of the pre-Revolutionary Russian applied arts. Once again, Russia was sharing a Western practice, because the application of Art Nouveau to ecclesiastical buildings in Europe was certainly not exceptional— from England (the Church of St. Mary the Virgin at Great Warley by William Reynolds Stephens in 1904) to Spain (Gaudí's Church of the Sagrada Familia).

To comment on foreign influences on the Russian Style Moderne is difficult, not because of any lack of visual and theoretical communication between Russia and the West, but rather because of the sporadic and selective ways in which this communication was maintained via the press, exhibitions, study tours, or personal preferences. The World of Art group, for example, manifested a strong interest in the British heritage, particularly in the journal, making frequent reference to Beardsley and running obituaries on Edward Burne-Jones, Ruskin, and Oscar Wilde, as well as advertisements for Russian translations of Ruskin's books *Art and Reality* and *Lectures about Art*. *Mir iskusstva* carried reproductions of furniture and accessories by Mackintosh, Joseph Simpson, and other Arts and Crafts members, a visual source that left a deep imprint on the young generation of Russian designers such as Korovin and Fomin—some of whose contributions to the Contemporary Art enterprise and "Exhibition of Architecture and Industrial Design in the 'New Style'" bear an uncanny resemblance to the forms and motifs of their British colleagues. Perhaps the most influential British import, however, was

Above:
282. *Princess Mariia Tenisheva. Maquette for The Church at Talashkino, near Smolensk (built 1903–07). Princess Tenisheva, aided by Nicholas Roerich, produced several maquettes for her Church at Talashkino. The dome of the actual church, consecrated in 1903, was decorated by the Fabergé Workshops, the interior by Roerich.*

Right:
283. *The Church at Talashkino showing the exterior mosaic by Nicholas Roerich, 1903–07 (see ill. 135).*

Opposite bottom left:
284. *Aubrey Beardsley. Illustration for Oscar Wilde's play* Salomé, *first published in Paris in 1893 and in London in 1894. The Russian reaction to Beardsley's bold and provocative black-and-white illustrations for* Salomé *was deep, if delayed, affecting the second generation of Moscow and St. Petersburg Symbolists in particular. Léon Bakst and Konstantin Somov, for example, were certainly aware of Beardsley's graphic suite, but a stronger resonance can be felt in the work of Nikolai Kalmakov, who was responsible for the spicy costumes and sets for the 1908 production of* Salomé *(see ill. 484) and for the rich illustrations to* Princess Lera *(see ill. 314).*

the art of Beardsley, eulogized and copied in numerous publications—and Moscow even boasted its own Beardsley, Nikolai Feofilaktov, whose ample nudes and saucy cupids Briusov, as editor, reproduced in the review *Vesy*[16] [ills. 285, 286], while Beardsley's illustrations for Wilde's *Salomé* left an indelible impression on many Russian playwrights and scenographers [ill. 284]. Russian artists also acknowledged the graphic mastery of the Continental illustrators such as Otto Eckmann, Max Klinger, and Vallotton and looked carefully at the work of Julius Dietz, Thomas Theodor Heine, and other artists of Der Simplicissimus.

If Great Britain was accepted as the philosophical founder of the new movement and its chief practitioner in specific areas such as book and furniture design, France, with her more enticing interpretations of Art Nouveau, was recognized as the purveyor of luxury goods for the wealthy home such as lamps by Emile Gallé

Above right:
285. Nikolai Feofilaktov. Design for a special issue of the journal Vesy *(Scales) dedicated to the work of Aubrey Beardsley, 1905.*

Right:
286. Nikolai Feofilaktov. Idol, 1905.

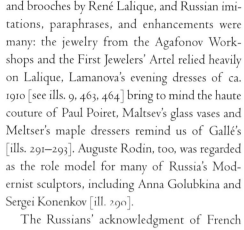

and brooches by René Lalique, and Russian imitations, paraphrases, and enhancements were many: the jewelry from the Agafonov Workshops and the First Jewelers' Artel relied heavily on Lalique, Lamanova's evening dresses of ca. 1910 [see ills. 9, 463, 464] bring to mind the haute couture of Paul Poiret, Maltsev's glass vases and Meltser's maple dressers remind us of Gallé's [ills. 291–293]. Auguste Rodin, too, was regarded as the role model for many of Russia's Modernist sculptors, including Anna Golubkina and Sergei Konenkov [ill. 290].

The Russians' acknowledgment of French Post-Impressionist and Symbolist painting and sculpture was enhanced by a parallel interest in Japan and japonaiserie, and in this, once again, the Russians were following, rather than guiding, a Western fashion. True, Russia had no Félix Bracquemond or James McNeill Whistler (even though he had spent his childhood in St. Petersburg) and, generally speaking, there was a broader public sympathy for Siam and China than for Japan, as the Russo-Japanese War of 1904–05 demonstrated so clearly. Even so, Russian artists and critics, especially those of the World of Art, cultivated an interest in the Japanese graphic arts, reproduced them in their magazines, included them in their exhibitions, and published a number of scholarly articles on the subject. Bakst, for example, collected Japanese colored engravings, including Hokusai. Ivan Bilibin, too, made a diligent study of Hokusai, expressed in his combination of Japanese and Slavic ornaments in his illustrations for the episode of the Thirty-Three Knights in the 1907 edition of *The Tale of Tsar Saltan* [ill. 289].

Scandinavian culture also exerted a formative influence on the early development of the Russian Style Moderne, owing in part to Diaghilev's "Exhibition of Scandinavian Artists" in St. Petersburg in 1897 and the "Exhibition of Russian and Finnish Artists" the following year, both of which showed modern Russian and Finnish painters in tandem. A similar artistic confrontation between Russia and Scandinavia took place at the 1900 "Exposition Universelle" in Paris, where the Russian and Finnish pavilions, for example, were remarked upon for their common styles and aesthetic concerns, and Golovin's and Korovin's installations in the Style Russe, looking like boyars' chambers and accommodating artifacts from Abramtsevo

and Talashkino, carried the same organic, folkloric exuberance as Eliel Saarinen's and Akseli Gallen-Kallela's designs for the Finnish representation [ills. 287, 288]. It is perhaps for this reason that the Art Nouveau stoves with their swirling plant motifs produced by the Finnish factory of Aabo & Co. enjoyed such a phenomenal success in St. Petersburg homes.[17]

Whether exemplified by a mantelpiece clock, an Ericsson telephone produced in St. Petersburg, or a mushroom pen cleaner, it is clear that the Style Moderne developed in a highly eclectic and diversified way, assimilating both indigenous and foreign elements. There are many instances of the marriage between East and West, such as the silver *kovsh* (traditional Russian ladle), manufactured in

Opposite top:
287. Aleksandr Golovin and Konstantin Korovin, designers. Russian pavilion at the "Exposition Universelle," Paris, 1900.

Opposite bottom:
288. Eliel Saarinen, architect. Finnish pavilion at the "Exposition Universelle," Paris, 1900.

Above:
289. Ivan Bilibin. Thirty-Three Knights. Illustration to Alexander Pushkin's fairy tale The Tale of Tsar Saltan, 1905. Watercolor and Indian ink on paper, 10 x 27.5 cm (4 x 10 7/8 in.). State Russian Museum, St. Petersburg. The book was published by the prestigious Department for the Preparation of State Papers, St. Petersburg, in 1907.

Left:
290. Anna Golubkina. Portrait of the Writer Andrei Belyi, 1907. Bronze, height 42 cm (16.5 in). State Russian Museum, St. Petersburg.

Opposite:
291. *Sideboard in the Style Russe, or Neo-Russian style, after a design by Sergei Maliutin, 1900. Talashkino. Carved wood and brass. State Hermitage, St. Petersburg.*

Top left:
292. *The "Iris" Vase, 1900s. Imperial Glass Factory. State Hermitage, St. Petersburg.*

Top right:
293. *The "Poppy" Vase, 1900s. Kuznetsov Corporation, Tver. Faience, color glaze. State Hermitage, St. Petersburg.*

Above:
294. *Aleksandr Golovin. Platter with Firebird motif produced at Petr Vaulin's Artistic Ceramic Manufactory in Kikerino near St. Petersburg, 1896–99. Majolica. State Hermitage, St. Petersburg.*

Center right:
295. *Fountain in the form of the head of Bacchus, 1903. Ceramic atelier of the Stroganov Institute, Moscow. Majolica. State Hermitage, St. Petersburg.*

Bottom left:
296. *Mikhail Vrubel. Spes, vase, early 1890s. Abramtsevo Ceramic Factory, Moscow. Majolica, height 49 cm (19 1/4 in.). Abramtsevo Museum and Reserve.*

Bottom right:
297. *Mikhail Vrubel. The Poet, vase, early 1890s. Abramtsevo Ceramic Factory, Moscow. Majolica, height 52.5 cm (20 5/8 in.). Abramtsevo Museum and Reserve.*

1910, which sports the head of a *bogatyr*, or medieval Russian heroic warrior, with its body ornamented in a typical Art Nouveau scrolling vine motif [ill. 299]. On the other hand, many items of middle-class consumption—ice buckets, family magazines, phonograph record labels, hand mirrors, belt buckles, door handles, restaurant menus, and bathroom accessories—sold at department stores (such as Miur and Meriliz in Moscow [ill. 302]) borrow wholly from Western models, even if manufactured in St. Petersburg, Moscow, Saratov, Yalta, or Kiev [ills. 298, 300, 301].

Above left:
298. Price list for items produced at the Einem Sweet and Biscuit Factory, Moscow, 1906.

Above right:
299. Kovsh (bowl), Moscow, ca. 1910. Silver, length 35.5 cm (14 in.). The prow bears the head of a bogatyr, or medieval Russian warrior.

Below:
300. Menu for the Hermitage Corporation Restaurant, Moscow, dated 11 September 1904.

Opposite bottom right:
*301. Anatolii Gunst. Bathroom in Nina
Konshina's residence, Moscow, ca. 1910.*

Above:
*302. Roman Klein, architect. Miur and Meriliz
Department Store in Moscow, 1906–08. Today this
is the premises of TsUM (Central Universal Store).*

Above:
303. Fedor Shekhtel, designer. The Central (foreground) and Mining Pavilions for the Russian Section of the "International Exhibition" in Glasgow, 1901.

Opposite top:
304. Electric lamp, 1910s.

Opposite bottom left:
305. Armchair with carved lyre back and single elbow rest. State Hermitage, St. Petersburg.

Opposite bottom center:
306. Ivan Fomin, designer. Office armchair, 1910s. State Hermitage, St. Petersburg.

Opposite bottom right:
307. Singer sewing machine poster, ca. 1910.

It would be wrong to assume, however, that the industrial multiplication of objects bearing Art Nouveau motifs represented the same aspiration toward synthesis that can be associated with Talashkino or with Shekhtel's pavilions for the "International Exhibition" in Glasgow in 1901 [ill. 303]. That the same elongated plant forms and maiden's tresses can be found on a mass-produced belt buckle, a lamp with imitation precious stones [ill. 304], or a copper clock stand of ca. 1910 does not mean that the respective owners professed a deep faith in the virtues of artistic synthesism. Obeisant to the pressures of social convention, they ordered what was fashionable from their mail-order catalogues, but whether or not the Russian bourgeois consumer gave credence to deeper philosophical meanings, these trade directories were clear evidence of the rapid diffusion of the Style Moderne. The respectable St. Petersburg or Moscow family could now surround itself with a stylistic constant in which, like some gigantic fresco, a uniform, ornamental rhythm extended from one element to the next: wallpaper, tables and chairs, telephones, sewing machines, clocks, lamps, cutlery, tea-glass holders, tea caddies, sweetmeat baskets, picture frames, cushions, drapes, kitchen scales, gas stoves—the most innocuous appurtenance was now affected by the linear abandon of the Style Moderne [ills. 305–312].

However tempting such bagatelles, their buyers were limited, coming from the still tiny percentage of Russian society which in 1910 was literate, cultivated, and solvent. The exhibitions, the conferences, the publications, and the commercial outlets were intended for a discrete clientele (one of the key journals of the Silver Age was actually called *Moi zhurnal dlia nemnogikh* (My journal for the few)—in the same way that the collection of esoteric poetry or folio of erotic drawings was intended only for the connoisseur. Similarly, the actual manufacture and promotion of the Style Moderne lay in the hands of the privileged few who held the monopoly on construction materials, publishing houses, advertising services, and often the very commissions which brought projects to fruition—including Shekhtel's buildings and the lavish Symbolist editions. The Abramtsevo Ceramic Factory, founded by Mamontov at Abramtsevo in 1889 and then transferred to Moscow in 1896, also welcomed special, customized orders, commissioning artists such as Golovin, Kuznetsov, Matveev, and Vrubel to fulfill them. Supervised by Vaulin, the Moscow factory produced some of the most experimental pottery in the Art Nouveau style and fulfilled many prestigious commissions, such as the details for the Yaroslavl Station. Vrubel, the most original of the Abramtsevo ceramicists, tended to use his vases and tiles as settings for literary or mythological narratives: the *Angel* plaque for Kuchuk-Koi, the *Mikula Selianinovich and Volga* fireplace surround, the prince pulling a mermaid out of the water in the form of a bowl, and the platter of amorous couples. He often borrowed his motifs from the Neo-Nationalist lexicon. Vrubel also conducted bold experiments in the actual manufacture of ceramics, especially in the glazing processes. The particular iridescence which he attained in works such as the Spes vase (1899) [ill. 296] and the *Poet* vase (ca. 1900) [ill. 297]

Top left:
308. Eduard Bolin, designer. Cutlery set, St Petersburg, 1908–17. Silver.

Top right:
309. Mikhail and Semeon Grachev, designers. Traveling cutlery set, St. Petersburg, 1899–1908. Silver.

Bottom left:
310. Henrik (Heinrich) Wigström, designer. Translucent buckle, ca. 1910, Fabergé Workshops. St. Petersburg. Silver, gold, and enamel, length 7 cm (2 3/4 in.).

Bottom right:
311. Anonymous designer. Buckle, ca. 1900. Fabergé Workshops, Moscow. Silver, enamel, and nephrite, width 7 cm (2 3/4 in).

Opposite bottom left:
312. Nikolai Zverev and a second maker, designers. Two tea-glass holders and two tea-spoons, Moscow, ca. 1900. Silver and enamel, heights 9.8 and 8.9 cm (3 7/8 in. and 3 1/2 in.).

Opposite top:
313. Aleksandr Golovin. Set design for Act IV (Donna Anna's Chamber) of Alexander Pushkin's The Stone Guest with music by Aleksandr Dargomyzhsky, produced by Vsevolod Meierkhold at the Mariinsky Theater, Petrograd, 1917. Tempera on plywood, 77.5 x 112.5 cm (30 1/2 x 44 1/4 in.).

and his choice of greens, purples, and carmines left a deep imprint on an entire generation of Russian artists such as the Murava community, the studios of the Stieglitz and Stroganov Institutes, and Vaulin's Ceramic Manufactory near St. Petersburg [ills. 294, 295].

The Style Moderne reached its zenith in the first decade of the twentieth century, when the shining examples of its architecture, painting, and applied arts were produced. Certainly, it continued through the 1910s and into the 1920s, but the brilliance and originality of its initial accomplishments (e.g., Shekhtel's villa for Riabushinsky) yielded to the plainer and more canonical industrial items produced en masse for the broader market. There were, of course, striking exceptions such as Kalmakov's extravagant illustrations in silver, green, and red for Nikolai Kronidov's private edition of the fairy tale *Princess Lera* in 1912 [ill. 314] and Golovin's sets and costumes for Meierkhold's production of *The Stone Guest* at the Mariinsky Theater, Petrograd, in 1917 [ill. 313]. But by then the Style Moderne had lost ground to the competing styles of the avant-garde and the new Neo-Classicism, and its rhetorical forms and excessive ornaments seemed

strangely out of place in a society now plagued by the deficits of war and revolution. Finally, after 1910 a central part of the infrastructure which had protected and promoted the Style Moderne, i.e., the Symbolist societies, magazines, and exhibitions, had terminated or shifted allegiances. Chief among the propagators of the Style Moderne had been the World of Art group.

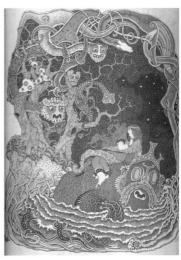

Above:

314. Nikolai Kalmakov. Illustration for Nikolai Kronidov's fairy tale Princess Lera. *St. Petersburg: Kronidov, 1911. Evidence suggests that "Nikolai Kronidov" was the pseudonym of Nikolai Kalmakov, i.e., that Kalmakov was both author and illustrator of this book.*

THE WORLD OF ART
Sergei Diaghilev and His Circle

"In art we are now living through all ages and all nations; the art of the past races before us. This is because we are standing before a grand future."[1] That is how Belyi described the cultural spectrum of the Russian fin de siècle. Colleague of Benois and Diaghilev and sitter for Bakst and Somov, Belyi was well aware of the eclecticism of his age, of its extraordinary diapason of ideas and disciplines, even if, paradoxically, a strong aspiration of the Russian Silver Age was to restore aesthetic unity to the disparate disciplines. To this end, poets and painters sought a common philosophical and formal denominator, often exploring more than one medium simultaneously.[2]

In keeping with this "interdisciplinarity" is the fact that the principal artistic and intellectual society with which many of the Symbolist writers and artists were associated was the St. Petersburg group known as the World of Art (*Mir iskusstva*)[3] [ill. 321], which, to some extent, may be regarded as Russia's counterpart to the various European secessions of the same period, especially the Munich Simplicissimus. Certainly, the World of Art was not the only cultural organization of the Silver Age which encouraged change in the established codes of aesthetic consensus—mention might also be made of the Union of Russian Artists, the Moscow Association of Artists, and the Moscow Salon[4]—but it was the most resolute and the most influential.

Hostile toward both the Academy and nineteenth-century Realism, the World of Art owed its singular vision, practical organization, and public success largely to Diaghilev, who in November 1898 launched the celebrated magazine of the same name (*Mir iskusstva*, St. Petersburg, 1898–1904 [ills. 316–320]), sponsored a cycle of important national and international art exhibitions (1899–1906), and, with great aplomb, propagated Russian art and music in the West [ill. 315]. The World of Art artists and writers never issued a written manifesto, but their attention to artistic craft, cult of retrospective beauty, and assumed distance from the ills of sociopolitical reality indicated a firm belief in "art for art's sake" and in a sense of measured grace which they identified in particular with the haunting beauty of St. Petersburg.

A cosmopolitan at home in St. Petersburg, Paris, Venice, and London and in touch with the social, literary, and artistic luminaries of his time, Diaghilev emphasized the need for a distinctive nationalism in Russian art, one which would compensate for the apparent anonymity of the nineteenth century—which is one reason why he gave

315. From left to right: Igor Stravinsky, Ruzhena Khvoshchinskaia, Sergei Diaghilev, and Léon Bakst, in Lausanne, 1915. Neutral territory during World War I, Lausanne was a favorite retreat for Diaghilev and other associates of the Ballets Russes. Diaghilev and Stravinsky found momentary respite from the tensions of the ballet company, while the hypochondriac Bakst took the cures. Even so, a number of important projects were also elaborated in Lausanne, including Goncharova's designs for Liturgie *and Larionov's for* Le Soleil de Nuit *and* Chout. *Khvoshchinskaia, often erroneously referred to as Mme. Kvochinsky and sometimes misidentified as Tamara Karsavina, was the wife of an attaché at the Russian Embassy in Rome.*

Opposite:
316. Mariia Yakunchikova. Study for the cover of the magazine Mir iskusstva *(World of Art), St. Petersburg, 1898. Watercolor, gouache, and bronze paint on paper, 35 x 28 cm (13³/₄ x 11 in.).*

Top:
317. Mariia Yakunchikova. Cover of the magazine Mir iskusstva *(World of Art), St. Petersburg, Vol. 1, 1898.*

Center:
318. Elena Polenova. Headpiece for article on Elena Polenova by N. Borok (= Natalia Davydova) in Mir iskusstva *(World of Art), St. Petersburg, November 1899, no. 18–19, p. 97.*

Bottom left:
319. Konstantin Somov. Cover for the journal Mir iskusstva *(World of Art), St. Petersburg, November 1900, no. 21–22.*

Bottom right:
320. Léon Bakst. Cover for the journal Mir iskusstva *(World of Art), St. Petersburg, November 1902, no. 3.*

321. Boris Kustodiev. Group Portrait of the Artists of the World of Art Society,
*1920. Oil on canvas, 52 x 89 cm (20 ¹/₂ x 35 in.). State Russian Museum, St. Petersburg.
From left to right: Igor Grabar, Nikolas Roerich, Evgenii Lancéray, Ivan Bilibin, Alexandre
Benois, Georgii Narbut, Nikolai Milioti, Konstantin Somov, Mstislav Dobuzhinsky,
Kuzma Petrov-Vodkin, Anna Ostroumova-Lebedeva, and Boris Kustodiev.*

particular, even disproportionate, attention to the Neo-Nationalist artists in exhibitions and publications, especially to Korovin, Maliutin, Roerich, Vasnetsov, and Vrubel [ills. 322–324, 327, 328]. In their evocations of Ancient Russia, Diaghilev recognized a move to liberate Russian painting from the rigid conventions of didactic Realism on the one hand, and from the Imperial Academy of Arts on the other. Such artists belonged to the first wave of Russia's decorative revival, accommodated within the Neo-Russian or Neo-Nationalist school and nurtured at the artistic retreats of Abramtsevo [ills. 325, 326] and Talashkino, which provided a vital stimulus to the later, more celebrated designs by Bakst, Benois, and Roerich for the Ballets Russes.

The World of Art group and its eponymous magazine embraced a multiplicity of artistic phenomena—the demonic art of Vrubel and the stylizations of the early Kandinsky, the graphics of Beardsley and the German Simplicissimus group, the Art Nouveau designs of Mackintosh and the poetry of Konstantin Balmont, the exoticism

Opposite top:
322. Konstantin Korovin. Northern Idyll, 1886. Oil on canvas, 113 x 153 cm (44 1/2 x 60 1/4 in.). State Tretiakov Gallery, Moscow.

Opposite bottom:
323. Viktor Vasnetsov. Flying Carpet, 1880. Oil on canvas, 165 x 297 cm (65 x 117 in.). Nizhnii-Novgorod State Museum of Art.

Below:
324. Nikolas Roerich. Idols, 1901. Gouache on cardboard, 49 x 58 cm (19 1/4 x 22 7/8 in.). State Russian Museum, St. Petersburg.

Right:
325. Interior view of a wooden teremok *(chamber) at Abramtsevo.*

Below left:
326. Ivan Ropet (pseudonym of Ivan Petrov). Tiled ceramic stove for a teremok *(chamber), 1892. The central panel shows Sirin, a bird which traditionally predicts misfortune.*

Below right:
327. Sergei Maliutin, designer. Interior of the Pertsov House in Moscow, 1905–07.

Opposite top:
328. Sergei Maliutin. Illustration for a deluxe edition of Alexander Pushkin's poem Ruslan i Liudmila. *Moscow: Mamontov, 1899, p. 32.*

of Bakst and the necromancy of Somov [ills. 329–331]. Although not a painter, Diaghilev was a perceptive critic and an indefatigable organizer, and it was thanks mainly to his efforts that the group's magazine won the financial support of Mamontov (the owner of Abramtsevo) and Princess Mariia Tenisheva (the owner of Talashkino) and that the first cycle of "World of Art" exhibitions took place [see ills. 281, 482]. These two enterprises fulfilled the double function of propagating Russian art at home and abroad and of

presenting the first comprehensive surveys of modern Western art to the Russian public.

The founding members, Bakst, Benois, Diaghilev, Serov, and Somov, not to mention later arrivals such as Bilibin, Dobuzhinsky, Lancéray, Anna Ostroumova-Lebedeva, and Roerich, shared, above all, the desire to recapture that formal discipline lost, allegedly, with

Below:
329. Vasilii Kandinsky. Motley Life, 1907.
Tempera on canvas, 130 x 162.5 cm
(51 ¹/₈ x 64 in.). Städtische Galerie,
Lenbachhaus, Munich.

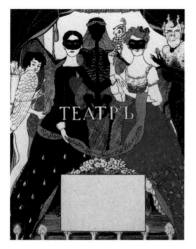

the technical laxity of Russia's late-nineteenth-century Realist painters known as the Wanderers.[5] Thus we find that some of the greatest achievements of the World of Art painters are to be seen in art forms which dictate intensive concentration on line and, in general, require extraordinary concentration and finesse—the miniature, the embroidery, the silhouette, the book illustration, and the diminutive watercolor and pastel [ills. 332–334, 340]. This is not to say, of course, that the *miriskusniki* (World of Art artists) neglected other areas of painting: Somov produced some remarkable portraits of his contemporaries, such as Blok and Dobuzhinsky, as did Bakst (e.g., of his wife, Liubov Gritsenko, Belyi, and Zinaida Gippius), and most members were fine landscapists [ills. 335–339, 350].

The *World of Art* represented a catholic mix of styles and attitudes. It was, as Benois himself admitted, "not this, that, or the other in isolation, but everything together."[6] According to Dmitrii Filosofov, Diaghilev's cousin and literary factotum of the magazine, the *World of Art*, therefore, examined "everything": "Gainsborough and Beardsley,

Above left:

332. Alexandre Benois. Azbuka v kartinakh (ABC in pictures), 1904. The letter "A"—"Arap" (Blackamoor). Benois's charming ABC book was published by the Department for the Preparation of State Papers, St. Petersburg, in 1905.

Above right:

333. Alexandre Benois. Azbuka v kartinakh (ABC in pictures), 1904. The letter "T"—"Theater."

Right:

334. Vera Vulf. Winter Twilight, 1913. Appliqué on fabric, 77 x 62 cm (30 3/8 x 24 1/2 in.).

Above left:
335. Konstantin Somov. Portrait of the
Artist Mstislav Dobuzhinsky, 1910. *Pencil
and sanguine on paper, 44.5 x 31 cm
(17 ¹/₂ x 12 ¹/₄ in.). State Tretiakov Gallery,
Moscow.*

Above right:
336. Léon Bakst. Portrait of Andrei Belyi,
1906. *Paper, color pencil, chalk.*

Levitsky and Briullov, Velázquez and Manet, German woodcuts of
the sixteenth century and Goya's prints, steel engravings and lithographs of 1830, Orlovsky's sketches and those of Daumier."[7] True,
this emphasis on the eighteenth century was only one stratum in the
historical digest of the World of Art publications and exhibitions, a
primary hope being to create a new artistic code through the recognition and rediscovery of bygone cultures in general.

Diaghilev, for example, identified the apogees of civilization as
"Egypt, Greece, and the Middle Ages," and the gods of his age as
"Giotto, Shakespeare, and Bach."[8] Bakst was passionate about
Greece, Egypt, and the Orient,[9] Benois and Somov were drawn to
the epoch of Versailles, Aleksandr Golovin looked to the traditions of Spain, while Dobuzhinsky, Lancéray, and Ostroumova-
Lebedeva were captured by the charm of eighteenth- and nineteenth-
century St. Petersburg [ills. 341–343, see also 425]. In any case, the
retrospective tendency of the World of Art was not confined to
the praise of canonical legacies such as the culture of Classical
Greece. A profound interest in popular myth and in the primordial
state of man also occupied artists like Roerich and Vrubel whose
paintings such as *The Kiss to the Earth* (1912) [ill. 344] and *Demon Cast
Down* [see ill. 6], respectively, were regarded as embodiments of an
archaic and cohesive strength lacking in the disrupted society of
pre-Revolutionary Russia.

Opposite bottom:
337. Konstantin Somov. Portrait of the
Poet Aleksandr Blok, 1907. Crayons and
gouache on paper, 38 x 30 cm
(15 x 11 3/4 in.). State Tretiakov Gallery,
Moscow.

Above:
338. Léon Bakst. Portrait of a Princess,
1899–1901. Oil on canvas, 89 x 68 cm
(35 x 26 3/4 in.).

Right:
339. Léon Bakst. Portrait of Zinaida
Gippius. 1906. Pencil, chalk, and sanguine on
paper on cardboard, 54 x 44 cm
(21 1/4 x 17 3/8 in.). State Tretiakov Gallery,
Moscow.

Above:
340. Elizaveta Kruglikova. Portrait of Léon
Bakst, *1914. Silhouette, 10.2 x 7.4 cm
(4 x 3 in.). State Russian Museum,
St. Petersburg.*

Right:
341. Léon Bakst. Décor for the ballet L'Après-
midi d'un faune, *1912. Gouache on paper,
75 x 105 cm (29 ¹/₂ x 41 ³/₈ in.), Musée
National d'Art Moderne, Centre Georges
Pompidou, Paris, France.*

Not without a measure of desperation, Diaghilev and his col-leagues were looking to past epochs for a corroborative cultural flowering that could be studied and perhaps emulated, among them the late seventeenth and eighteenth centuries. Two of Diaghilev's ear-ly triumphs—his deluxe catalogue raisonné of Dmitrii Levitsky's portraits[10] and his supervision of the "Historical and Artistic Exhi-bition of Russian Portraits" at the Tauride Palace in St. Petersburg in 1905 [ill. 345]—are primary examples of what at once was an undis-guised nostalgia for Russia's Imperial glory and, at the same time, an awareness that such glory was fast fading. Diaghilev said as much in his celebrated speech, entitled "At the Hour of Reckoning," which he delivered after the opening of the exhibition:

Above:
344. Nicholas Roerich. Kiss to the Earth
(also called Adoration of the Earth*), study.*
Second version of the decor for Igor Stravinsky's
ballet Le Sacre du printemps, *1912. Tempera on*
cardboard, 62 × 94 cm (24 ¹/₂ × 37 in.). State
Russian Museum, St. Petersburg.

Below:
345. Evgenii Lancéray. Poster for the "Historical
and Artistic Exhibition of Russian Portraits,"
St. Petersburg. 1905.

Do you not feel that the long gallery of portraits of
people great and small . . . is but a grand and
convincing reckoning of a brilliant, but, alas,
mortified, period of our history? . . . We are witnesses to
a great historical moment of reckoning and ending in the
name of a new, unknown culture.[11]

The social and cultural effect of the exhibition was profound:[12] for the first time the public at large sensed the "great skill of Levitsky, the extraordinary gift of Rokotov, the charm of Borovikovsky, and the mastery of Kiprensky and Briullov."[13] The exhibition prompted Konstantin Stanislavsky to transfer the historical setting of his production of Gerhart Hauptmann's *Schluck und Jau* at the Moscow Art Theater from the Middle Ages to the eighteenth century; and it corroborated Serov's interest in the imperious salon portrait of such subjects as Nicholas II at the moment of his coronation, Prince Felix Yusupov, and Princess Olga Orlova [ills. 346–348]. Open during the tragic events of the Revolution of 1905, the Tauride Palace exhibition was a visual metaphor for the brilliant majesty of an era long passed, one that "exuded the might and power of land ownership and the full-dress uniform."[14]

Arguing that the nineteenth century had lacked technical prowess
and ignored formal beauty, Diaghilev professed the urgent need to
recapture the mastery and artisanship of the Russian eighteenth century. To the World of Art artists, painting, sculpture, and the
applied arts required reasoned imagination and technical control,
salient features which they identified, in turn, with the high artistic
culture of Russia's eighteenth century. Finally, the World of Art
accused the nineteenth century of "vandalizing" much of Catherine's cultural legacy by changing, demolishing, or simply neglecting
architectural monuments such as the Mikhailovskii Palace in St.
Petersburg;[15] and Diaghilev himself was quick to criticize the newly
established Museum of Alexander III in St. Petersburg (now the
State Russian Museum) for focusing on the Realist painters at the
expense of eighteenth-century Russian portraiture.

Such vociferousness encouraged a veritable campaign to promote
and save Russia's eighteenth-century heritage in the specialist journals *Khudozhestvennye sokrovishcha Rossii* (Art Treasures of Russia, St.
Petersburg, 1901–03) and *Starye gody* (Bygone years, St. Petersburg,

348. *Valentin Serov.* The Coronation. The
Anointing of Nicholas II in the Uspensky
Cathedral, Moscow, *1896. Oil on canvas,
43 x 64 cm (17 x 25 ¹/₈ in.). State Tretiakov
Gallery, Moscow.*

1907–16), which the World of Art members supported. Both of
these journals, (the first edited by Benois until 1903, the second by
him throughout), attracted a number of astute historians and collectors such as Georgii Lukomsky and Baron Nikolai Vrangel, who
contributed essays on painting, architecture, the decorative arts, and
material culture. Benois identified their mission as follows: "We
believe that the forms which once upon a time grew naturally from
the Russian soil are closer to the Russian heart. . . . However, to cease
being a European now, to shelter from the West behind a wall, would
be odd, even absurd. . . . That is why, alongside works of our own
national art, we will not fear to present all things foreign and European preserved within the borders of Russia."[16]

Such sentiments demonstrate that, for the *miriskusniki*, Russia's
eighteenth century meant not only the grandeur of Catherine's
"painterly St. Petersburg,"[17] but also the "genuine magic"[18] of Russia's
first professional portrait painters such as Aleksei Antropov, Ivan
and Nikolai Argunov, and Levitsky, the modest Classical buildings
of pre-Napoleonic Moscow, the noble knickknacks of snuffboxes,
miniatures, teacups, fans, screens, figurines, and ribbons (cf. Somov's
languishing young ladies [ill. 349]) and the hieratic rituals which

accompanied the ambassadorial reception, the grand ball, and the royal hunt (cf. Serov's *Emperor Peter II and Elizaveta Petrovna Going out to Hunt*).[19] The chinoiserie of the eighteenth century also returns in Benois' fanciful *Chinese Pavilion* (1906) [ills. 351, 352], in his designs for Diaghilev's production of *Le Rossignol* (1914) [ill. 353], and in his essay on the Chinese Palace at Oranienbaum.[20]

A man of independent means with a casual degree in law, Diaghilev acted autocratically and egoistically, because he believed in a preordained order of things—that's the way it was—and the ego was to be borne, adorned, and communicated unashamedly and forthrightly, a tenet which informs many of his early publications. For example, in his article "Complicated Questions. Our Imaginary Decline" of 1898, Diaghilev spoke of his generation as one which "seeks only the personal and believes only in its own cause. This is one of our great qualities, and whoever wishes to know us—may he cease thinking that, like Narcissus, we love only ourselves. We are greater, broader than anyone else."[21]

Diaghilev's unconcealed homosexual affection for the "architecture of the male physique,"[22] his impeccable appearance and pragmatic, brusque, and calculating attitudes toward most men and women were all part of a desire to express and affirm a strong

349. Konstantin Somov. Young Lady Asleep, 1909. Watercolor and gouache on paper on fabric, 30.2 x 41.5 cm (11 7/8 x 16 3/8 in.). State Tretiakov Gallery, Moscow.

individuality [ill. 354]. As he wrote to his stepmother in 1895: "Firstly, I'm a great charlatan, albeit a brilliant one; secondly, I'm a great *charmeur*; thirdly, a great lout; fourthly, someone with a great amount of logic and very few principles."[23] Perhaps in conscious emulation of Peter the Great and Catherine the Great, Diaghilev exercised an autocratic prerogative in his selection of artists and works of art, dancers and repertoires, lovers and friendships. Self-confident and ambitious, Diaghilev had no qualms about attaching his name or signature to endeavors which promoted his own talent or taste: as early as 1895 he proposed founding a national gallery "in his own name,"[24] he ordered his clothes from Savile Row, and he dyed his forelock silver to affect greater wisdom and maturity.

The fame of several World of Art painters, particularly Bakst and Benois, rests—in Europe and America at least—on their set and

Below:
353. Alexandre Benois. A dancer in the procession of the Chinese Emperor. Costume design for Igor Stravinsky's opera Le Rossignol, *produced by Sergei Diaghilev in Paris in 1914. Watercolor and pencil on paper, 47.8 x 30.5 cm (18 7/8 x 12 in.). State Russian Museum, St. Petersburg.*

costume designs for Diaghilev's greatest enterprise, the Ballets Russes (1909–29), which, with its emphasis on artistic synthesis, archaic and exotic cultures, and new choreographic, musical, and visual systems, can be regarded as an extension of the Symbolist platform. The ease with which painters transferred pictorial ideas from studio to stage (productions such as *Cléopâtre* of 1909 and *Schéhérazade* of 1910 designed by Bakst, *Petrouchka* of 1911 designed by Benois, and *Le Sacre du Printemps* of 1913 designed by Roerich come to mind [ills. 355–357; see also 344, 425, 563–565]) was indicative of a general tendency toward "theatricalization" evident in the culture of the Silver Age. Here was an exaggerated sensibility as well as a conviction that movement, artistically composed and expressed, was the common denominator of all "great" works of art. This could take the form of physical movement such as dance and eurhythmics or of abstract equivalents such as poetry and music, which, for the Symbolists, was the highest form of expression, the least material and yet the most intense.

Above:
354. Sergei Diaghilev, New York, 1916.

Below:
355. Léon Bakst. Set design for Schéhérazade, *1910. Watercolor and gouache on paper.*

FINE LIMITED EDITIONS

For many of the World of Art artists, the ballet was not the only, or even the primary, synthetic discipline. Haute couture, architecture, and especially book design were also regarded as rich avenues of artistic endeavor which by their very nature could integrate several media. As a synthetic work of art, the book enjoyed no less attention than the opera and the ballet, and its capitals, headpieces, tailpieces, and vignettes attracted the foremost artistic talents [ills. 358, 361]. Like the ballet, too, the book was regarded as a laboratory for sophisticated technical experimentation, and the substantial improvements in printing technology at the end of the nineteenth

century helped reinforce this impetus toward formal perfection. The clarity of typeface and diversity of fonts, the accurate color superimposition of chromolithography, and the wider accessibility of fine papers provided the book with a new, mechanical permanence which must have appealed even more to the Russian tendency to accept the word as truth.

Right:

*358. Alexandre Benois. Illustration for
Alexander Pushkin's poem* The Bronze
Horseman, *1916. Indian ink, brush, pencil,
and white paint on paper, 30 x 47 cm
(11 3/4 x 18 1/2 in.). All-Russia Museum
of Alexander Pushkin, St. Petersburg.*

Below:

*359. Sergei Chekhonin. Illustration for Evgenii
Chirikov's story "About What?" (1913).*

In some sense, the book (as well as the journal)—each with its own libretto, decoration, and audience—was a theater in miniature, and artists such as Benois, Bilibin, Dobuzhinsky, Somov, and their younger disciples such as Dmitrii Mitrokhin and Sergei Chekhonin supported this argument, accepting the book as a Gesamtkunstwerk which could gratify both sense and sensibility [ills. 359, 360]. Their approach was supported by individual book collectors and special-interest groups such as the St. Evgenia Society and Vasilii Vereshchagin's Circle of Lovers of Russian Fine Editions, both in St. Petersburg, which propagated the various print media of engraving, etching, xylography, zincography, and lithography by sponsoring

exhibitions devoted to book design, underwriting handsome editions (e.g., *1812 v basniakh Krylova* [1812 in the Fables of Krylov] with
silhouettes by Narbut in 1912 and Nikolai Gogol's *Nevskii Prospekt*,
illustrated by Dmitrii Kardovsky in 1905), and publishing literature
on the subject—an expanding appreciation of the deluxe edition
which coincided with the general refurbishment of Russian arts and
crafts [ills. 362–364].

The period ca. 1900–1925 witnessed a phenomenal collecting
activity in St. Petersburg and Moscow, a particular orientation of
which was toward the rare book and the original engraving. Limited
deluxe editions of books of poetry, albums, and folios were printed
as collectors' items, often evoking a nostalgia for the exploits of Russia's

Imperial past such as Nikolai Kutepov's grandiose *Tsarskaia i imperatorskaia okhota na Rusi* (The Tsarist and Imperial hunt in Russia, St. Petersburg, 1902) with illustrations by Benois, Serov, and others. Books treating taboo subjects such as erotica and demonism, corporal punishment and psychic phenomena multiplied during this time, attracting a new generation of illustrators, many of whom deserve to be more widely known, including Feofilaktov, Masiutin, and Zamirailo [ills. 365, 366, see also 87].

In any case, by the late nineteenth century the printing arts and publishing industry in Russia had reached new heights of professionalism and sophistication, witness to which is the proliferation of luxury magazines such as *Mir iskusstva* and *Zolotoe runo*, superb examples of visual and verbal synthesis. There were also prestigious publishing houses such as Knebel and Skorpion (Moscow) and the Department for the Preparation of State Papers and Golike and Vilborg (St. Petersburg), responsible for such masterpieces as the enchanting series of fairy stories illustrated by Mitrokhin, the celebrated set of Russian fairy tales illustrated by Bilibin [ill. 378, see also 289], and Pushkin's *Pikovaia dama* (Queen of spades) designed by Benois (1911) [ill. 367]. Last but not least, there were specialist journals devoted to the art of the book[25] and avid collectors of ex-libris designs and first editions, including Benois, Diaghilev, Somov, and Vasilii A. Vereshchagin.[26]

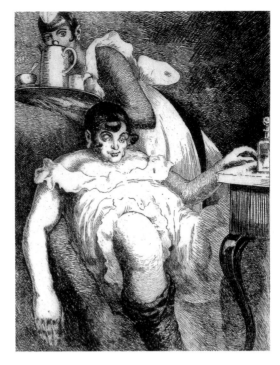

Below:
366. Viktor Zamirailo. Wolves, ca. 1910.
Black and brown ink on paper, 20.5 x 25 cm
(8 x 9 7/8 in.).

Opposite top:
362. Vladimir Arnold. Illustration for his story Unpeger.
Legenda poliarnykh stran *(Unpeger. A legend of the polar countries), St. Petersburg: Obshchestvennaia polza, 1910, p. 12. Arnold's color zincographs were incised and printed by Sergei Prokudin-Gorsky, the pioneer of color photography in Russia.*

Opposite bottom left and right:
363 & 364. Georgii Narbut. Frontispiece (left) and illustration for the fable "The Fox and the Vine" (right) in the book Tri Basni Krylova *(Three fables of Krylov). Moscow: Knebel, 1913.*

Above:
365. Vasilii Masiutin. The Gracious Lady, plate from the cycle Sem smertnykh grekhov *(Seven deadly sins). Moscow: 1918. Lithograph, 21.5 x 16.2 cm (8 1/2 x 6 3/8 in.).*

Above:

367. Alexandre Benois. Illustration for Alexander Pushkin's story Pikovaia dama *(Queen of spades), 1910. Watercolor and Indian ink on paper, 25.6 x 16.3 cm (10 x 6 ¹/₂ in.). All-Russia Museum of Alexander Pushkin, St. Petersburg.*

Of course, book design of the Silver Age was not always proper and demure, for many artists were drawn to the erotic, the occult, and the necrological, Feofilaktov's femmes fatales for the journal *Vesy* and Somov's piquant illustrations for *Le Livre de la Marquise* being cases in point[27] [ill. 368, see also 286]. What is especially interesting in this context is that women artists, including Olga Amosova and Miss (pseudonym of Natalia Remizova), were also prominent contributors to this trend, drawing amorous caprices for a variety of lighter journals such as *Stolitsa i usadba* (Town and country) and *Zhurnal dlia khoziaek* (Housewives' journal),[28] and other publications [see ill. 112]. The flirtation with sex and violence was expressed further in an unexpected context, namely, in the radical caricature journals of 1905–06, which, being socially conscious and humanitarian, can ostensibly be regarded as organs of the revolutionary cause. Closer investigation of journals such as *Adskaia pochta* (Hellish post) and *Zhupel* (Bugbear), however, indicates that their numerous images of death and disease, freaks and monsters, serpents and wild beasts may have been dictated not necessarily by an artist's particular political ideology, but rather by a psychological fascination with Decadent motifs. In other words, contributors such as Boris Anisfeld, Bilibin, Isaak Brodsky, Sergei Chekhonin, Dobuzhinsky, Zinovii Grzhebin, Boris Kustodiev, and Lancéray were using the satirical journals as convenient vehicles for the depiction of subjects which, in another context, would have been socially taboo[29] [ills. 369–376].

This is not to say that such artists were politically naïve or indifferent to the events of 1905 or to the need for social reforms. Most of the Symbolists were discontent with the status quo, especially after Russia's ignominious defeat in the Russo-Japanese War, but their stance was by no means uniform. Gorky saw the insurrections of 1905–06 as an opportunity to destroy the "stupid gluttons and syphilitics from the House of the Romanovs who have ruined and shamed Russia."[30] Diaghilev saw the events as a "wild bacchanalia" and wanted to "get the hell out of here."[31] Dobuzhinsky, in the manifesto entitled "The Artists' Voice," consigned by Benois, Lancéray, and Somov, welcomed social change, but feared that "beauty will be abolished and forgotten in the mighty wave of urgent, practical needs."[32] Some of the artists who promoted reform and who moved swiftly from an aesthetic passivity to a more engaged position in 1905 did, indeed, begin to use caricature and cartoon to express dissatisfaction and contempt. Works such as Dobuzhinsky's *Pacification* (showing the Kremlin almost immersed in a sea of blood) and *October Idyll* or Kustodiev's *Moscow 1. Entry* (showing a gigantic skeleton rushing from behind the workers' barricades on to the Imperial troops) and Grzhebin's

Opposite bottom:
368. Konstantin Somov. Illustration for Le Livre de
la Marquise *by Franz Blei. St. Petersburg: Golike and
Vilborg, 1918, p. 45. The corresponding illustration for
the unexpurgated edition of* Le Livre de la Marquise
*(also St. Petersburg, 1918) shows parts of a more
private nature.*

Above left:
369. Sergei Chekhonin. The Editor-in-Chief
Has the Amnesty Just about Ready, but It's
Covered Up by a Flag, *1906. Drawing for the
satirical journal* Maski *(Masks), St. Petersburg,
1906, no. 9, p. 7. The Imperial Russian flag is
draped over the donkey's muzzle. The caption
accompanying the composition incorporates the
Russian expression* na nosu *(lit. "on the nose,"
meaning "very soon").*

Above right:
370. Ivan Bilibin. A Donkey ¹/₂₀ Natural Size,
1906. Drawing for the satirical journal Zhupel
*(Bugbear), St. Petersburg, 1906, no. 3, p. 9. The
ass or donkey replaces the coat of arms of the
Romanov dynasty.*

Left:
371. Zinovii Grzhebin. Eagle-Werewolf *or*
Domestic and Foreign Policy, *1905. Drawing
for the satirical journal* Zhupel *(Bugbear),
St. Petersburg, 1905, no. 1, p, 4. The censor
omitted to turn the page upside down—and, to the
consternation or joy of many, ratified reproduction
of the image.*

Above left:
372. Isaak Brodsky. Worn
Out, 1906. Drawing for the
satirical journal Leshii
(Wood goblin), St.
Petersburg, 1906, no. 1, p. 12.

Above right:
373. Mstislav Dobuzhinsky.
October. Idyll, 1905.
Drawing for the satirical
journal Zhupel (Bugbear),
St. Petersburg, 1905, no. 1, p. 4.

Right:
374. Boris Kustodiev.
Moscow 1. Entry, 1905.
Drawing for the satirical
journal Zhupel (Bugbear),
St. Petersburg, 1905, no. 2, p.
4. The symbology is simple:
Death advances upon the
government troops in the
foreground from the workers
behind the barricades.

Above:

*375. Nikolai Feshin (Nicholas Fechin). Before the
Police Constable, 1906. Drawing for the satirical
journal Leshii (Wood goblin), St. Petersburg, 1906,
no. 2, p. 4.*

Right:

*376. Evgenii Lancéray. Funeral Repast, 1906.
Drawing for the satirical journal Adskaia pochta
(Hellish post), St. Petersburg, 1906, no. 2, p. 4.*

Eagle-Werewolf, or Domestic and Foreign Policy, all of which appeared in *Zhupel*, are clear examples of this new political commitment.

Adskaia pochta, edited by Lancéray and named after the satirical journal of the same name published under, and eventually closed by, Catherine the Great, maintained the same high artistic and intellectual standard as *Zhupel*. One of its most effective images, for example, was Lancéray's *Funeral Repast*: this title not only held a symbolic meaning, but also interpreted an actual episode when officers of the Semeonov Regiment went on a drinking binge after massacring workers. In the process of transmitting a forceful political message, this cartoon—and many others like it—uses an unwarranted measure of bestial distortion, indicating that perhaps the artist had been inspired as much by a morbid fascination with the macabre and the bizarre as by social indignation. In other words, the monsters of Anisfeld, the corpses of Brodsky, the coffins of Nikolai Feshin, and so on, may derive not only from civic concern, but also from a more deeply expressionistic and psychological urge—as was the case, for example, with Alfred Kubin's and Frantisek Kupka's contributions to *L'Assiette au beurre* or Heine's to *Simplicissimus*.

Certainly, the First Revolution represented a clear condition wherein the forces of good (liberation) and evil (reaction) could be identified immediately with the qualities of the insurgents on the one hand and the Tsarist order on the other, and, therefore, the imagery of monsters, snakes, chains, skeletons, cemeteries, bloodbaths, and so forth could be applied "legitimately," even though some observers felt that such a sinister iconography might deflect attention from the higher cause of social justice.[33] In any case, this kind of imagery was not entirely new to Russian art, with curious precedents in the more sinister pictures and illustrations of Elena Polenova and Mariia Yakunchikova of the 1890s [ills. 377, 379, 380]. But perhaps the most haunting extensions of Decadent imagery appeared after the revolutionary episode, i.e., during the period ca. 1908–1920, captured, for example, in the lithographs of Vasilii Masiutin such as his editions of *Sem smertnykh grekhov* (The Seven mortal sins) of 1909 with its *Woman-Mask, Woman on a Beast, Woman with Tails, Life*, and *Sickness*. Inspired by Honoré Daumier, Francisco Goya, and Félicien Rops, Masiutin possessed a faultless technique and highly charged imagination, and his monstrous visions are among the most disturbing of the Silver Age [ill. 381, see also 365].

The journals which supported this tendency, especially *Satirikon* (Satyricon, St. Petersburg, 1908–13) and *Novyi Satirikon* (New Satyricon, St. Petersburg, 1914–18), provided a fertile training ground for younger illustrators and caricaturists such as Yurii Annenkov [ill. 382], Vladimir Lebedev, and Nikolai Remizov (Re-mi) [ill. 383],

Opposite:
377. Elena Polenova. Illustration for the fairy tale Zver *(Beast), 1898. Oil on canvas, 144 x 103 cm (56 5/8 x 40 1/2 in.). Abramtsevo Museum and Reserve.*

Above:
378. Ivan Bilibin. Vasilisa in the Forest. Illustration for the Russian folk tale Vasilisa prekrasnaia *(Vasilisa the beautiful), 1900.*

Below:
379. Elena Polenova. The Ducks Save Filipko. Illustration for the fairy tale Synko-Filipko *(Little Boy Filipko), 1890s. Gouache, Indian ink, brush, and pencil on paper, 30.8 x 22.3 cm (12 1/8 x 87 3/4 in.). State Tretiakov Museum, Moscow.*

whose posters and illustrations in both lighter and more serious genres just after the October Revolution cannot be fully understood without due reference to this strong graphic heritage. Some artists of the older generation such as Kalmakov and Somov pursued their demonic and erotic visions in emigration, but they withdrew into internal worlds, reiterating subjects which they had already drawn and painted many years before, while at home, in the new Russia, they were soon rejected out of hand for their "bourgeois hedonism, Decadent Romanticism . . . and refined aestheticism united by a common cult of individualism taken to extremes."[34]

The art of the book also received the unprecedented attention of professional critics and theorists, a concern that lasted well into Soviet times. New concepts and definitions of the book were elaborated by outstanding specialists such as Vladimir Adariukov, Pavel Ettinger, Erik Gollerbakh, Aleksandr Larionov, Aleksei Sidorov, and Vereshchagin, while artists, poets, and philosophers such as Vladimir Favorsky and Belyi offered new and often provocative interpretations of book design, of the act of reading, and of the correlations between the spoken, the written, and the printed word.

Opposite:
380. Mariia Yakunchikova. Fear, 1893–94. Colored etching, 30 x 20 cm (11 7/8 x 7 7/8 in.). Clearly, Yakunchikova was inspired by Edvard Munch's painting The Scream *of 1893.*

Above:
381. Vasilii Masiutin. Death, 1911. Engraving, 38 x 27.5 cm (15 x 10 7/8 in.).

The priest, mathematician, and art historian Pavel Florensky, for example, even wrote an essay on the relationship between a book cover and its text.[35] The bibliophilic passion of the Silver Age also informed many intellectual activities in Moscow and Petrograd in the early 1920s, inspiring collections and studies of ex-libris designs, theories of book design, and specialist journals and exhibitions devoted to the art of the book such as "The Graphic Arts in the USSR 1917–1927," which Gollerbakh and Vsevolod Voinov organized in Moscow in 1927. A powerful laboratory for the investigation into and promotion of the book as artifact was the Russian (State) Academy of Artistic Sciences (RAKhN) in Moscow, with which both A. Larionov and Sidorov were associated.[36] RAKhN (founded by Kandinsky in 1921) not only organized lectures on the art of the book, mounted exhibitions of ex-libris designs, and developed theories of book design, but also, like its Symbolist precedents, regarded the book as a synthetic—and liberating—exercise in colors and words.[37]

*383. Attributed to Miss
(pseudonym of Natalia
Remizova, sister of Nikolai
Remizov). Poster for the
Theater of Miniatures, St.
Petersburg. St. Petersburg:
Golike and Vilborg, 1911,
lithograph, 106 cm x 72 cm
(41³/₄ x 28³/₈ in.).*

FLOWERS, FLOWERS TO COVER THE TOMB!
Blooms of Decadence[1]

MIKHAIL VRUBEL

The most original artist of the Russian Silver Age was Mikhail Vrubel, whose fertile imagination produced paintings, designs, and ceramics of extreme power and originality such as the disconcerting *Demon Cast Down* [see ill. 6] and *Vision of the Prophet Ezekiel*. While Art Nouveau or the Style Moderne and its Russian precedent, Neo-Nationalism, are terms which come to mind in this context, Vrubel approached the act of painting as a constant process of experimentation, returning to his major canvases again and again, erasing, repainting, modifying. His tireless restructuring of forms, his release of ornamental energy, and his intense elaboration of the surface prompted critics to speak of the crystalline formations and "Cubist" faceting[2] of his painting, to which the strangely lapidary flowers in his *Demon Seated* [see ill. 170] bear strong testimony.

That flowers held a fatal attraction for the painters and poets of Russia's cultural efflorescence is demonstrated no more clearly than in Vrubel's sinister canvas *Lilacs* (1900) [ill. 385]. Painted at the very equinox of the nineteenth and twentieth centuries, *Lilacs* exposes an eerie and unequal struggle between the encroaching mass of flowers and the wan, emaciated human figure. Here is an image of decay surrounded by the deep purple, mauve, and green of the lilacs, almost out of control in this crepuscular hush.

Opposite:
384. Sergei Chekhonin. Cornflowers, *1916. Oil on canvas, 68 x 59 cm (26 3/4 x 23 in.). State Museum and Reserve of History, Art, and Architecture, Pskov.*

Below:
385. Mikhail Vrubel. Lilacs, *1900. Oil on canvas, 160 x 177 cm (63 x 69 3/4 in.). State Tretiakov Gallery, Moscow.*

There would seem to be an organic and disturbing connection
between *Lilacs* and the birth of Russian Modernism, for the image of
the flower was among the most strident symbols of the Russian Silver Age. Here was a flowering of all the arts, and the activities and
cultural manifestations of its primary exponents bear witness to this,
whether we think of the Decadent writers with their flowers of the
night and poetical *fleurs du mal* or the ominous and animated blooms
of Sergei Chekhonin [ill. 384, see also 359], the green carnations of
Oscar Wilde,³ the Blue Rose group of painters, or the annual poetical miscellany *Severnye tsvety* (Northern flowers). In a metaphorical
sense, too, the circles in which the Symbolists moved can be regarded
as hothouses in which subtle horticulturalists tended their exotic
blooms—the studio paintings, book illustrations, stage designs,
poems, and creative prose of their imagination.

The notion of full flowering, of fruit decaying, and of putrefac-
tion was central to the sensibility of the Silver Age, the Decadents
even referring to their artistic productions as flowers cast upon the
tomb. Indeed, the idea of the work of art as a wreath placed over the
void of death—the "wreath" and "garland" are recurrent motifs in
the Symbolist vocabulary as in the paintings of Viktor Borisov-
Musatov [ill. 386]—functions well, because, in some sense, the artists
and writers of Russia's fin de siècle were engaged in a highly ritual-

387. *Viktor Borisov-Musatov. Gobelin, 1901. Tempera on canvas, 103 x 141.2 cm (40 ¹/₂ x 55 ¹/₂ in.). State Tretiakov Gallery, Moscow.*

ized dance of death. All were aware of the transformation, if not demise, that awaited Imperial Russian society, and the Russo-Japanese War, the First Revolution, and World War I were accepted as harbingers of Russia's ultimate decomposition. The almost hysterical energy with which Russian artists and writers tried to disguise this rupture with their ornaments and facades expressed a desperate attempt to ignore the impending doom.

THE BLUE ROSE

The Russian Silver Age was not confined by strict geographical or social boundaries, for it flowered well beyond the two capitals. Even Saratov, then a small town to the south of Moscow, became a major center of Symbolist enquiry, thanks, in particular, to the activities of the painter Borisov-Musatov. Impressed by Puvis de Chavannes and the Nabis—especially Maurice Denis—during his residence in Paris, Borisov-Musatov incorporated their monumental style and subdued palette into his elusive depictions of phantasmal women, as in *Gobelin* (1901) and *Reservoir* (1902) [ill. 387, see also 271].[4]

In contrast to the more rigid, architectonic linearity of artists such as Benois, Bilibin, and Somov, Borisov-Musatov presented a formal flexibility which helped to ease Russian painting from the graphic

388. *Arkhip Kuindzhi. Birch Grove, 1879. Oil on canvas, 97 x 181 cm (38 ¹/₈ x 71 ¹/₄ in.). State Tretiakov Gallery, Moscow. Although Kuindzhi's experiments in pigmentation ofen resulted in brilliant light effects, many of his paintings darkened very quickly. With its prismatic clarity and arresting contrast between light and shadow,* Birch Grove *is one of the happy exceptions to this accelerated aging process.*

discipline of the World of Art. Evoking a gentler and more tranquil age, Borisov-Musatov shared the Symbolists' desire to escape from their troubled time, and one of his central motifs, the Eternal Feminine, aligned him with writers such as Belyi, Blok, and Soloviev in their search for cosmic harmony and moral intactness.

> *Dear friend, don't you see*
> *That all that is seen by us*
> *Is only a reflection, only shadows,*
> *Of what the eye cannot see?*[5]

In evoking diaphanous vestal maidens languishing at melancholy country estates, Borisov-Musatov concentrated on the purely painterly elements of color, mass, and texture, prompting critics to dismiss his elusive imagery as a "morbid illusion . . . a mere mass of rough blots with no outline at all."[6]

Willy-nilly, Borisov-Musatov was also drawing on a lyrical or Luminist tradition in later nineteenth-century Russian painting represented by Isaak Levitan and especially Arkhip Kuindzhi, celebrated for his *Birch Grove* (1879), nocturnal landscapes, and spectacular sunsets [ills. 388, 389]. It is, of course, hazardous to attempt to establish in retrospect the existence of a Russian Luminist or "proto-Symbolist" school. However, a number of Russian artists (e.g., Nikolai Ge,

Kuindzhi, Levitan, Repin, and Vereshchagin) were deeply interested
in the newest photographic technology and discoveries of Russian
physicists, and, perhaps, the very vastness and flatness of the
steppe could not have failed to affect optical perception and
reception. For example, as if using a wide-angle lens to observe
changing cloud formations and aquatic reflections, Levitan
evoked the endlessness and melancholic serenity of the Russian

391. *Alfred Eberling. Illustration for Mikhail Lermontov's poem* Demon. *Moscow: Volf, 1910, between pp. 2 and 3.*

landscape in his *Above Eternal Peace* (1894) [ill. 390], one of the most suggestive Russian paintings of the time and certainly prescient of the lyrical visions of Borisov-Musatov in particular.

Such elements generated qualities readily identifiable as Luminist: brilliant and refractive light, strong horizontal structure, and panoramic space, qualities especially manifest in the work of Kuindzhi. The audacious spectral contrasts and light effects of his epic landscapes both separate his art from the usual tendentious work of so many of his contemporaries and anticipate the experiments of Russian Modernism. In using nature expressively rather than narratively, Kuindzhi imbued his art with a sense of timelessness.

Somewhat like his contemporaries, the pantheistic poets Afanasii Fet and Konstantin Fofanov, Kuindzhi presaged the highly subjective, oneiric evocations of the Symbolist movement. Perhaps there is some truth in Benois's description of Kuindzhi as the "Russian Monet,"[7] and certainly Kuindzhi's "stereoscopic" tones seem to have cast a strong reflection upon other, younger lyrical painters of his era, including Alfred Eberling [ill. 391].

On one level, like Levitan, Kuindzhi was reacting against the Positivist interpretation of reality common to the Realists, epitomized in the tenets of the engaged social critics Nikolai Chernyshevsky and Nikolai Dobroliubov for whom "that object is beautiful which displays life in itself or reminds us of life."[8] Kuindzhi abstracted or synthesized the natural world so that his epic landscapes, devoid of human figures, come forth as the ultimate distillation of nature herself and of the divine energy "dispersing into infinity,"[9] i.e., they are neither narrations nor protocols, but pictures of mood and states of mind.

However different their subjects and psychological attitudes toward nature, such artists as Kuindzhi and Levitan were united in their awareness of the deeper, symbolic essence of the surrounding world, suggesting a parallel with Ralph Waldo Emerson's Transcendentalism and the Luminist movement in America. Borisov-Musatov equated this condition with the force of music:

> The endless melody which Wagner found in
> music is also present in painting. This melody
> is in the lugubrious, northern landscapes of
> Grieg, in the songs of the medieval troubadours,
> and in the Romanticism of our native, Russian
> Turgenevs. . . . In frescoes this leitmotif should
> correspond to line. Endless, monotonic, impassive,
> without angles.[10]

Borisov-Musatov also established a short-lived but crucial "school" of painters, for he was the vital instigator of the Golubaia roza (Blue Rose), a Moscow group which might well be considered as the real beginning of the avant-garde in Russian art.[11] Apologists for Belyi's aesthetics and Blok's poetry, the Blue Rose artists, especially their leader, Pavel Kuznetsov, explored a particular repertoire of symbols (blue-green foliage, fountains, vestal maidens, embryonic forms) to evoke the global orchestra beyond the world of appearances [ill. 392]. Concerned with the oblique and the intangible, they dematerialized

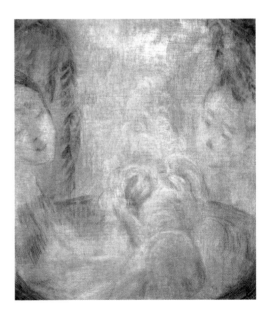

392. *Pavel Kuznetsov. Birth, 1906–07. Pastel on canvas, 73 x 66 cm (28 3/4 x 25 3/4 in.). State Tretiakov Gallery, Moscow. Along with Sudeikin, Utkin, and, at this time, Malevich, the Symbolist Kuznetsov was fascinated by the Eternal Feminine, motherhood, and the cycle of life. According to rumor, he even spent time in a maternity hospital, painting from nature.*

Алая Роза

Алая Роза

Выставка Картинъ

Above:
393. Sergei Sudeikin. Cover of the "Crimson Rose" exhibition catalogue, Saratov, 1904.

Below:
394. Nikolai Riabushinsky, ca. 1906.

nature and thereby heralded the radical concept of the picture as a self-sufficient, abstract unit. The Symbolist journals *Vesy, Iskusstvo* (Art, 1905), and *Zolotoe runo*, in particular, did much to promote their ideas and imagery.[12]

In May 1904 an untitled group of artists, for the most part students at the Moscow Institute of Painting, Sculpture, and Architecture, organized an exhibition called the "Crimson Rose" *(Alaia roza)* in Saratov [ill. 393]. The tone of the exhibition was set by the leaders of the group, Kuznetsov and Petr Utkin, both former pupils of Borisov-Musatov; their pictures, in the main landscapes, lacked bright color and strict delineation, elements which would be identifiable with the whole output of the Blue Rose. Perhaps paying homage to Savva Mamontov, who had written a fairy story called *The Crimson Rose*, the Saratov group, still tentative and desultory, emphasized the lyrical element of painting in their restrained and intimate depictions of earth, foliage, and water. In so doing, they avoided the retrospectivism of the World of Art, the didactic emphasis of the Wanderers, and the formulaic schemes of the academicians, confirming that the true purpose of art was not to represent material bodies but to summon their essence. This aesthetic privilege became the guiding principle of the Blue Rose group, founded in 1907 in the wake of the Saratov episode; its very name elicited the celestial, the silent, the exotic, and the unattainable (in 1907 a blue rose was still a fiction).

In March–April 1907, under the financial auspices of Nikolai Riabushinsky, banker, poet, painter, collector, editor of *Zolotoe runo*, and patron of the arts [ill. 394], the "Blue Rose" exhibition opened. Sixteen artists led by Kuznetsov presented their essays in pictorial Symbolism. Essentially, the group—which also included Anatolii Arapov, Nikolai and Vasilii Milioti, Nikolai Sapunov, Martiros Sarian, Sergei Sudeikin, Petr Utkin, and the sculptor Aleksandr Matveev, and which maintained close ties with Petrov-Vodkin—was a Symbolist one, both in its collective aspiration to depict an ulterior reality and in its association with the Symbolist writers, especially Belyi and Blok [ills. 395–398].

Belyi's comprehension of music as the fundamental and essential form of reality was but another symptom of the general aspiration toward harmony in its widest sense, but his development of the basic concept into a theoretical premise—and hence his imposition of a philosophical purpose upon art—brought him especially close to Blok and to the Blue Rose group. In this respect, the fact that one of the last literary contributions to the *World of Art* magazine was by Belyi creates a convenient bridge from the first Symbolist generation to the second. In this article Belyi continued to talk of the intensity of "musical symbols" and of the "approach of inner music to the

Above:
395. Nikolai Sapunov. Still Life with
Self-portrait, *1910–11. Tempera on
cardboard, 78 x 97.5 cm
(30³/₄ x 38³/₈ in.).*

Left:
396. Sergei Sudeikin. Ballet (Three
Ecossaises), *1907. Oil on cardboard,
21.5 x 26 cm (8¹/₂ x 10¹/₄ in.). State
Literary Museum, Moscow.*

397. *Martiros Sarian. Lake of the Fairies,
1905. Gouache on paper, 24.5 x 24.5 cm
(9 5/8 x 9 5/8 in.). State Tretiakov Gallery,
Moscow.*

398. *Aleksandr Matveev. Headstone of the grave
of the artist Viktor Borisov-Musatov in Tarusa,
1912. Granite.*

399. *Mikalojus Čiurlionis.* Sonata of the Stars (Chaos). Allegro, *1908. Tempera on paper, 72.2 x 61.4 cm (28 3/8 x 24 1/8 in.). Mikalojaus Čiurlionis Art Museum, Kaunas. A synesthesiac, Čiurlionis gave musical titles to his paintings and evoked strong visual imagery in his musical compositions (see ill. 551).*

surface of the consciousness."[13] Such mystical, abstracted thinking would explain his admiration for the musical and translucent allusions of the Blue Rose painters, already far removed from the formal accuracy of the World of Art artists: "In painting we are not concerned with the projection of reality on to a plane. . . . It is not the picture itself which should come to the fore, but the veracity of the emotions and moods being experienced which this or that picture of nature evokes in us."[14] The idea that in art evocation of mood was more important than the representation of a given part of reality was especially relevant to the art of the Blue Rose artists. Indeed, it was their reaction against both the reportorial purpose of the Realists and the formal refinement of the World of Art painting, and their interfusion of mass, subtle gradations of pastel colors, and loss of contour which recalled the musicality of the Lithuanian painter and composer Mikalojus Čiurlionis, and the cosmic force of Kandinsky's improvisations [ill. 399, see also 20].

The Blue Rose artists owed much to the art of the Nabis, especially Denis, as well as to their mentor, Borisov-Musatov. They

400. *Pavel Kuznetsov.* Blue Fountain, *1905.*
Tempera on canvas, 127 x 131 cm
(50 x 51 ¹/₂ in.). State Tretiakov Gallery,
Moscow.

applied their system of images or symbols to transmit that primordial spirit which, like Belyi and Blok, they felt lay beyond the world of
appearances. Just as their colleagues concentrated on music in their
poetry to summon the superior reality, so the Blue Rose artists
resorted to a melody or rhythm of pictorial construction based on
curves and circles. This counterpoint of forms, especially evident in
Kuznetsov's compositions, parallels the delicate phonic schemes of,
for example, Blok's descriptions of his Beautiful Lady (1901–02), and
connects immediately with Borisov-Musatov's "endless melody."
Furthermore, if the dominant form in the Blue Rose paintings is the
curve and the dominant color blue, then the result is strangely reminiscent of Kandinsky's conclusion regarding the correspondence of
forms to colors, according to which "blue develops a centrifugal
movement (like a snail retreating into its shell) and moves away from
you."[15] In turn, the muted colors and lack of contours and outlines in
the Blue Rose works produce the impression of ethereality, other-
worldliness, and silence, which undermine the academic perception
of perspective, spatial definition, and proportion.

The escape from a photographic naturalism to a mystical fantasy
or, as one critic commented aptly, the "dematerialization of
nature,"[16] was expressed most forcefully in the work of Kuznetsov:
his *Blue Fountain* [ill. 400], not shown at the "Blue Rose," but typical
of his contribution, not only depicts a subjective vision but also
points to the artist's deliberate neglect of formal delineation. In his

review of the "Blue Rose" exhibition, Sergei Makovsky wrote:

> [The artists] are in love with the music of
> color and line. They have heralded that
> primitivism to which modern painting has
> come in its search for a rebirth at its very
> sources—in spontaneous creation
> unweakened by the weight of historical
> experience.[17]

This distinct trend toward the abstract, balanced by exquisite combinations of cold colors and contrasting textures, is peculiar to the best work of the Blue Rose and heralds the radical concept of the picture as a self-sufficient unit.

401. Dmitrii Merezhkovsky, Dmitrii Filosofov, and Zinaida Gippus, early 1900s. It is not easy to dispel the rumors and legends which now surround these three Symbolist writers—Merezhkovsky the novelist, Filosofov the critic, and Gippius the poetess—to the effect that they constituted a ménage à trois, or that Gippius and Merezhkovsky, guided by lofty ideals, chose not to consummate their marriage, or that Filosofov's genuine passion was neither for Merezhkovsky nor for Gippius, but for Sergei Diaghilev. On the other hand, this kind of extended family or, rather, convoluted relationship was an organic part of the Symbolists' behavior and demonstrated a strong desire to test boundaries not only of artistic form, but also of life itself.

DECADENCE

The image of the celestial bloom or the full and wilting flower or the mulch which nurtures blossoms of incredible beauty connects immediately with the notion of Decadence. In turn, it connects with states of mind, often altered through experimental lifestyles promoting homosexuality (Mikhail Kuzmin),[18] lesbianism (Olga Glebova), the ménage à trois (Filosofov, Gippius, and Merezhkovsky),[19] open marriage (Pallada Bogdanova-Belskaia), and pedophilia (Vrangel),[20] or through the use of alcohol and drugs (Balmont, Briusov, Vsevolod Maskimovich, Vrubel) [ills. 401–403].

The Russian or, strictly speaking, Ukrainian Decadent Maksimovich, is a case in point. Drawing upon a heady mix of Symbolist sources, he was a startling representative of the Style Moderne, albeit

Right:
402. Konstantin Somov. Portrait of the Poet Mikhail Kuzmin, *1909. Watercolor, white paint, and pencil on paper. 32.8 x 24.5 cm (13 x 9 5/8 in.). State Tretiakov Gallery, Moscow. Somov's portrait introduces us to a richly physical and sensual human being: the ear is large (indicating Kuzmin's love of music), the eyes are large (indicating a love of art), the hair is disheveled (indicating the rush of poetical inspiration), the lips are red and full (indicating a bon vivant), and the moustache and beard are trimmed meticulously (indicating the same kind of cosmetic self-representation which Diaghilev achieved with his dyed silver forelock).*

Opposite:
403. Olga Glebova, right, and Anna Akhmatova, 1910s.

belated and derivative. On one level, the clinging tentacles of his compositions define spaces of amber luminescence inhabited by distraught ephebi and corrupt Apollos, Dionysian nymphs and voluptuous Argonauts. Living in the same crepuscular zone as his friend and mentor Ivan Miasoedov, Maskimovich seemed literally to put the *zhiznetvorchestvo* (life creativity) of the Symbolist poets into practice. True, Maksimovich created his most haunting works such as *Self-Portrait, Lovers, Banquet,* and *The Kiss* only in 1912–14 [ills. 404, 405], i.e., more than a decade after the Decadent poetry of Briusov and Zinaida Gippius and two decades after Merezhkovsky's Symbolist manifesto.[21] On the other hand, Maksimovich's compositions subsume many intertexts and points of reference. The filigrees of Beardsley, Julius Dietz, T. T. Heine, and Somov come to mind, as do those of their Moscow counterparts such as Nikolai Feofilaktov and Vasilii Milioti [see ill. 286].

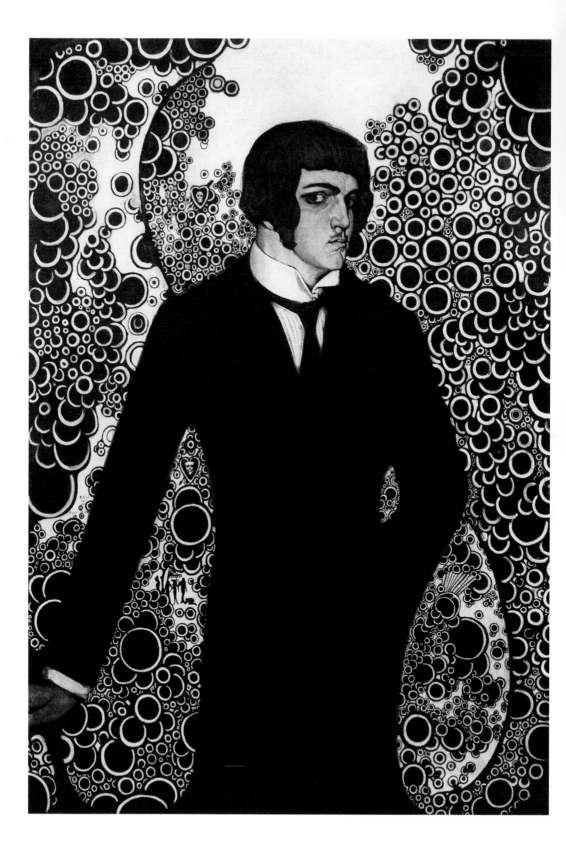

But there was also the strong appeal to the Classical repertoire of the Academy of Arts, which Maksimovich must have seen in the pictures of the Russian, Polish, and Ukrainian salon painters such as Stepan Bakalovich, Vilgelm Kotarbinsky, and Genrikh Semiradsky [ill. 406], or their loyal progeny such as Isaak Brodsky [ill. 407] and Ivan Miasoedov, the latter his close friend. As in the case of these and other Russian and Ukrainian practitioners of the Style Moderne, Maksimovich's artistic individuality strikes by its sheer force: his desperate attempt to assume the mantle of genius, his submission to drugs and alcohol, and his flirtation with the nocturnal prodigality of Kiev and Moscow both inspired his haunting pictures and contributed to his self-destruction. In 1914, following the failure of his one-man exhibition in Moscow and experiences of alleged sexual

Opposite:
404. Vsevolod Maksimovich. Self-Portrait, 1913. Oil on canvas, 142 x 105 cm (56 x 41 3/8 in.). National Art Museum of the Ukraine, Kiev.

Above:
405. Vsevolod Maksimovich. The Kiss, 1913. Oil on canvas, 100 x 100 cm (39 3/8 x 39 3/8 in.). National Art Museum of the Ukraine, Kiev.

inadequacy, he committed suicide, soon after appearing in the lead role, or so it would seem, of the avant-garde movie *Drama in the Futurists' Cabaret No. 13*[22] [ill. 408].

Prenatal and posthumous experiences and illness were also perceived as psychic conditions which could establish immediate contact with the ulterior world—Belyi, for example, confusing the stars, his mother's voice, and the wall of his room when he was ill with scarlet fever,[23] and Kandinsky seeing an abstract painting when he was ill with typhus.[24] That the Symbolists held Vrubel and Čiurlionis, both victims of grave psychiatric disease, in high regard is also symptomatic of their belief that altered states of mind could bring spiritual illumination. The prodigal behavior and bizarre experiences which poets such as Blok and Briusov described in their poetry were often equated with alleged sensual excess and moral looseness, which, in turn, became emblematic of the Symbolist movement in general. The art of the Decadents, with its fixations, neuroses, and often embarrassing exaggerations, is, to say the least, uneven in achievement and at times can seem trite, if not absurd, in its flirtation with Medusas and Madonnas. Although the aesthetics of Decadence may strike us sometimes as lax or forced, the historical reasons for its advent and its peculiar world view still deserve scrutiny.

By around 1910 the flower of Decadence in the Symbolist garden had become a consumer product—advertised, promoted, and anthologized. In Russia, Nikolai Evreinov and Sidorov were publishing handsome monographs on Félicien Rops and Beardsley[25] [ill. 409]. Makovsky was including Odilon Redon and Kees van Dongen in his exhibitions of contemporary European graphics,[26] Belyi was preparing his synoptic *Simvolizm* for press, the Russian translation of Otto Weininger's *Geschlecht und Charakter* (1903) was already sold out, every boudoir sported a reproduction of Arnold Böcklin's *Isle of the Dead*, while movie posters, perfume labels, and even soap wrappers carried alluring images of exotic climes, swooning females, and satanic beasts [ills. 410–412]. In other words, by the 1910s the educated public had been primed to accept "Decadence" and was not as provoked as it might have been, for example, by the first appearance of the *poètes maudits* many years before. The Russian Decadents, however, argued that, far from being degenerate, they themselves were testing boundaries and charting foreign waters in search of the new, the vigorous, and the vital, and that it was other sections of society which were in decline. As Diaghilev asserted in his 1898 essay

"Complicated Questions. Our Imaginary Decline," the real decadents were not the new artists of the Silver Age, but, rather, the epigones of established styles, i.e.:

1) *decadents of Classicism, our most decrepit and hence incorrigible enemies.*
2) *sickly sentimentalists, fainting away to the sounds of Mendelssohn Lieder. . . . They are the decadents of Romanticism, terrible enemies.*
3) *a very recent group which imagined that it had amazed the world with its audacious discovery—dragging peasant shoes and rags on to the canvas—whereas this had already been done incomparably bettter and with much more vigor fifty years before by the great Balzac and Millet. . . . They are the decadents of Realism.*[27]

Of course, there were many symptoms of social malaise and psychiatric imbalance during the Russian Silver Age and, no doubt, the upright petit bourgeois, comfortable with the status quo, would have been disturbed by what must have seemed excessive cultural and social change. The First Revolution in 1905, the alleged depravity of the aristocracy, the political scandals, the unseemly all-night parties of Moscow's gilded youth, the incomprehensible poetry and painting of the Symbolists and Futurists, the absurdity of World War I, the dark machinations and murder of Rasputin in 1916—to many these things must have seemed sinister, unwholesome, and decadent. In contrast, Diaghilev and his colleagues apprehended a healthier condition in the new artistic and intellectual expressions of their time, finding therein an unsullied source of cultural sanity and renewal. If a healthy mind is to be found in a healthy body, then surely the Russian Silver Age, with its veritable cult of the corporeal arts (ballet, dramatic theater, *danse plastique*, nudism, martial arts), should be regarded as a moment not of Russia's decadence, but of her renaissance.

Above:
411. Postcard advertising Rose de Noël perfume, which was produced by the Brokar (Brocard) Company, Moscow, ca. 1910.

Left:
412. Advertisement for Leda soap, which was produced by A. Ralle & Co., Moscow, ca. 1910.

BODY ART
Ballet, Theater, Cabaret, Nudism

THE BALLETS RUSSES

Not surprisingly, it was the Russian theater in its widest sense which appealed most immediately to the Decadent sensibility and which recognized and appropriated, perhaps more than any other discipline, the manifest freedom of the Style Moderne, especially in the sets and costumes for Diaghilev's Ballets Russes, and several of the World of Art members attained international recognition through their involvement in the performing arts [see ill. 1]. The achievements of the Russian avant-garde theater, for example Exter's Cubist Baroque designs for Aleksandr Tairov's Chamber Theater [ill. 413] and Popova's *prozodezhda* (uniform industrial clothing) for Vsevolod Meierkhold [ill. 414], would not have been possible without the exuberant precedents of Bakst, Benois, Golovin, and Roerich, especially within the context of Diaghilev's Ballets Russes.

Opposite:
413. Alexandra Exter. Costume design for a Bacchante in Thamira Khytharedes, *produced by Aleksandr Tairov at the Chamber Theater, Moscow, 1916. Gouache and gold paint on paper, 50.8 x 33.3 cm (20 x 13 1/8 in.).*

Below:
414. Liubov Popova. Prozodezhda (uniform industrial clothing) for Actor No.7, 1921. Gouache, ink and collage on paper on wood, 34 x 25.1 cm (13 3/8 x 9 7/8 in.).

The Ballets Russes was one of the most dazzling cultural enterprises of the twentieth century. Not only did the company transform critical and public perceptions of the performing arts in general, but it also placed the Russian Silver Age within the international arena, emphasizing the essential, interdisciplinary engagement of the new ballet with painting, poetry, photography, cinema, plastic movement, haute couture, literary criticism, music, and many other media. Furthermore, even if the primary heroes of the Ballets Russes were born in the Russian Empire (Diaghilev, Bakst, Benois, Michel Fokine, Anna Pavlova, Tamara Karsavina, Serge Lifar, Nijinsky, and Stravinsky, among others) [ills. 415–421, 423, 424], the company also attracted many European and American talents, especially in the late 1910s and 1920s—from Fernand Léger and Pablo Picasso to Cyril Beaumont and Erik Satie.

Ever since Richard Buckle's pioneering exhibition in Edinburgh and London in 1954,[1] there has been an increasing public awareness

Above:
415. Aleksandr Golovin. Costume design for a Knight in The Firebird, *1910. Watercolor and pencil on paper. Glinka Museum of Theatrical and Musical Art, St. Petersburg.*

Right:
416. Michel and Vera Fokine as Ivan Tsarevitch and The Beautiful Tsarevna in The Firebird, *1910.*

Opposite:
417. Mikhail Bobyshev. Michel Fokine in the Ballet "Carnival," 1918. Gouache and tempera on cardboard. Bakhrushin State Central Theater Museum, Moscow.

Below:

421. Valentin Serov. Poster advertising the inauguration of the first "Russian Season" at the Théâtre du Chatelet, Paris, May–June, 1909. Lithographic poster in black and white on a blue background. 231 x 177.7 cm (90 7/8 x 69 7/8 in.). Incorporating Serov's interpretation of Anna Pavlova dancing, the poster was produced to coincide with the premiere of Michel Fokine's ballet Les Sylphides.

BAKST

Opposite:
425. Léon Bakst. Costume for Cleopatra worn by Ida Rubinstein in Sergei Diaghilev's production of Cléopâtre, Paris, 1909. Pencil and watercolor on paper, 28 x 21 cm (11 x 8 1/4 in.).

Top left:
426. Léon Bakst. Costume design for Vaslav Nijinsky as Iskandar in La Péri, 1911. Watercolor, 67.6 x 48.9 cm (26 5/8 x 19 1/4 in.).

Top right:
427. Léon Bakst. Costume design for a bacchante in Narcisse, 1911. Pencil and watercolor on paper. 22 x 18.5 cm (8 5/8 x 7 1/4 in.). Musée National d'Art Moderne, Centre Pompidou, Paris.

Center:
428. Léon Bakst. Costume design for two Béotiennes in Narcisse, 1911. Watercolor and pencil, 40 x 27.5 cm (15 3/4 x 10 7/8 in.). Glinka Museum of Theatrical and Musical Art, St. Petersburg.

Bottom:
429. Léon Bakst. Costume of an odalisque in Nikolai Rimsky-Korsakov's ballet Schéhérazade, 1910. Watercolor on paper, 67 x 49 cm (26 3/8 x 19 1/4 in.).

and appreciation of the Diaghilev era—its dancers, artists, intrigues, and scandals. Visual and documentary materials abound, and much has been written about Diaghilev as impresario; the great dancers such as Karsavina and Nijinsky; the patrons such as Gabriel Astruc, Lady Juliet Duff, and Misia Sert; and the designers, especially Bakst and Benois.[2] In fact, European and American—as well as Russian—artists were also much responsible for the wider aesthetic reception and projection of the Ballets Russes, which is to say that if the primary set and costume designers were Russian, the "ethnographers" and educated observers tended to be foreign; Georges Barbier, Paul Iribe, and Arabella Yorke among them [ills. 422, 430–32].

Above:
430. Georges Barbier. Tamara Karsavina as Columbine, Vaslav Nijinsky as Harlequin, and Adolph Bolm as Pierrot in Carnaval, *1910. Pochoir printed in 1914.*

Right:
431. Georges Barbier. Vaslav Nijinsky in Schéhérazade, 1912. Watercolor on paper.

Opposite:
432. Arabella Yorke. Lydia Lopukhova as the Firebird. Hand-colored photograph-relief, 1920.

Right:
433. Léon Bakst. Costume design for Natalie Trouhanova as the Péri in La Péri, *rehearsed but not produced, by Sergei Diaghilev in Paris, 1911. Gouache, gold paint, and pencil on paper, 68 x 48.5 (26 3/4 x 19 in.).*

Below:
434. Vaslav Nijinsky in Le Dieu bleu, *Paris, 1912.*

Opposite:
435. Léon Bakst. Costume design for a temple dancer in Le Dieu bleu, *1912. Drawing dated 1922. Watercolor, gouache, gold, charcoal, and pencil on paper. 64.8 x 47 cm (25 1/2 x 18 1/2 in.). Marion Koogler McNay Art Museum, San Antonio.*

These individuals and their visual interpretations demonstrate that the Ballets Russes relied for its success not only upon the brilliant technique of its own dancers and designers, but also upon an entire network of external enthusiasts and sympathizers who, with their various skills and faculties, disseminated the ideas and ideals of Diaghilev's company to the community at large. Some of them such as Beaumont, Cocteau, and the photographer Emil Otto Hoppé are celebrated; others such as the musicologist Michel Dimitri Calvocoressi have fallen from critical grace; still others, once central to the running of the ballet productions such as the scene painter Vladimir Polunin,[3] have receded into the mists of history.

The surfeit of colors and forms identifiable with ballets such as *Schéhérazade* (1910) and *Le Dieu Bleu* (1912) [ills. 429, 434, 435–437, see also 24, 25, 355], evoking "all the cruelty and voluptuousness of the East,"[4] titillated a blasé, complacent Edwardian public, bemused it

Above:
436. *Léon Bakst. Costume design for the Blue Sultana in the ballet* Schéhérazade, *produced by Sergei Diaghilev, Paris, 1910. Watercolor on paper, 29.5 x 23 cm (11 ¹/₂ x 9 in.).*

Right:
437. *Adolf Bolm as the Shah Shahriar and Tamara Karsavina as Zobeida in* Schéhérazade.

with a heady mix of vaguely ethnographic appendages,[5] and shielded it from the dramatic social and political changes taking place outside. In addition, such ballets served a function similar to that of the Hollywood movie during the Golden Age of film, offering momentary oblivion to a weary populace by alluding to transgressive indulgences which few would ever savor. To a considerable extent, the productions of *Cléopâtre* and *Schéhérazade* also maintained the laden tradition of Imperial etiquette, for they were all about privilege and rank, luxury and fantasy, magic and mystery. In turn, the majesty of the Imperial productions—and of the Ballets Russes—extended well beyond the theater to the domestic extravaganzas of Russia's nobility and plutocracy, whose parties and celebrations often assumed the quality of theatrical productions. Serov captured this mood and moment in some of his salon portraits of the 1900s such as the *Portrait of Princess Olga Orlova* [see ill. 347]. Bakst, too, designed the gowns and wigs for a number of society evenings in St. Petersburg, including Countess Mariia Kleinmikhel's Costume Ball and Countess Elizaveta Shuvalova's Ball of the Colored Wigs in January and March 1914, respectively [ill. 438].[6]

Most discussions of the Ballets Russes concentrate on the innovative, the experimental, and the provocative, a focus which is reasonable

438. Ball of the Colored Wigs, held at the palace of Countess Elizaveta Shuvalova in St. Petersburg on March 22, 1914, during the last social season before the outbreak of World War I. The women's wigs were designed by Léon Bakst.

Above:

439. *Alexandre Benois. Stage design for Armide's Garden in Scene II of* Le Pavillon d'Armide, *produced by Sergei Diaghilev, Paris, 1909. Watercolor and collage on paper,* 45 x 63 cm (17 3/4 x 24 3/4 in.).

Left:

440. *Tamara Karsavina as Armide and Mikhail Mordkin as the Viscount in* Le Pavillon d'Armide, *Paris, 1909.*

Left:
441. Vaslav Nijinsky in the costume of Armide's favorite slave in Le Pavillon d'Armide, *Paris, 1909.*

Above:
442. Alexandre Benois. Costume for Armide's favorite slave, danced by Vaslav Nijinsky in Le Pavillon d'Armide, *1909.*

Left:

443. Léon Bakst. Hunting Costume for the Duchess in Sergei Diaghilev's production of The Sleeping Princess, *London, 1921. Gouache, watercolor, and gold on paper, 63 x 48 cm (26 1/2 x 19 in.).*

Above:

444. Léon Bakst. Set design for The Awakening *in Scene 4 of Sergei Diaghilev's production of* The Sleeping Princess, *London, 1921. Pencil and watercolor on paper. 48 x 66.8 cm (18 7/8 x 26 1/4 in.).*

Opposite bottom:
445. The arrival of the wicked fairy in Scene 1
of Sergei Diaghilev's production of The
Sleeping Princess, London, 1921.

Left:
446. Edmund Dulac. "The Good Fairy Bakst
Leads Prince Charming Diaghilev to the Shrine
of the Sleeping Princess." Drawing published in
The Sketch, London, 28 December 1921.

and understandable, given the power of such spectacles as *Le Pavillon d'Armide*, *Petrouchka*, and *Le Sacre du Printemps* [ills. 439–442, see also 344, 356, 357]. Such an approach may emphasize the inventive energy and prescience of Diaghilev's company, but, inevitably, it maligns or neglects those productions which either lacked originality and novelty (e.g., *Midas*, 1914) or public success at the time (e.g., *Les Biches*, 1924). Another ballet which suffered a similar fate was *The Sleeping Princess*, produced by Diaghilev in 1921, designed by Bakst, and choreographed by Marius Petipa, an example of what Evreinov called the "theater of excess"[7] [ills. 443–445]. In fact, what was one of Diaghilev's resounding commercial failures may have been one of his most glamorous productions; at any event, *The Sleeping Princess* remains one of the strongest aftershocks of the Russian Silver Age within the cultural emigration [ill. 446].

The Sleeping Princess—and the *Dames de Bonne Humeur* of 1917—were not isolated cases of visual abundance. Suffice it to recall that also in 1917, but in Petrograd and on the eve of the February Revolution, Meierkhold, now celebrated for his Constructivist productions of *The Magnanimous Cuckold* (1922) and *Earth on End* (1923), was organizing one of the most opulent extravaganzas in the history of the Russian theater: this was his production of Mikhail Lermontov's play

Masquerade for the Alexandrinsky Theater, which, though not a ballet did include a major dance component (the *ballo in maschera* in Act III) Golovin, for many years artist in residence for the Imperial theaters created more than four thousand sketches for *Masquerade*, regarding the commission as a tour de force in his more than fifty stage engagements.[8] In size and extravagance *Masquerade* even surpassed Golovin's notable successes in *Carmen* (Mariinsky Theater, 1908) and *L'Oiseau d feu* (The Firebird; he collaborated with Bakst on the 1910 production in Paris) [ills. 447, 448]. *Masquerade* anticipated Golovin's magnificent, albeit anachronistic, designs for *Le Chant du Rossignol* the following year at the Mariinsky, also produced by Meierkhold.

Be that as it may, the inexorable, chronological development of the set design, choreography, and music within the Ballets Russes seems to have been from "more" to "less," beginning with the emotional and visual splendor of *Le Pavillon d'Armide*, *Cléopatre*, and *Schéhérazade* and ending with the industrial efficiency of *La Chatte* [ills. 449, 450] and *Le Pas d'acier* in 1927 [see ills. 161, 162]. Such an evolution paralleled the trajectory of early-twentieth-century Russian art in general, at least as mapped by historians who are tempted to accept the heady mix of Symbolism as the starting point of "modern" and the formal severity of Constructivism as its destination. Along this pathway Malevich's *Black Square* (1915) [see ill. 215] and

Right:
449. Serge Lifar as the Young Man, here being borne away by his comrades, in La Chatte, *1927.*

Below:
450. Naum Gabo and Anton Pevsner. Set design for La Chatte, *produced by Sergei Diaghilev in Monte Carlo and Paris, 1927. La Chatte was one of the rare occasions when the two artist brothers, Gabo and Pevsner, applied their abstract principles of Constructivism to a utilitarian context, and the result was astonishing. By using light instead of color as a main artistic force and by constructing transparent and refractive surfaces from mica, celluloid, black oilcloth, etc., they created a mobile and variable decor that reflected and magnified the movements of the dancers.*

451. *Vladimir Tatlin.* Material Assemblage. Counterrelief, 1916. *Rosewood, spruce, sheet and galvanized iron, and zinc, 100 x 64 x 24 cm (39³/₈ x 25 ¹/₈ x 9 ¹/₂ in.). State Tretiakov Gallery, Moscow.*

Vladimir Tatlin's abstract material reliefs (1914–18) [ill. 451] are offered as indisputable proof of the advance from maximum to minimum, from external Realism to aesthetic independence, and are praised precisely for this momentum. Consequently and conversely, the upholders of established ideas who refused to adjust to newer trends—such as Anisfeld or Kalmakov, who continued to offer their languid delights throughout the time of Cubism and Constructivism—are often considered to be derivative and retrograde. For example, Anisfeld's designs for Michel Fokine's production of *Islamey* at the Mariinsky in 1912 won praise for their waft of Oriental spice, yet his studio paintings, exhibited a mere ten years later, were "without the element of beauty; in some instances even unsightly and incomprehensible"[9] [ill. 452]. Similarly, Kalmakov's bizarre resolutions for Vera Komissarzhevskaia's *Salomé* [see ill. 484] were all that a Symbolist design should have been in 1908—"grotesque, bestial, fluorescent, voluptuous"[10]—and were, therefore, "legitimate," but his later, analogous pictures are often regarded as labored and vulgar.

In 1914 Bakst published a review of the state of the performing arts, entitled, appropriately enough, "On Contemporary Theater. In the Theater No One Wants to Listen Anymore, but Wants to See." In this telling essay Bakst not only emphasized the new and general orientation toward the pictorial on stage under the encroaching pressure of the cinema and at the expense of real sound and real movement, but also described this visual extravagance as a "dramatic art" born within a "mute form."[11] Seven years later Bakst himself fell victim to this triumph of the trompe l'oeil with his luxurious sets, costumes, and props for Diaghilev's production of *The Sleeping*

452. Boris Anisfeld. Set design for Milii Balakirev's ballet Islamei *at the Mariinsky Theater, St. Petersburg, 1912. Gouache, bronze, and silver paint on cardboard.*

Princess at the Alhambra Theatre, London (a three-hour version of Charles Perrault's *Sleeping Beauty* with music by Peter Tchaikovsky and choreography by Marius Petipa).

In some sense, *The Sleeping Princess* marked the culmination not only of the strong visual tendency to which Bakst had referred in his article, but also to an entire direction within the Ballets Russes: throughout its vigorous life, Diaghilev's company investigated many musical and choreographic ideas vested in calculated decoration, sometimes spare, sometimes lush. The year 1913, for example, had witnessed both the sensual hyperbole of *La Tragédie de Salomé* (designs by Sudeikin) and the sober geometry of *Jeux* (designs by Bakst), two parallel but very different productions [ills. 453–455]. The former attracted by its satiety of color and elaborate haberdashery, the latter by its monochromatic reduction and highly controlled movements, a counterpoint which testified to the broad

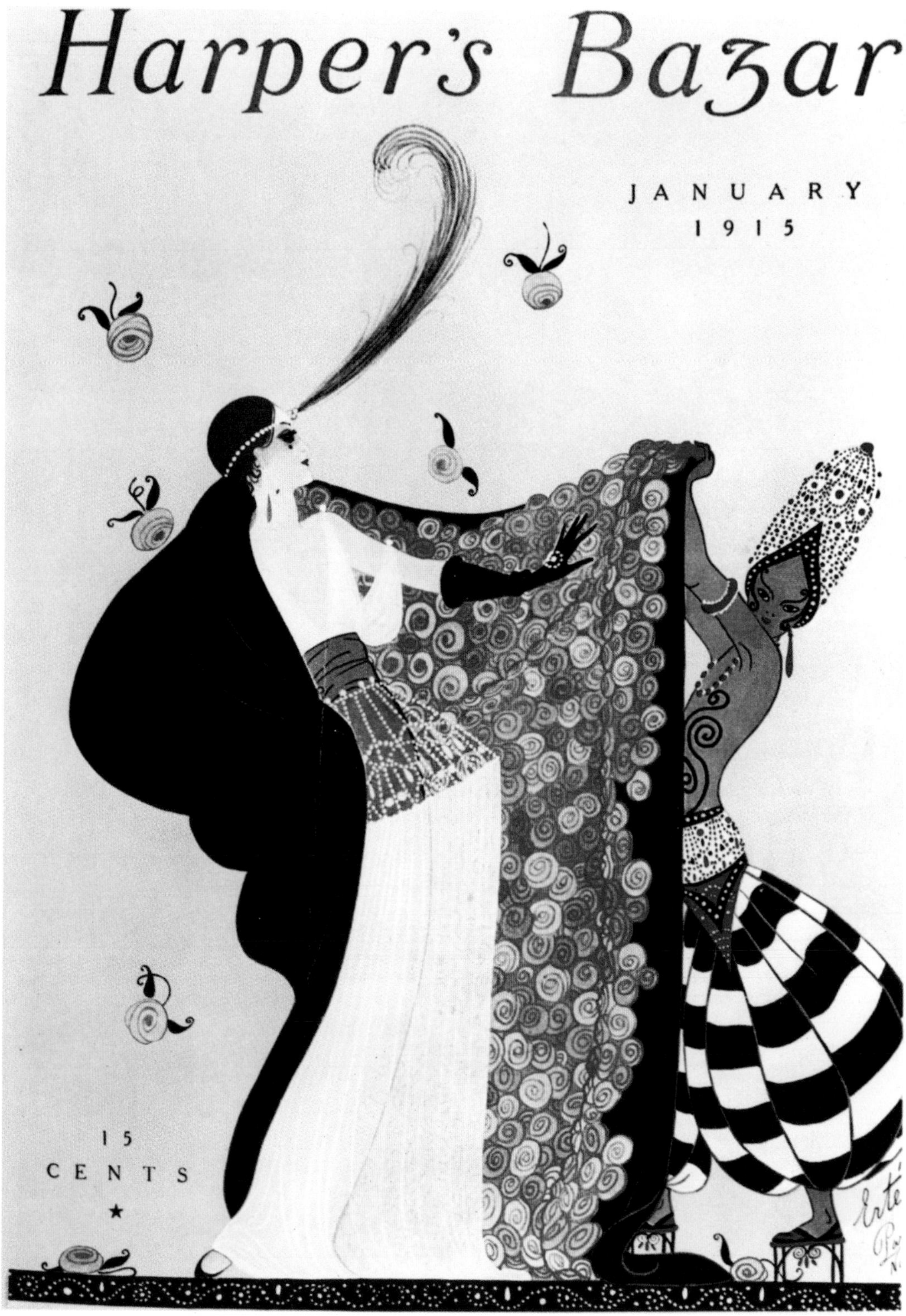
Harper's Bazar
JANUARY
1915
15
CENTS
★
Erté

repertoire of the Ballets Russes, to the aesthetic tolerance of Diaghilev, and to the versatility of his designers. Incidentally, in *Jeux* Nijinsky wanted to have an airplane fall onto the stage—just as the Cubo-Futurists did in their *Victory over the Sun* of 1913, for which, incidentally, Malevich, too, designed the costume for a sportsman.[12] Both pieces paralleled the emerging interest in time and motion studies, championed in Russia by Aleksei Gastev,[13] and also presaged Meierkhold's application of biomechanics to the dramatic theater.

If *The Sleeping Princess* was a brilliant but falling star in the firmament of the new postwar, postrevolutionary world, it was not the only one, and the more brittle fantasies of Bakst's epigones such as Boris Bilinsky, Erté (Roman de Tirtoff), Vladimir Jedrinsky, and Georges Pogedaieff persisted well into the twentieth century, promoting ideas, motifs, and designs of the Silver Age in the 1920s and onward in many Western capitals [ills. 456, 457, see also 44]. Logically enough, some of these artists turned to the silver screen for further inspiration, especially Bilinsky, whose vivid style suited the effervescent scenarios of the émigré producers working in the French movie business at Montreuil. Erté, too, worked in Paris and Hollywood, although more as a designer of fabulous evening gowns, and the luminous colors and elegant silhouettes of his outlandish designs tell us immediately of Bakst's influence.

Opposite:
456. Erté (Roman de Tirtoff). Cover of Harper's Bazar, *New York, January 1915.*

Above:
457. Georges Pogedaieff. Costume designs for two male performers in the Polovtsian Dances *from* Prince Igor, *1920s. Watercolor, charcoal, gold, and silver on paper, 42 x 44 cm (16 1/2 x 17 3/8 in.).*

IN THE WINGS

Adjacent to, but often at loggerheads with the Ballets Russes were the many other Russian dance companies established during the 1910s and 1920s, for the most part transitory, that rode on the crest of Diaghilev's success, but moved "en marge des [on the margins of the] Ballets Russes."[14] Anna Pavlova, Ida Rubinstein, Alexandre and Clotilde Sakharoff, and Natalie Trouhanova [ills. 458–460], among many other dancers, pursued individual, professional careers outside the Diaghilev orbit, organizing their own troupes and inviting prestigious designers such as Anisfeld and Bakst. Pavlova, the Imperial diva, appeared at many venues, not least the Palais du Trocadéro in Paris in 1921, while Trouhanova, a star of lesser brilliance, tried to outwit both Pavlova and Diaghilev by arranging her own "Concerts de Danse" in Paris in 1912.

The renovation of the classical ballet coincided with the development of a countermovement known as free or plastic dance, which in Russia owed much to the expressions in gesture, step, and body of Olga Desmond, Isadora Duncan, and Ruth St. Denis, in particular. Duncan was especially popular in Russia from her several tours [see ills. 76, 77] and, in the 1910s and early 1920s, inspired a large following of dancers,

clotilde &
alexandre
SAKHAROFF

ANNA PAVLOVA

N.REMISOFF.

Opposite:
458. Georges Barbier. Program cover for a recital by
Clotilde and Alexandre Sakharoff at the Théâtre des
Champs-Elysées, Paris, 1921.

Above:
459. Nicholas Remisoff (Nikolai Remizov;
pseudonym: Re-mi). Lithographic cover for the
program advertising Anna Pavlova's solo appearance
at the Palais du Trocadéro, Paris (June 1921).

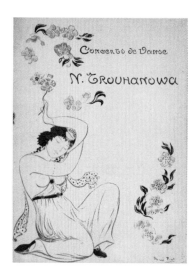

female and male, in St. Petersburg and Moscow. These *bosonozhki* (lit., barefooters) elaborated variants of free dance into new and original systems or schools such as Geptakhor and Liudmila Alekseeva's School of Harmonious Gymnastics, perhaps the closest to the Duncan method. Parallel to these experiments in free dance, and drawing heavily on the Symbolist concern with rhythm, Prince Sergei Volkonsky founded his Institute of Rhythm in Petrograd in 1921, one of the several curious aftershocks of the Silver Age during the first years of the Bolshevik regime [ill. 462]. Arguing that bodily movement should be stimulated and controlled by rhythm in concert with the symmetry of the body itself, Volkonsky developed a theory of aesthetic motion which, in some perverse way, may be regarded as the artistic counterpart to Gastev's ergometric gymnastics at his Institute of Labor.[15]

Above:
460. René Piot. Program cover for Concerts de Danse: Donnés par Mlle. N. Trouhanova. *Paris: Maquet, 1912.*

Right:
461. Natalia Goncharova. Poster for the Grand Bal de Nuit at the Grand Bal des Artistes, Paris, 1923. Color lithograph, 119 x 79 cm (43 3/4 x 31 1/2 in.).

462. Prince Sergei Volkonsky, Director of the Imperial Theaters, St. Petersburg, 1899–1901. A major force in Russian theatrical life, Volkonsky was purposeful and self-willed, qualities which sometimes antagonized people, for example, Sergei Diaghilev. A theorist of gesture and speech and an adept of Emile Jaques-Dalcroze, Volkonsky directed the Institute of Rhythm in Moscow before emigrating to Italy in 1921.

Above left:
463. The artist Mak (pseudonym of Pavel Ivanov) and his partner Elza Kriuger dancing the tango of death, Moscow, 1913. The artist and actor Mak was also a celebrated ballroom dancer, and he and his constant partner, Kriuger, were widely considered to be the best pair of tango dancers in Moscow (see ill. 553). Kriuger is wearing a dress designed by Nadezhda Lamanova.

Above right:
464. Mak and Elza Kriuger dancing the tango, Moscow, 1913. The dress is by Nadezhda Lamanova.

That the passion for the new dance was not confined to balletomanes and cognoscenti during the Silver Age is demonstrated by the fact that the Russian avant-garde also cultivated an eager interest in the tango, which, between 1912 and 1914 was the "in" dance in Moscow. One could learn the tango in a variety of Moscow dance studios, primarily that of the caricaturist and stage designer Pavel Ivanov (pseudonym: Mak) [ills. 463, 464]. Ivanov, whose portrait Goncharova painted in 1913, and his main partner, Elza Kriuger, moved closely with the bohemia, especially Goncharova and Larionov. Encouraging rhythmical abandon and the wearing of masks, they offered the tango as an iconoclastic emblem of social and cultural emancipation, as if to confirm Duncan's belief that "with her dance . . . the dancer of the future . . . will sing the freedom of woman"[16]— which, no doubt, is why a photograph of *tangisty* accompanies

Larionov's 1913 manifesto on face painting.[17] Much later, in Paris, Goncharova, Larionov, Ilia Zdanevich, and others organized an elaborate cycle of costume balls, including the Grand Bal des Artistes Travesti/Transmental of 1923, which also celebrated the tango [ill. 461].

DRAMATIC THEATER

A central reason for the ready inculcation of the Style Moderne into the Russian theater lies in its synthetic impulse. If the artists and writers of both the Symbolist and the avant-garde movements called for an aesthetic common denominator which would unite all the arts into what Kandinsky called a "monumental art or art as a whole,"[18] the Style Moderne catered to this demand. Its elongated forms and exuberant gestures elicited associations with music, free dance, and the mellifluousness of poetry; its architectural service conducted energy to concomitant objects such as tableware, clothes, and jewelry; and it was but a short step from the waves of

Above:
465. Konstantin Somov. Portrait of Evfimiia Nosova, 1911. Oil on canvas, 138.5 x 88 cm (54 1/2 x 34 5/8). State Tretiakov Gallery, Moscow.

Right:
466. Mstislav Dobuzhinsky. Ceiling fresco on the grand staircase in the Nosovs' winter residence, Moscow, 1900–10.

Opposite top:
467. Fedor Shekhtel and Ivan Fomin, architects. Moscow Art Theater, 1901–02.

Opposite bottom:
468. Fedor Shekhtel and Ivan Fomin, architects. Vestibule of the Moscow Art Theater, 1901–02.

Shekhtel's ceiling and staircase for Stepan Riabushinsky's villa [see ill. 264] to the serpentine grace of a Moscow hostess such as Evfimiia Nosova in her Lamanova dress (cf. Somov's portrait of 1910–11) [ills. 465, 466].

In the spirit of the times, Stanislavsky and Vladimir Nemirovich-Danchenko ratified Shekhtel's elaborate design for the new Moscow Art Theater (MKhAT), completed in 1902–03 [ills. 467, 468]. True, Stanislavsky's basic orientation was toward the Realist aesthetic, as he demonstrated in his productions of Chekhov's plays and in his 1909 production of Ivan Turgenev's *A Month in the Country*, designed by Dobuzhinsky: for Stanislavsky [ill. 471], the actor remained the dominant and dynamic force, while the decor was intended to complement the speech and the gesture, a perception which, essentially, contravened the new scenic principles espoused by Adolf Appia, Edward Gordon Craig, Vera Komissarzhevskaia, Meierkhold, and Tairov. On the other hand, with its febrile facade by Anna Golubkina paraphrasing that of

August Endell's for the Atelier Elvira in Munich [ills. 469, 470], the new Art Nouveau premises of MKhAT on Kamergerskii Lane symbolized the revolution affecting the dramatic stage and its repertoire (Leonid Andreev, Chekhov, Fedor Sologub), dance (Duncan was a frequent visitor to Russia), the circus, the cabaret, even sports and the martial arts.

Suddenly, everyone wanted to "play and to play merrily,"[19] but they could do so only in a theater liberated of its tendentious nineteenth-century gravity and academic routine. Founded on the ancient conventions of tragedy and comedy, the dramatic theater had developed into a mature and sophisticated medium in Russia only in

Above:
469. Anna Golubkina. The Billow, high relief on the front facade of the Moscow Art Theater, 1901.

Right:
470. August Endell. Facade of the Atelier Elvira in Munich, 1898.

Below:
471. Konstantin Stanislavsky, 1910s (see ill. 237).

Opposite:
472. Valentin Serov. Portrait of Maxim Gorky, 1905. Oil on canvas, 126 x 91 cm (49 1/2 x 35 7/8 in.). Maxim Gorky Museum, Moscow.

the first half of the nineteenth century with plays such as Aleksandr Griboedov's *Woe from Wit*, Pushkin's *Little Tragedies*, and Nikolai Gogol's *Inspector General*. In the later nineteenth century, assimilation of the Classical and then Romantic repertoires prepared the way for the complex dramas of Alexei K. Tolstoi and Aleksandr Ostrovsky, such as *Tsar Fedor Ioannovich* and *There Was Not a Penny and Suddenly There Was a Pound* with their prompting for social change, and then for the more experimental plays of Chekhov, Blok, and Gorky, all of whom emphasized the role of the spoken word (or eloquent silence) as an expression of individual polemic and social conflict [ills. 472, 473]. The focus on the hero, moral crisis, and the private deliberation in much of the dramatic tradition favored the appearance of the diva or star, and actresses such as Mariia Ermolova, Vera Komissarzhevskaia, and Alisa Koonen, in particular, left a stong imprint on the perception of the dramatic theater in modern Russia. Tairov's Classical restorations such as *Phèdre* and *Thamira Khytharedes* in the 1910s and 1920s catered well to this condition.

473. Maxim Gorky with actors of the Moscow Art Theater, ca. 1900. Co-founded in 1898 by Konstantin Stanislavsky (see ills. 237, 471) and Vladimir Nemirovich-Danchenko, the Moscow Art Theater developed and maintained a broad international repertoire, embracing such disparate playwrights as Maurice Maeterlinck and Anton Chekhov, Gerhart Hauptmann and Maxim Gorky. Gorky (standing, right), socially committed and a staunch Realist, believed that art should not disguise the ills of society but, on the contrary, be concerned with problems of inequality and injustice. His stories such as Twenty-six Men and a Girl *and plays such as* The Lower Depths *represented a reportorial and didactic trend much at odds with the brittle dreams of the Symbolist dramatists.*

Fedor Komissarzhevsky, artistic director of the Imperial theaters and brother of Vera, summarized the Modernist development of the dramatic theater by suggesting that there were two distinct methods at the disposal of the contemporary producer and designer: the "psychological" and the "spectacular."[20] Rejecting the latter, he concluded that:

> with all these thousands of meters of canvas for
> productions, with these props and apparatuses . . .
> we have reached the stage where the decor storage areas
> of our theaters are much bigger than the theaters
> themselves. We must lighten the theater.[21]

According to Komissarzhevsky, the design system that was to replace "these thousands of meters of canvas" was the economical, "psychological" one, which "does not disperse the viewer's attention all over the stage, but concentrates it on the actor or the action"[22]—and it

Left:
474. Fedor Shekhtel, architect. Stage at the Moscow Art Theater.

Below:
475. Staging of The Cherry Orchard *at the Moscow Art Theater, 1904.*

was MKhAT, founded in 1898, which helped to move the art of the stage toward a deeper, more psychological conception.

While the first MKhAT productions were much obliged to the Realist tradition, the very fact that Chekhov's "psychological dramas" debuted there (with designs by Viktor Simov) testifies to the refreshingly different approach of Stanislavsky's theater, even if there were close parallels with Western trends. Inevitably, not

NIEMIROVITSCH...ENKO ...SCHINLAWSKI LUSCHSKU KNIPPER, STANISLAWSKI, TSCHECHOW ARTEM ANDREJEWA ANDRLIEFF LUINA GRIGORIEVA TICHOMIROV ROKSANOVA MEIERHOLD

476. *Anton Chekhov (holding book) with cast members of his play* The Seagull *at the Moscow Art Theater in 1899, including director Konstantin Stanislavsky, seated next to Chekhov; Olga Knipper-Chekhova (Chekhov's wife), standing to the left of Stanislavsky; and Vsevolod Meierkhold, seated far right.*

everyone was pleased with the progression from physical to psychological, and the 1896 premiere of *The Seagull*, for example, was a disaster, critics complaining of desultory action and obscure plot. But the die was cast and by the time *The Cherry Orchard* premiered in 1903, Stanislavsky was acknowledged as Russia's leading director and MKhAT as a bold laboratory of theatrical solutions [ills. 474–476]. Indeed, if Stanislavsky's presentation of Chekhov's plays portrayed the "reality" of people and things, it also emphasized the intangible, the invisible, and the oblique. Both Chekhov and Stanislavsky understood that no one speaks the same language, that dialogues often operate at cross-purposes, the interlocutors never really communicating, and that there are other sign systems operative beyond our everyday grammar and syntax. In particular, *The Seagull* with its Maeterlinckian imagery and *The Cherry Orchard* with its recurrent, but inexplicable sound from far away elicited this sense of otherwordliness.

Of course, "psychology" also lay at the basis of the scenographic theories of Adolphe Appia and Edward Gordon Craig, disseminated in Russia by Prince Sergei Volkonsky (one-time director of the Imperial theaters), the critic Mikhail Babenchikov, the historian Evgenii Znosko-Borovsky, and—in a practical way—Tairov at his Chamber Theater.[23] Appia's and Craig's—and Max Reinhardt's—new concepts, therefore, finding an enthusiastic audience in St. Petersburg and Moscow, helped to cleanse Russian stage design of the more cumbersome elements of the nineteenth-century heritage.

Craig's co-production with Stanislavsky and Leopold Sulerzhitsky of *Hamlet* at MKhAT in 1911 was one result of this international cooperation, even if by then Craig's Symbolist principles were somewhat passé.

All this is to say that Russian directors, producers, and actors were well aware of Western European innovations through publications and frequent travel to Berlin, Munich, and Paris. Meierkhold, for example, encouraged his artists to produce psychological designs based on Appia's sparse, emotive forms, an instruction confirmed by his 1907 production of Leonid Andreev's *Life of a Man* at Komissarzhevskaia's theater. But not all Russians regarded the English, German, and Austrian influences as beneficial and some, including Komissarzhevsky and Meierkhold, even maintained that German "bad taste" was ruining the Russian theater.[24] As if to counter this insurgence, Russian producers and stage designers, including those of the avant-garde, turned to their own heritage for artistic inspiration, in some cases creating a vigorous and exotic product which Western audiences, in particular, accepted immediately as "Russian" or "oriental." Diaghilev's productions of *Schéhérazade* and *Les Orientales* in Paris in 1910 are cases in point [ills. 477, 478].

The marriage of East and West may have been consummated during the Diaghilev epoch, but the betrothal occurred much earlier, for the Russian theater witnessed many attempts to bridge the gap between high and low, between the studio and the street. That is why no discussion of the modern Russian theater can be complete

Above and below:
477 & 478. Eugène Druet. Vaslav Nijinsky in the Danse Siamoise from Les Orientales, *1910.*

479. *Boris Kustodiev.* Fairground Booths, *1917. Oil on canvas, 80 x 93 cm (31 ¹/₂ x 36 ⁵/₈ in.). The State Russian Museum, St. Petersburg. Kustodiev is remembered for his vigorous evocations of merchant Russia. Growing up in a merchant's house in Astrakhan and a student of theology, Kustodiev treasured the customs, dress, and sensual abundance of Russia's middle class. His portraits of merchants and, more pressingly, of merchants' wives, often presented as Russian Venuses, carry strong pictorial references to quaint churches, bright store signboards, bustling priests, and busy fairgrounds. Even after the October Revolution, Kustodiev continued to describe Old Russia in this reassuring and engaging manner.*

without ample reference to the tradition of the *balagan* (fairground booth) as a theatrical form. Benois recalled the *balagany* of his St. Petersburg childhood [ill. 479]:

> The *balagany served as the main attraction of that promenading that, "since time immemorial," or more exactly since the eighteenth century, had been the most important popular pastime in Russia, especially in the two capitals. This promenading corresponded to what are called foires or fairs in Western Europe. In many respects, our entertainments were copies of what had been elaborated in the West, but still, whatever came from overseas was imbued with a specifically "Russian spirit." The merriment in these promenades was of a more tempestuous, more elemental character. Apart from that, it was possible to see much of a distinctive, local flavor, something ultra-amusing and picturesque. And there were more drunks around here than anyplace in Europe, and they were noisier, more tempestuous, and also terrifying. The general drunkenness of the simple folk who in the evening remained behind as the real proprietors of the squares that were allotted to these amusements, gave them some kind of downright demonic, dashing character—communicated so wonderfully in Scene IV of Stravinsky's* Petrouchka *[ills. 480, 481].*[25]

The *balagan* was just one part of a popular cultural tradition in Russia which included bazaars and buffoons, minstrels and hawkers, and quacks and Punch-and-Judy shows, even though by the late nineteenth century much of this was disappearing or, rather, interfusing with the circus, the traveling prestidigitator, the flea market, and, subsequently, the cinema. Presenting folk dramas, especially Punch-and-

Above:

480. Alexandre Benois. Set design for the Butter Week Fair in Scenes 1 and 4 of Petrouchka, *1911. Graphite, tempera and/or watercolor, and crayon on paper, 44.8 x 61.5 cm (17 $^{11}/_{16}$ x 24 $^3/_{16}$ in.).*

Left:

481. The Butter Week Fair in Petrouchka *with Enrico Cecchetti, Tamara Karsavina, and Vaslav Nijinsky in the puppet booth, Paris, 1911.*

482. *Ilia Repin.* Portrait of Savva
Mamontov, *1878. Oil on canvas, 71 x 58 cm
(28 x 22 ⅞ in.). Abramtsevo Museum and
Reserve.*

Judy shows, to an eager audience, the *balagany* depended for their effect on rude actions, colorful language, simple cues, and rough décor—making the spectacle not so much a "theater of movement in general, but a theater of verbal dynamics," as literary critic Viktor Shklovsky wrote in 1920.[26] The *balagan*, therefore, contained strong theatrical possibilities—a mobile stage, a wide variety of acts, audience participation—which the Modernists adapted to their own productions such as *Victory over the Sun* and to theatrical forms such as the avant-garde cabaret.

After the exclusive Imperial monopoly on the Russian stage was lifted in 1882, a number of important private companies were established, among them Mamontov's opera company in 1885. In managing the so-called Krotkov Private Opera Troupe in Moscow, Mamontov [ill. 482] implemented his desire to integrate the arts and, more egocentrically, to build a monument that would help him overcome the identity crisis which he had suffered as a young man:

> *I am not a writer. I'm not a philosopher yet, not a great*
> *social do-gooder. After me nothing will remain that*
> *might remind people that there once lived Savva*
> *Ivanovich Mamontov and that this is how he lived.*[27]

True, Mamontov's opera company drew on a theatrical experience going back to the early 1870s, when the Abramtsevo circle of artists, writers, and actors had begun to stage plays and charades, some of them written by Mamontov himself. These tableaux vivants were in the tradition of Victorian family entertainment, except that the "family" included professional artists such as Levitan, Polenov, Vasnetsov, and Vrubel. For example, Vasnetsov designed the production of Aleksandr Ostrovsky's play *Snegurochka*, (The Snow Maiden) in the winter of 1882–83, and Polenov made the decorations for Mamontov's own play *The Crimson Rose* in January 1883. Furthermore, as in the case of *Snegurochka*, the circle often used genuine peasant costumes, which lent a special vitality and immediacy to the productions.

The Abramtsevo circle worked in the spirit of true amateurs, and their productions carried none of the tedious schemata of the Imperial stage, although the musical organization and acting for the first productions in Abramtsevo and Moscow (e.g., *Rusalka* and *Snegurochka* with décor by Vasnetsov [ill. 483]; *Aida*, designed by Polenov; and *Carmen*, designed by Ilia Ostroukhov), encountered criticism rather than praise. In 1896 the company reopened, inaugurating its second and more successful phase and witnessing, for example, the appearance of Nadezhda Zabela (Vrubel's wife) in *Hansel and Gretel*, designed by Vrubel, and Fedor Chaliapin in Mussorgsky's *Khovan-*

483. *Viktor Vasnetsov. Stage design for the Chambers of Tsar Berendei in Nikolai Rimsky-Korsakov's opera* Snegourochka, *produced at Abramtsevo in 1885. Watercolor, gouache, gold, and pencil on paper, 35.5 x 48.8 cm (14 x 19 1/4 in.). State Tretiakov Gallery, Moscow.*

shchina, designed by Korovin and Maliutin. Just like his German contemporary, the duke of Saxe-Meiningen, Mamontov encouraged his designers to deemphasize the extravagant and to allow the actor freedom of movement while still respecting historical accuracy. Within these parameters, Korovin and Polenov, in particular, helped to create a "revolt in stage design."[28]

The enterprises of Mamontov's rival, Princess Tenisheva [see ills. 276, 281], especially the artistic retreat she established at her estate, Talashkino, were also pertinent to the development of the new ideas in the Russian theater. Sharing Mamontov's aspirations, Tenisheva felt her vocation to be the revival and propagation of Russian peasant art. To this end, she invited artists and writers to visit her estate, among them Diaghilev, Golovin, Korovin, Sergei Makovsky, Maliutin, Roerich, Dmitrii Stelletsky, and Vrubel. She also established workshops for training young peasants in traditional crafts and opened a theater that gave particular attention to the dramatization of fairy tales. Unlike Mamontov, Tenisheva did not run a private opera (in spite of her own training as a singer) and her theater was of modest dimensions (seating only two hundred), but she ensured that the dramatic repertoire consisted of Russian titles based on legends and fables and that they were acted by peasants—one example being

Above:
484. Nikolai Kalmakov. Costume design for
Salomé for the production of Oscar Wilde's
Salomé at Vera Komissarzhevskaia's Theater,
St. Petersburg, 1908. Watercolor on paper, 32.5
x 21 cm (12 3/4 x 8 1/4 in.).

the opera *The Tale of the Dead Tsarevna and the Seven Bogatyrs*. Tenisheva
also founded a balalaika orchestra and invited Vrubel and other
artists to decorate the sounding boards of the instruments. It was in
the "primitive" ambience of Talashkino and in consultation with her
sometime curator there, Roerich, that Stravinsky found essential
ideas and materials, both ethnographical and musical, for *Le Sacre du
printemps* [see ill. 344].

Naturally, both Tenisheva and Mamontov superimposed personal
taste upon their respective activities, bringing the professional conventions of high art and the theater to their perceptions of peasant
culture so as to create the kind of amalgam later developed by
Diaghilev in productions such as *Le Sacre du printemps*, *Coq d'or*, *Soleil de
nuit*, and *Contes Russes*. The repertoires may have featured village
maidens, monsters, and witches, yet the key prop was no longer the
imagination of the sympathetic crowd of villagers or humble towns-
folk, but, at least in the case of Mamontov's opera company, a
mechanical complex which changed scenes, dropped curtains, and
modified lighting. The costumes and sets may have incorporated
mythic *sirin* birds and ears of wheat, but they were painted by studio
artists conversant with the ideas of Art Nouveau. In any case, the
audiences of Mamontov's opera and Tenisheva's theater consisted of
literati, students, critics, and professional artists who, through a con-
spiracy of methods, were encouraged to view the performances not
as rowdy entertainment, but rather as an aesthetic experience. Indeed,
it was the presence of a sophisticated audience—educated, solvent,
and curious—as much as the new methods and perceptions on stage
which inspired the theatrical renaissance of the Russian Silver Age.

Of primary importance in this context was the theater which the
actress Komissarzhevskaia founded in St. Petersburg in 1906 [ill.
485], for which she commissioned a number of experimental productions, staged by Meierkhold, who joined her after a brief collab-
oration with Stanislavsky in Moscow, including Ibsen's *Hedda Gabler*
(designed by Sapunov and Vasilii Milioti), Maeterlinck's *Soeur Béatrice*
(designed by Sudeikin), and Blok's *Balaganchik* (Fairground booth),
designed by Sapunov [ill. 486]. As if to contest Stanislavsky's Realist
priorities, Meierkhold and Komissarzhevskaia selected plays and
artists with a strong inclination toward the radical and the unortho-
dox. For example, Komissarzhevskaia was responsible for the notorious production of *Salomé* in 1908 with Kalmakov's perverse designs
which, after the dress rehearsal, was banned by the Holy Synod
because of alleged pornography [ill. 484]. The production of
Maeterlinck's *Soeur Béatrice* also elicited harsh criticism both for its
"conditional" acting and for its "abstract" sets and costumes, leading Walter Nouvel to dismiss it as a "sad and hopeless" production.[29]

Sapunov's decorative arrangement for *Hedda Gabler* in 1906 was no less provocative, the action taking place not within the usual three walls of the proscenium, but against a single, monochrome backdrop located close to the front of the stage and leaving only a narrow area of the stage for the actors. Fedor Komissarzhevsky described the effect: "Everything was like a phantom. The stage seemed to be enveloped in a bluish-green, silver smoke. The back curtain was blue."[30] Also in 1906, Komissarzhevskaia, Meierkhold, and Sapunov expressed their new attitude in the interpretation of Blok's *Balaganchik*—a psychological drama which reflected both Appia's and Edward Gordon Craig's psychological theories of stage design. At his Chamber Theater in Moscow Aleksandr Tairov and his designers, especially Exter, were ready to follow the lead, as the productions of *Thamira Khytharedes* (1916) [see ill. 413] and *Salomé* (1917) in particular indicate so clearly.[31]

If the Style Moderne graced the surfaces of the new villas, Meltser furniture, and Kikerino ceramics, the whirls of Fabergé jewelry and Kuznetsov porcelain, and the intricate patterns of Lamanova custom-made dresses and anonymous manufactured chintzes, it also affected the theater—and in the most obvious and obtrusive manner. In some sense, the audaciously florid buildings of Kekushev and Shekhtel could themselves be regarded as theatrical laboratories—with their soirées, *jours fixes* (salon visiting days), dinner parties, charades, and the often pretentious deportment of the owners, some of the houses turned into veritable miniature theaters.

Opposite bottom:
485. Actress Vera Komissarzhevskaia in her St. Petersburg home, ca. 1908. A professional actress with a forceful personality, Komissarzhevskaia founded her theater in St. Petersburg in 1906 with the express aim of encouraging and promoting young playwrights, and, to this end, she invited Vsevolod Meierkhold to be her first director. Until her untimely death in 1910, Komissarzhevskaia assembled a rich Symbolist repertoire, including plays by Leonid Andreev, Aleksandr Blok, Gerhart Hauptmann, Hugo von Hofmannsthal, Aleksei Remizov, and Fedor Sologub, with set design by up-and-coming artists such as Nikolai Kalmakov, Nikolai Sapunov, and Sergei Sudeikin. Balaganchik (Fairground booth) was among Komissarzhevskaia's most important productions.

Above:
486. Nikolai Sapunov. Mystical Meeting, 1907. Gouache, bronze, gold and silver paint, and charcoal on paper, 42 x 84 cm (16 1/2 x 33 in.). State Tretiakov Gallery, Moscow. Sapunov based his picture on Aleksandr Blok's play Balaganchik *(Fairground booth), which Vsevolod Meierkhold produced at Vera Komissarzhevskaia's Theater, St. Petersburg, in 1906.*

487. *Evening dress, 1910s. From the atelier of Anna Gindus, St. Petersburg. State Hermitage, St. Petersburg.*

In this regard, the rapid development of what one may call the Russian fashion industry or, rather, Russian haute couture, may be seen as a logical appendage to the social life of the *osobniak* (mansion). If the Imperial family continued to dictate taste in haberdashery, Russia's new and expanding middle class called for a faster, often more flamboyant style of dress, and ateliers run by Lamanova and Anna Gindus catered to their sometimes rather ostentatious taste [ill. 487, see also 9]. Among the decorative sources exploited by these women were the Russian Neo-Nationalist, or Neo-Russian, style, the latest Parisian fads, and, in the 1910s, the Ballets Russes, especially the costumes of Bakst.[32] In keeping with the station of the nouvelles riches, Bakst, for example, enhanced sexuality and, not without the influence of sports and gymnastics, freed the modern woman from the strictures of the bustle, the hoop, and even the corset. Bakst regarded dress design as one of the most original fields of artistic endeavor, affirming that an evening gown could be just as inspiring and as beautiful as a painting of the Madonna. Furthermore, for Bakst, fashion, including the fashion parade and the costume ball, was a synthetic discipline which, like the opera, the ballet, and the deluxe edition, whether book, poster, visiting card, or menu, relied upon the simultaneous elicitation and gratification of at least two of the senses (particularly sight, touch, and sound, and sometimes even smell). This theatricalized quality of the plutocratic and intellectual élite, both in St. Petersburg and in Moscow, should not be underestimated—and not only because it extended the *zhiznetvorchestvo* of the Symbolist generation, but also because it inspired and informed actual experiments in the performing arts.[33]

THE BUSINESS OF CULTURE

During the Silver Age the *jour fixe* was a key component of literary and artistic life in St. Petersburg and Moscow. Balmont's "Tuesdays," Briusov's "Wednesdays," Belyi's "Sundays," Diaghilev's Wednesday teas, and V. Ivanov's receptions at his Tower apartment provided time and space for the debate of countless intellectual, political, and occult subjects. These personal salons were enhanced by the activities of several clubs and salons, above all the Society of Free Aesthetics founded in Moscow in 1906 as an exhibition, lecture, and performance venue [ill. 488]. Under the auspices of Belyi and Briusov, the Society did much to promote Symbolism, although after about 1910, it broadened its interests considerably when mercantile members began to "raise their voices."[34] Actually, the intellectual membership of the Society was dominated by painters and musicians, including Leonid Sabaneev, Serov, and Scriabin, the Blue Rose artists, as well as Goncharova and Larionov,

whose one-man exhibitions Briusov organized there in 1910 and 1912, respectively. Among the foreign visitors were Henri Matisse, Émile Verhaeren, and Vincent d'Indy. The Society lasted until 1917, by which time, as Belyi recalled, its membership was suffering from an "excess of lady millionaires."[35]

Later on, describing his impressions of the Society of Free Aesthetics and of Moscow's café culture in general, Belyi wrote: "Savva Mamontovs, lots of them, suddenly caught on to us. . . . Such couples (the Girshmans) turned up everywhere: the husbands would give subsidies to societies trying to obtain something from us with the persistence of goats; the wives were languorous and, like Venuses, issued forth from a beautiful foam of muslin and diamond constellations."[36] But in spite of Belyi's sardonic tone, these "goats" and "Venuses" were positive forces in the dissemination of new artistic ideas, not least through their purchases of works of art. The wealthy Genrietta and Vladimir Girshman, for example, collected paintings by the Milioti brothers, Sapunov, Somov, and Sudeikin and inspired a number of portraits by Serov and Somov.

Of great importance to the development of Moscow's Modernism were the activities of two businessmen and collectors in particular,

488. *Leonid Pasternak. A Recital by Wanda Landowska at the Society of Free Aesthetics, Moscow, on 7 March 1907, 1907. Pastel on paper, 43.5 x 64 cm (17 1/8 x 25 1/8 in.). State Tretiakov Gallery, Moscow. Sergei Diaghilev sits on the right, his head turned toward the art critic Pavel Ettinger, who is sitting on the far left; the lady in white is Genrietta Girshman.*

489. *Valentin Serov.* Portrait of Ivan Morozov, 1910. *Tempera on cardboard, 63.5 x 77 cm (25 x 30 3/8 in.). State Tretiakov Gallery, Moscow.*

that is, Ivan Morozov and Sergei Shchukin [ills. 489, 490]. Ivan Morozov, owner of textile mills, was the most celebrated member of his dynasty, at least as far as the arts were concerned, thanks to his collection of modern French paintings. But in addition to his interest in the French masters (especially Denis), Morozov acquired works by young Russians, including Goncharova, Sarian, and Utkin—and Serov's 1910 portrait of him demonstrates the high regard in which artists held him. Starting his collection of French Impressionists and Post-Impressionists in 1903, Morozov soon owned one of the greatest collections of such art, rivaled only by that of Shchukin. His villa in downtown Moscow, which he restructured to resemble an art gallery, boasted examples of Bonnard, Cézanne, Denis, Gauguin, Matisse, and Renoir, and by 1917 the number of such pictures reached 250. Morozov was in personal contact with many of these artists and on his invitation, for example, Denis came to Moscow to create his wall paintings for the villa, including the story of Psyche for the music room [ill. 491]. In 1912 Morozov's French paintings were catalogued by Sergei Makovsky, who published the inventory in *Apollon* (no. 3–4).

Shchukin started his equally famous collection of modern European paintings in about 1897 and by the early 1900s had acquired examples by all the leading Impressionists, including Degas, Monet, and Renoir, housed in his eighteenth-century villa [ills. 492, 493]. The most valuable part of his collection was a room devoted to Gauguin, although in later years he focused on the Cubists, including Braque, Derain, Le Fauconnier, and Picasso. Like Morozov, Shchukin cultivated personal acquaintance with Western artists, inviting Matisse to visit Moscow in October 1911, under the auspices of the Society of Free Aesthetics. The catalogue of Shchukin's Western masters was published in 1913 and, like Morozov's, the entire collection was inventoried upon its nationalization and transference to the Museum of New Western Painting (now the Pushkin Museum of Fine Arts) in 1918.

Thanks to their unique collections, Morozov and Shchukin exerted an appreciable influence upon the development of Modernist art in Russia, and Moscow artists, Goncharova and Larionov in particular, paraphrased a number of the Gauguin and Matisse canvases which they saw in Morozov's and Shchukin's homes. But both men, somewhat aloof from Moscow's bohemia, favored a traditional, patriarchal way of life. In this respect they differed markedly from Nikolai Riabushinsky, the prodigal son of the banking family and, surely, the most colorful of the Moscow Maecenases [see ill. 394]. To a considerable degree, Riabushinsky was typical of that generation—passionate, eccentric, often dictatorial, sometimes very generous—and convinced of his role as first emissary of the Russian artistic renaissance.

Above:
490. Sergei Shchukin, ca. 1900.

Below:
491. Photograph of the music room in Ivan Morozov's Moscow home showing the story of Psyche, which Maurice Denis painted in 1908–09.

492. This room in Sergei Shchukin's Moscow home displays paintings by Paul Cézanne, including Pierrot and Harlequin.

Below:

493. Interior of Sergei Shchukin's Moscow home. Twenty-one of the thirty-eight paintings in the salon are by Henri Matisse. The artist himself devised the hanging scheme for his works when he came to oversee the installation of the two immense panels of Dance *and* Music *on the main stair in 1911.*

494. *Vladimir Maiat, architect. Nikolai Riabushinsky's mansion, The Black Swan, in Petrovskii Park, Moscow. Interior, ca. 1910.*

Riabushinsky was a playboy and a dilettante, possessing neither the business acumen of his brothers, Stepan (a banker) and Pavel (owner of the newspaper *Utro Rossii*), nor the cultural refinement of Diaghilev, whom, ostensibly, he chose to emulate. Nevertheless, Riabushinsky was fascinated by the new art and did much to propagate it—his luxurious review, *Zolotoe runo*, being a powerful vehicle of the Symbolist movement and the early avant-garde [see ill. 86]. Riabushinsky also rendered a valuable service to modern art by financing and organizing four major exhibitions: the "Blue Rose" (1907) [see ills. 83, 84], the international "Salon of the Golden Fleece" (1908), and the two "Golden Fleece" exhibitions (1909, 1910). In addition to collecting works by Russian and French artists, he painted profusely, contributed to exhibitions, wrote critical reviews, and even published a book of poetry under his pseudonym, N. Shinsky.[37] To indulge his pleasures, Riabushinsky built himself a mansion called the Black Swan, which, behind its Neo-Classical facade, hosted the most outlandish events [ill. 494]: there were cages for lions and tigers in the garden, at Christmas a huge fir tree would be erected and decorated with electric lights, and the interior boasted an array of

Above:

495. Konstantin Somov. Portrait of Viacheslav Ivanov, *1906. Pencil, sanguine, and gouache on paper on cardboard, 42.4 x 26.6 cm (16 3/4 x 10 1/2 in.). State Tretiakov Gallery, Moscow.*

Right:

496. Nikolai Riabushinsky in the doorway of his antique store on the Avenue Kléber in Paris, ca. 1930.

exotic souvenirs. Riabushinsky's maxim, "I love beauty and I love a lot of women" betrayed the kind of lifestyle which he conducted.[38]

Whatever his personal quirks, Riabushinsky was liberal with his financial assets. For example, in 1906 he commissioned a gallery of portraits of contemporary writers, which resulted in masterpieces such as Somov's renderings of Blok and Ivanov [ill. 495, see also 337]. That same year he sent paints and brushes to the ailing Vrubel, then resident in Usoltsev's mental asylum, so that he could finish the portrait of Briusov [see ill. 222], and organized a competition with a cash prize for the most convincing portrait of the Devil (the prize was not awarded). Riabushinsky's merits as a patron, while doubted in some quarters, were recognized even by Tsar Nicholas, who, in October 1906, received him, accepting the nine issues of *Zolotoe runo* in handsome bindings designed by Riabushinsky himself.[39]

Riabushinsky was interested not only in promoting magazines and exhibitions, but also in enjoying the profits that the buying and selling of art could generate. This prompted him to entertain the idea of a so-called Palace of the Arts in Moscow supported through a shareholder scheme of five hundred shares at 1,000 rubles per share. The Palace of Arts was to have included a permanent exhibition hall, a museum of modern Russian art, and auction facilities, but, although Riabushinsky himself bought twenty-five shares, the project was never realized, owing to his own financial collapse. To cut his losses, Riabushinsky auctioned off part of his own art collection in 1911 (and also in 1916), and much of what remained was destroyed by a fire which gutted the Black Swan in 1914. After the October Revolution Riabushinsky emigrated to France and spent the remainder of his life commuting between Paris and Nice, where he ran antiques stores [ill. 496]. The one in Nice was called, appropriately enough, La Rose Bleue.

The activities of the Moscow merchants, especially the Girshmans, Morozov, Riabushinsky, and Shchukin, played a central role in the propagation of aesthetic and intellectual values. The diversity and rapid expansion of their private collections, their ready sponsorship of cultural initiatives, their individual commissions and consignments, and their personal friendships with artists and writers were symptomatic of the energy and inventiveness of the Moscow art scene—driven by private enterprise, self-confidence, and a profound belief in the need to restructure and renew Russian society and culture. Quite literally, the Moscow Maecenases turned their homes into artistic laboratories, entertaining, networking, creating, collecting—and, thereby, exerting a profound influence on the ideas and ideals of the Russian Silver Age. In some sense, theirs was a theatrical action where the salon was the stage; the *jour fixe*, the day of performance; the reception, the drama; and the guests, the audience.

CABARET

This "in-home" variant of the theater coincided with a strong proclivity for the intimate theater and the cabaret. After all, Baron Nikola Drizen opened his Antique Theater in St. Petersburg in the winter of 1907, just a few months before Nikita Baliev established his Bat cabaret in Moscow (known later on in the West as the Chauve-Souris); Aleksandr Fokin (brother of celebrated dancer and choreographer Michel Fokine) used the profits from his automobile and bicycle business to establish the Troitskii Theater of Miniatures in St. Petersburg in 1911 [see ill. 383]; and Aleksandr Tairov opened his Chamber Theater in Moscow in 1913. Many of the primary stage directors and producers of the time such as Evreinov, Komissarzhevskaia, Meierkhold, and Tairov made their early advances in intimate theater. Evreinov, for example, founded his theater of satire—the Crooked Mirror—in 1908, while as early as 1904 Ivanov had turned his *bashnia*, or Tower, apartment in St. Petersburg into a virtual forum for acting, declaiming, and dancing with scenic contributions by Kuzmin, Meierkhold, and Sudeikin, among others.[40]

Many artists of the Russian Silver Age, including Benois, Evreinov, Kalmakov, Meierkhold, Nina Simonovich-Efimova, Somov, and Sudeikin, were also drawn to the puppet theater, regarding it, not without the influence of Craig and Reinhardt, as a "primitive" or "infantile" source of artistic inspiration. They felt similarly about the old Shrovetide *balagany* (fairground-booth shows) and the conventions of the Punch-and-Judy show or, rather, Petrouchka—the indigenous interpretation of the commedia dell'arte. Professional artists and directors had much to say about this local tradition and, to a considerable extent, used the puppet theater as a workshop for

497. *Nikolai Kalmakov. Design for a Devil in the puppet play* The Power of Love and Magic *by Tirso de Molina, produced at Yuliia Slonimskaia's Marionette Theater, Petrograd, 1916. Gouache on paper, 24 x 33 cm (9 7/16 x 13 in.).*

Right:
498. Mikhail Bobyshev. Stage design for Nikolai Evreinov's play In the Side Scenes of the Soul, *produced at the Crooked Mirror cabaret, St. Petersburg, 1912. The action of the play takes place inside the human body.*

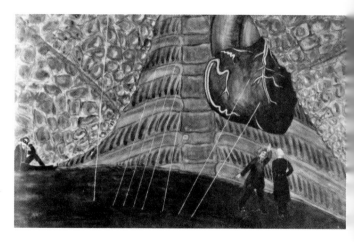

Below:
499. Interior of the Bat cabaret, Bolshoi Gnezdnikovskii Lane, Moscow. 1910s. On February 29, 1908 (a leap year), Nikita Baliev, an actor with the Moscow Art Theater, opened a tiny theater called the Bat, in Moscow. The idea of establishing such a cabaret derived from the kapustniki, or "cabbage parties" (from the Russian word kapusta, *meaning "cabbage") at which supporters of the Moscow Art Theater used to celebrate Shrovetide. At first, the Bat was housed in the cellar of the Pertsov House (see ill. 327), but in 1910 Baliev moved the enterprise to another cellar on Miliutinskii Lane and from there, in 1915, to more spacious premises on Bolshoi Gnezdnikovskii Lane, where it flourished until 1919. Before Morris Gest brought the Baliev company to the United States in 1922, the Bat or, as it was known abroad, the Chauve-Souris, toured France, Germany, and England, scoring a resounding success. Thereafter, the Roof Theater of the old Century Theater in New York became the more or less permanent home of the Chauve-Souris, and Baliev continued to welcome enthusiastic audiences there until his death in 1936. The kind of dramatic repertoire which Baliev commissioned was often the short skit, the parody of a famous classic such as Gogol's* Inspector General, *or a tinseled and sentimental dramatization of Old Russia.*

testing and adapting concepts of Symbolism and other aesthetic theories. Yuliia Slonimskaia and her husband, Pavel Sazonov, for example, even established an "adult" puppet theater in the private apartment of the painter Aleksandr Gaush in Petrograd, producing Tirso de Molina's *Power of Love and Magic* with designs by Kalmakov and music by Thomas von Hartmann in 1916 [ill. 497]. Supported by the Acmeist poets in particular, including Akhmatova, Georgii Ivanov, and Kuzmin, Slonimskaia was perhaps the most audacious and original puppeteer of the Silver Age, even publishing an explanation of her objectives in *Apollon*:

> *Just as algebraic signs substitute certain desired quantities, so the conditional flesh of the marionette substitutes real human flesh. . . . The infinite variety of the puppet repertoire has preserved one basic characteristic: indifference to the prose of everyday life and to the manifestation of the eternal qualities of the human soul.*[41]

In 1912 Evreinov staged a play called *In the Side Scenes of the Soul* at the Crooked Mirror. The distinguishing feature of this short piece, designed by Mikhail Bobyshev [ill. 498], was that the dramatic events took place inside the human body. Here you could actually see the mounting excitement through the inflating lungs and beating heart. This was intimate theater in the true sense of the word, and it symbolized a primary aspiration of Russian experimental theater of the 1910s—to move inward psychologically and physically.

Some of the Russian cabarets such as the Crooked Mirror, the Bat, the Stray Dog (founded in St. Petersburg in 1911), and the Comedians' Halt (founded in Petrograd in 1916) received wide recognition for their literary and artistic achievements; the collected names alone of these and others now constitute a kaleidoscope of the most exotic epithets: Bi-Ba-Bo, Blue Bird, Green Lampshade, Pink Lantern, Stable of Pegasus, Petrouchka, etc. The format of the Russian cabaret—a confined stage housed in a small restaurant or café providing amusement through a sequence of variety acts—owed much to Western models (Baliev's Bat, for example, carried an obvious reference to the Fledermaus in Vienna [ills. 499, 500]). However, the Russian cabaret also incorporated elements of domestic folk theater—quick repartee, a rapid sequence of numbers, clowning, the *pliaska* (Russian dance), and so on, providing, as Kandinsky remarked, a "very definite alogicality."[42]

More than their Moscow counterparts, the St. Petersburg cabarets, especially the Stray Dog and the Comedians' Halt [ills. 501, 502], attracted prominent intellectuals from all disciplines, because, in addition to presenting musical sketches and tableaux vivants, they commissioned lectures and recitations and led debates on topical issues. The Stray Dog, for example, compered by Nikolai Petrov and Boris Pronin, hosted many important cultural events during its brief active life (1911–15), encouraging discussions on the "Tarot, Theosophy, Alexandrian Christianity, the French magic revival, Russian Orthodoxy, neo-Platonism, Jacob Boehme, the monks of Athos" and many other subjects.[43] As artist-in-residence, Sudeikin often marked these meetings by designing special programs, décor, and even fancy-dress costumes [ill. 503].

BODY ART

One of the defining features of the artistic and philosophical

inquiry of the Russian Silver Age was a vigorous interest in "modern man," and both *Jeux* and *Victory over the Sun*, with their emphasis on streamlining, mechanical efficiency, and "men of the future," illustrated this tendency well [see ills. 213, 454]. But the intellectual interest was also part of a wider social concern with physical fitness and "beautification" evident from the surprising number of advertisements in Russian coffee-table magazines of the 1910s such as *Argus*, *Niva* (Field), and *Stolitsa i usadba* (Town and country) for cold creams, fragrances,

and beauty soaps guaranteed to improve looks or for sports equipment, the chiropractic re-formation of noses and paunches, potency pills—and contraceptives—to foster greater physical fitness and activity[44] [ill. 505].

Emblematic of this concern with the lean, efficient, and functional body is the famous portrait of Ida Rubinstein, which Serov, Bakst's rival and, incidentally, Larionov's mentor, painted in 1910 [ill. 504]. Serov's rendering of the dancer is startling precisely because it is not "beautiful," for, unlike Bakst's slave girls and bacchantes [ill. 506, see also 425–429], Serov's Rubinstein is awkward and strangely unerotic, and perhaps closer to the real Rubinstein than legend would have us believe. Serov presents this femme fatale, often compared to Mata Hari and Greta Garbo, as a graceful, constructive nude that, for all the nakedness and serpentine movement, has surpassed the temptations of the flesh (aptly enough, Serov painted his model in the disused chapel of a Catholic monastery in Paris). Here is the triumphant Saint Sebastian which Rubinstein interpreted in Diaghilev's 1911 production of Gabriele d'Annunzio's *Martyrdom of St. Sebastian*, a portrait of ascetic denial, moral sobriety, and physical efficacy [ill. 507].

The broader significance of Serov's *Ida Rubinstein* lies precisely in its emphasis on the bare mechanism of the nude body and on a physical structure independent of traditional beauty and erotic stimulus. In this sense, Serov was pointing to the avant-garde conception of the

Below:
505. Advertisements in Niva *(Field), Moscow, St. Petersburg, 1912, no. 51, p. 1024, for weight loss, dandruff control, the perfect bust, younger skin, musical instruments, and rubber soles.*

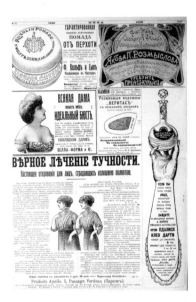

body as a source of primary energy and strength, a vitalist philosophy contrary to the Bakstian emphasis on seduction in favor of a puritanical health. Perhaps that is why, for the more radical artists and poets such as the Burliuk brothers, Goncharova, Kamensky, Petr Konchalovsky, Larionov, Aristarkh Lentulov, Malevich, and Ilia Mashkov, the wrestler, the boxer, and the weightlifter, often encountered at the circus and the fairground, were images central to their aesthetic and social vocabulary.[45] Goncharova's two versions of *Wrestlers* (1909) [ill. 508] and Larionov's portrait of Vladimir Burliuk with dumbbells come to mind here, as do the pastimes of wrestling, boxing, and weightlifting that some of the Jack of Diamonds artists pursued in the 1910s. Powerful witness to this body cult is the Mashkov double

Above:
506. Photograph of Ida Rubinstein as Zobeide in Schéhérazade, 1910. The costume was designed by Léon Bakst.

Right:
507. Léon Bakst. Costume design for Ida Rubinstein as St. Sebastien in Gabriele d'Annunzio's Martyrdom de St. Sébastien, produced by Sergei Diaghilev in Paris, 1911. Watercolor, pencil, gouache, and gold on paper, 44.5 x 25.5 cm (17 1/2 x 10 in.).

portrait of himself and Konchalovsky (1910) [ill. 510], in which the
two artists present themselves as strongmen, i.e., as the real-life
strongmen (silachi) whom Malevich reduced to robotic giants for Victory over the Sun [see ills. 562, 567–574].

Mashkov and Konchalovsky, like Larionov, modeled their physical prowess on the famous strongmen of the day such as Petr Krylov
and Aleksandr Znamensky (Viliams Moor-Znamensky) [ills. 509,
511, 512] and cultivated the body as a source of health and efficiency
and not necessarily as an instrument of sexual gratification.
Mashkov even kept dumbbells in his Moscow studio, where the sign
above the door read: "There is a place in my studio only for the
healthy and the strong." Lentulov also developed his muscles with

dumbbells, and contemporaries recall how dumbbells and weights graced the rooms of the Burliuks' country place, Chernianka, in Ukraine. Some of that generation, including the painters Fedor Krichevsky and Ivan Miasoedov, contributed vignettes to sports magazines such as *Gerkules* (Hercules) and *Vestnik zdorovia* (Herald of health) and engaged in real fistfights (as Malevich and Tatlin did at the "0.10" exhibition in December 1915).

The Futurists, Italian and Russian, were histrionic, the aesthetic of entertainment was crucial to their endeavor, and they made constant recourse to the theater in its widest sense as a laboratory for artistic experiment: the circus (Kamensky even recited his poetry while riding bareback in a ring), the martial arts (the Jack of Diamonds artists, Kamensky, Maiakovsky, and Zdanevich often attended

bodybuilding, boxing, and wrestling events), the opera *(Victory over the Sun)*, the cabaret, the café (the Café Kade and the Café Pittoresque in Moscow), and the cinema were important conduits of Modernist activity.

CINEMA

The Silver Age witnessed the rapid development of the Russian movie industry and its infrastructure of divas, movie houses, and promotional materials, especially the poster [ills. 513, 514]. By and large Russian cinematography was oriented toward the lower middle and working classes, whereas the intelligentsia seems to have cultivated only a limited interest in the subject, at least as a viable medium of artistic expression.[46] True, there are scattered and positive references to the cinema in the writings of Bakst, Belyi, and Malevich, but, in general, artists and writers seem to have regarded the cinema as little more than a source of entertainment, glamorous and engaging, but hardly "serious." This is in spite of the fact that the Russian cinema, even if it did prefer the detective, horror, and action movie, fostered a healthy concern with the classics, including *Evgenii Onegin* (directed by Nikolai Goncharov, 1911), *Anna Karenina* (directed by Vladimir Gardin, 1914) [see ill. 177], and *The Queen of Spades* (directed by Yakov Protazanov, 1916).

As was the case with the other arts, the Russian cinema divided its inquiries into various genres or fields of activity, functioning as an "Archive of Time," a "Torch of Knowledge," a living newspaper, and, of course, a dramatic narrative.[47] Not unexpectedly, the last category was the most popular and the most profitable, and the titles of some of the releases are gripping, indeed: *Chasm, Savage Force, We are Not Guilty of Their Blood!, A Mysterious Murder in Petrograd,* and so forth. Even the more audacious directors such as Evgenii Bauer and Wladislaw Starewicz seem to have chosen the drama as a preferred medium of experimentation, culminating in such cinematic masterpieces as *Silent Witnesses* (1914), *Child of the Big City* (1916), *After Death* (1916), and *In the Fire of Passions and Sufferings* (1916).

There can be no question that the particular formal devices of the cinema (if

515. *Olga Rozanova. "Moderne" Movie Theater on the Street, 1915. Oil on canvas, 99 x 75 cm (39 x 29 1/2 in.). Slobodskoi Art and Exhibition Center.*

not its anecdotal or reportorial purpose)—the reliance on black-and-white, the framing and cutting of action, the flickering of the screen, the staccato movements of the actors—informed other works of art during the Silver Age. It is tempting, for example, to regard Belyi's "monochromatic" novel *St. Petersburg* (1913) as an exercise in montage, Malevich's *Black Square* as a homage to the cinematic image on the screen, and Nijinsky's abrupt and episodic positioning of the figures in his *Jeux* as the repetition of a film sequence. Some artists tried to duplicate the effects of the projected film in their paintings, clear examples being Larionov's *Scene—Cinema* (1912) and Rozanova's *"Moderne" Movie Theater on the Street* (1915) [ill. 515]. The Cubo-Futurists even made a movie of themselves in a cabaret acting out a Futurist tango, a Futurist killing, and a Futurist funeral, i.e., the twenty-minute release called *Drama in the Futurists' Cabaret No. 13*, which, with such a crazy plot, is more suggestive of slapstick comedy and the circus than of the dark suspense of the cinema [see ill. 408].

CIRCUS

The circus appealed precisely because it enjoyed the license to upset, parody, and short-circuit conventional genres and disciplines. It tested emotional limits with its animal acts and high-wire acrobatics [ill. 516], and it was a spectacle that, like the avant-garde exhibition and debate, could surprise and sadden, entertain and alienate, while relying on an eclectic and improvisational arsenal of instruments, media, and narratives. In any case, the circus and other forms of "magic" enjoyed great popularity in Russia in the late nineteenth and early twentieth centuries: the circus troupe of Ciniselli, the clowns Anatolii Durov and Ivan Kozlov, and the magician Leoni (pseudonym of V. Larionov, not related to Mikhail) were household names [ills. 517, 518]. As the *skomorokhi*, or traveling buffoons, and the *balagany* (fairground booths) receded into history, new forms of mass

516. *Sergei Sudeikin,* Daring. *Illustration for the poem of the same name by Sergei Rafalovich in his miscellany* Speculum Animae. *Moscow: Siriius, 1911.*

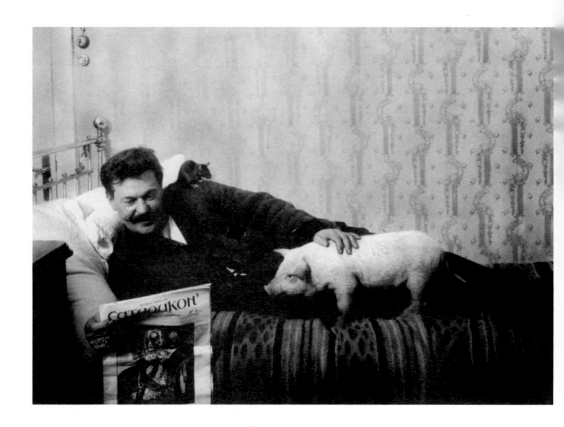

entertainment developed, including the professional circus (often staffed by Italians, Turks, and gypsies) and the movie industry [ill. 519]. Catering to an eager public, these recreations concocted and proffered "illusions" (the Russian word for "conjurer" is *illiuzionist* and the early cinemas in Russia were called *illiuziony*) which became ever more complex and spellbinding as technological possibilities advanced. Indeed, the making of these "factories of dreams" just before and after 1900 paralleled the development of other, more pragmatic wizardries, e.g., the telephone, the phonograph, the ozonator (an air purifier), the gas refrigerator, and various other mechanical and electrical apparatuses which, suddenly, performed miracles. Some of these inventions found an immediate application in the fairgrounds and circuses of early-twentieth-century Russia.

Trick photography, "levitations," "beheadings," "sawing ladies in half," face painting, dressing up, ventriloquism, fortune telling—these are just some of the tricks that can be associated with the great Russian circuses and also with the Modernist movement, and a

number of intriguing parallels can be traced. The scene of devils sawing a woman in half with which Malevich illustrated *Igra v adu* (A Game in hell) in 1914 brings to mind the traditional *lubok* (broadside) depicting an analogous action [ills. 520, 522]—and also the sensational acts of sawing by *illiuzionisty* in Moscow and St. Petersburg circuses; the weird clothes and painted faces of clowns return in the face painting of David Burliuk, Goncharova, Larionov, and Zdanevich [ill. 521, see also 110]. The "decapitations" and "displacements of heads" implemented by magicians bring to mind Cubo-Futurist paintings such as D. Burliuk's *Headless Barber* (a transcription of Larionov's *Officer at the Hairdresser* of 1909, which, in turn, is a paraphrase of the celebrated eighteenth-century *lubok* of an Old Believer having his beard cut off) [ills. 523–525]. Leoni's prestidigitations remind us of the magical vanishings in some of Larionov's paintings such as the chair with only two legs in *Officer at the Hairdresser*. The clown Durov used to enter the circus ring on a pig, shocking and amusing his public—just as

Opposite top:
517. Animal trainer and clown Anatolii Durov with one of his pet pigs, ca. 1910.

Opposite bottom:
518. Anatolii Durov, Jr., with his pet monkey, ca. 1920.

Above:
519. Aleksandr Shevchenko. Circus, 1913. Oil on canvas, 99 x 114 cm (39 x 44 7/8 in.). Nizhnii-Novgorod State Museum of Art.

Right:
520. Kazimir Malevich. Illustration of devils sawing a woman in half for the Futurist booklet Igra v adu *(A Game in hell) by Aleksei Kruchenykh and Velimir Khlebnikov. Moscow: Kuzmin and Dolinsky, 1914, unpaginated.*

Below left:
521. David Burliuk with face painted, Moscow, 1914.

Below right:
522. Lubok (broadsheet) showing punishments being inflicted upon a wicked rich man, 1850s. Lithograph.

Larionov did with the pig that trots in and out of his Neo-Primitivist paintings [ill. 527]—while Durov's top hat and colored vests were praised and imitated readily by Burliuk, Kamensky, and Maiakovsky, and Khlebnikov's laughter poem "Zakliatie smekhom" (Incantation by laughter, 1908) may have inspired the lecture "On Laughter," which Durov used to deliver to his circus audiences. It is also tempting to suggest that the Cubo-Futurists, in applying concepts such as verbal shift *(sdvig)* to their poems and paintings, as Larionov did, for example, with the word "blockhead" in his *Portrait of Vladimir Tatlin* [ill. 526], were also drawing on the art of the ventriloquist, i.e., the displacement and reimposition of voice.

The painter Ivan Miasoedov, son of the more celebrated nineteenth-century Realist painter Grigorii Miasoedov and friend of Evreinov, Kulbin, and Maksimovich, was a prizefighter, renowned less for his paintings than for the pokers that he could bend. In 1912 he

Right:
523. David Burliuk. Headless Barber (also called A Clean Shave), 1910s. Oil on canvas, 32.5 x 30 cm (12 ¾ x 11 ¾ in.). Philadelphia Museum of Art.

Below left:
524. Mikhail Larionov. Officer at the Hairdresser, 1908–09. Oil on canvas, 117 x 89 cm (46 x 35 in.).

Below right:
525. Broadsheet (lubok) showing an Old Believer having his beard cut off, 18th century. Lithograph.

Opposite
526. *Mikhail Larionov.* Portrait of
Vladimir Tatlin, 1913. *Oil on canvas, 90 x*
72 cm (35 3/8 x 28 3/8 in.). *Musée National*
d'Art Moderne, Centre Georges Pompidou,
Paris. Tatlin was 28 years old (hence the
number "28") when Larionov painted this
portrait, inscribed with the jovial, if
unflattering, word balda (*blockhead*).

Above:
527. *Mikhail Larionov.* Gypsy in Tiraspol,
1907. *Oil on canvas, 95 x 81 cm*
(37 1/2 x 31 7/8 in.). *For all her local color,*
Larionov's gypsy seems to have much in common
with Paul Gauguin's Polynesian beauties.

published the "Manifesto of Nudity," in which he argued that the naked body was superior to the clothed one, and had numerous nude photographic portraits made of himself [ill. 528].[48] Russian nudism even received an ideological justification after the October Revolution when in 1922 the first Soviet nudists organized Evenings of the Denuded Body in Moscow, declaring that nudity was the truly democratic form of dress. Miasoedov's naked romps, Mashkov's dumbbells, Serov's *Rubinstein*, and Larionov's Venuses can be accommodated easily within a nudist fashion and also emerge as experiments in radical corporeal design for the tough new century. The cult of bodybuilding, gymnastics, and the martial arts, and the "athletic" pictures such as Mashkov's *Self-Portrait and Portrait of Petr Konchalovsky*, Miasoedov's nude self-photographs as Hercules and Mercury, and perhaps even Malevich's robust peasants exude a Promethean and bellicose strength [ill. 530]. Further discussion of this context would take us into the still uncharted territory of Russian nudism and Naturalism, a lifestyle that attracted many converts during the Silver Age, including the writers Leonid Andreev and Maksimilian Voloshin [ill. 529].

Above:
528. Ivan Miasoedov posing as Hercules, ca. 1906.

Right:
529. Anonymous photographer. Photograph of Leonid Andreev and his son Savva by the Gulf of Finland, ca 1910.

Opposite:
530. Kazimir Malevich. The Mower, 1912. Oil on canvas, 113.5 x 66.5 cm (44 3/4 x 26 1/8 in.). Nizhnii-Novgorod State Museum of Art.

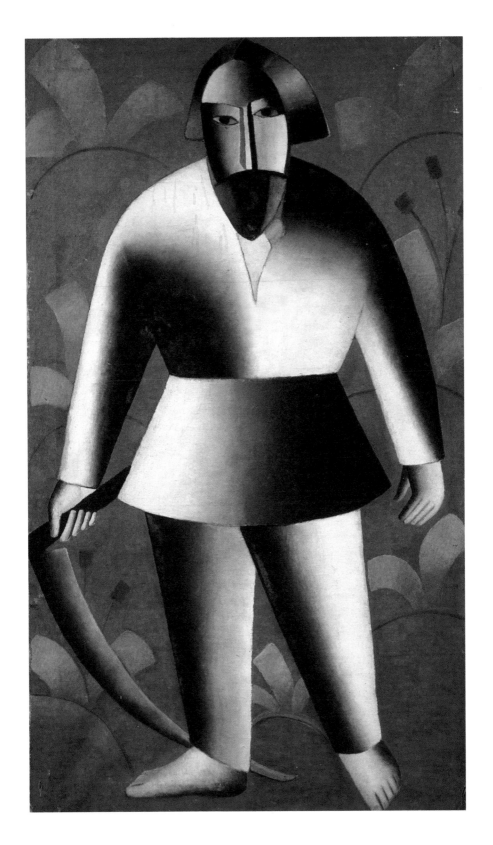

AESTHETES AND BARBARIANS
Apollo and the Suicide of Art

SERGEI MAKOVSKY AND *APOLLON*

After the closure of *Mir iskusstva* in 1904 and the conclusive "World of Art" exhibition in 1906, Diaghilev turned increasingly westward, preparing the way for his establishment of the Ballets Russes. If a major part of the World of Art circle, including Bakst and Benois, also followed Diaghilev and graced his new enterprise with their skills, some of their colleagues, such as Lancéray and Somov, stayed behind, miffed if not orphaned. Moreover, rival artistic and literary groups in St. Petersburg and Moscow, including the Acmeist movement and the nascent avant-garde, were now establishing their own platforms and intentions, no longer consonant with the aesthetic sensibility of the fin de siècle.

Even so, the World of Art, as a titled organization, did not die; on the contrary, it returned as a formal exhibition society in 1910, reinforced by a younger and more variegated generation of painters and designers, including Boris Grigoriev, Alexandre Jacovleff, and Vasilii Shukhaev [ills. 531–533, 536]. As an exhibition society, the new World of Art diversified, not only maintaining original members among its ranks (such as Benois and Dobuzhinsky), but also inviting Cubo-Futurists (such as D. Burliuk, Larionov, and Tatlin), and it continued its promotional activities in Russia until 1924. Still lacking in the latter years of its existence, however, were the charismatic leadership of Diaghilev and a reliable medium of information, promotion, and debate.

Ironically, the need for a new "arts administrator" was filled by the son of the Realist painter Konstantin Makovsky (one of Diaghilev's archenemies and target of abuse), i.e., the poet and esthete Sergei Makovsky. The younger Makovsky had made his debut as a critic of some insight in Nikolai Tarovaty's journal *Iskusstvo* (Art) in Moscow in 1905, when he had championed the new painting of the Moscow Symbolists; in 1906 he joined the staff of *Zolotoe runo*, demonstrating a keen interest in the new French art and, incidentally, in the work of Goncharova and Larionov. When he appeared in St. Petersburg society in 1908, he impressed people with his "artistic taste, artistic flair, and great energy"[1]—and it was natural that he would assume "certain of Diaghilev's functions."[2]

Above:
533. Vasilii Shukhaev. Portrait of Larisa Reisner, 1915. Oil and gold paint on wooden board, 107 x 75 cm (42 ¹/₈ x 29 ¹/₂ in.). State Literary Museum, Moscow.

Opposite top left:
534. Vladimir Levitsky. Title page of Apollon *(Apollo), St. Petersburg, 1913, no. 6.*

Opposite bottom left:
535. Georgii Narbut. Frontispiece for the journal Apollon *(Apollo), Petrograd, 1916.*

Opposite right:
536. Alexandre Jakovleff. The Violinist, 1915. Oil on canvas, 201 x 69 cm (79 ¹/₈ x 27 ¹/₈ in.). State Russian Museum, St. Petersburg.

In January 1909 Makovsky combined his critical and organizational talents to stage a comprehensive exhibition of modern Russian art called the "Salon" at the Menshikov Palace. Just as Diaghilev had brought together diverse trends of Russian art, so, at his "Salon," Makovsky assembled artists of the right and of the left— Bakst and David Burliuk, Benois and Kandinsky, Bilibin and Aleksej von Jawlensky, Dobuzhinsky and Georgii Yakulov, Čiurlionis and Sudeikin, Roerich and Petrov-Vodkin, and so on. The Salon provided the first Russian viewing of Bakst's *Terror Antiquus* after its triumph at the Paris "Salon d'automne" the year before [see ill. 165], gave ample space to the musical painting of Čiurlionis [see ill. 399],³ and arranged concerts of music by Čiurlionis, Medtner, and Scriabin while the exhibition was in progress. Makovsky's Salon coincided with the publication of his two-volume collection of critical essays *Stranitsy khudozhestvennoi kritiki* (Pages of art criticism) and with the extensive preparations for the first issues of his journal *Apollon* (Apollo), to which many of the *miriskusniki* (World of Art members), young and old, contributed [ills. 534, 535, see also 321].

There are many striking parallels between Makovsky/*Apollon* and Diaghilev/*Mir iskusstva*. *Apollon* was also published in St. Petersburg; it promoted the visual, literary, and performing arts; and it relied on private finance, being subsidized by a rich tea merchant, Mikhail Ushkov. Even on a more personal level, there are similarities: just as Repin attacked Diaghilev for his brazen artistic taste, so he attacked Makovsky and his "tasteless, illiterate, and nonsensical"⁴ promotion of certain young artists, especially Petrov-Vodkin; and just as Diaghilev lost no time in responding to Repin, so Makovsky was quick to publish a sober rebuttal.

Like Diaghilev, too, Makovsky was aware of the inner strength and potential of Russian culture and believed that it was standing on the threshold of a magnificent renaissance:

> *Over the last ten years Russian art has done the work of a whole generation. As for Russian culture in particular, I am deeply convinced that Russia has never before experienced such a fruitful era. What many people call by the derisive sobriquet of "modernism" is a symptom of the true advance of our aesthetic self-awareness.⁵*

Not surprisingly, Makovsky wished to export Russian art to the West and to import Western art to Russia, and his aesthetic preferences in this two-way transaction coincided to a considerable extent with Diaghilev's own tastes. When, for example, in 1910 the Belgian

Ministry of Arts and Sciences asked Makovsky to organize a Russian section for the "Exposition Universelle" in Brussels, Makovsky selected a substantial number of World of Art works, including Bakst's *Terror Antiquus*, drawings by Bilibin and Dobuzhinsky, St. Petersburg views by Ostroumova-Lebedeva, and archaic scenes by Roerich. In the same year Makovsky organized what was virtually a "World of Art" show at Bernheim-Jeune, Paris, sending works by nearly all the original World of Art members and by many of their younger disciples.

The august exhibition "One Hundred Years of French Painting," which Makovsky and Baron Nikolai Vrangel organized in St. Petersburg in 1912 was exactly the kind of enterprise which Diaghilev would have undertaken (although his name was absent from the advisory board). The catalogue, designed by Dobuzhinsky and with French and Russian texts, contained a long critical article by Arsène Alexandre (now remembered for his publications on Bakst) and a preface by Vrangel and Makovsky, emphasizing that this was the first exhibition outside France to present the development of nineteenth-century French painting in its entirety, from David and Ingres to Cézanne and Gauguin. Makovsky was an efficient organizer, and the intimate, one-man shows which he arranged regularly in the editorial offices of *Apollon* promoted many important artists and groups: Petrov-Vodkin and the *Satyricon* caricaturists in 1909, Dobuzhinsky and Nikolai Tarkhov in 1910. He also organized the "Exhibition of Female Portraits by Modern Russian Artists" in January 1910, which relied heavily on World of Art contributions, and he was responsible for the Russian selection at the international book-design exhibition in Leipzig in 1914.

If lacking the autocratic bearing of Diaghilev, Makovsky was still recognized as the leader or, at least, patron, of a renewed Classical, Alexandrine culture which countered the radical trends of the "new barbarians" in Moscow and St. Petersburg.[6] Symptomatic of this more reasoned inclination of *Apollon* is the fact that Kuzmin [see ill. 402] published his article "On Beautiful Clarity. Notes on Prose" in the January 1910 issue of the journal—the de facto manifesto of the Acmeist movement. Emphasizing the need to define the material world in a clear and graphic manner, to avoid the metaphysical and the abstract, and to present reality without capricious distortion and displacement, the Acmeists, formed by Nikolai Gumilev and Sergei Gorodetsky and including Georgii Ivanov, Osip Mandelshtam, Kuzmin, and Akhmatova [ill. 537; see also 13], used an economical and lucid language to describe the everyday. In other words, they cultivated a precious, subtle, and finely honed poetical style to evoke an amorous encounter, the Russian countryside, a church service, or an architectural monument. Their

Above:
538. Kuzma Petrov-Vodkin. Violin, *1918.*
Oil on canvas, 65 x 80 cm (25 ¹/₂ x 31 ¹/₂ in.).
State Russian Museum, St. Petersburg.

Opposite top:
539. Ivan Fomin, architect. Design for the
reconstruction of New St. Petersburg on Golodai
Island. Colonnade for a plaza, 1912. Etching
and aquatint on paper, 49 x 50 cm (19 ¹/₄ x 19
⁵/₈ in.).

Opposite bottom:
540. Ivan Zholtovsky, architect. Building of the
Horse-Racing Society, Moscow, photograph
1907.

verse was often inspired by the intimate and subjective experience, especially in the cases of Akhmatova, Ivanov, and Kuzmin, but they avoided the more metaphysical and occult dimensions of the Symbolists, favoring lucidity of meaning and constancy of structure.

Although there was no full visual counterpart to this literary trend, Petrov-Vodkin is often regarded as a sympathizer with the group, as his prismatic images, controlled and lapidary, would indicate [ill. 538]. To some extent, Natan Altman, Jacovleff, and Shukhaev, with their return to the physical world and the flesh of things, can also be accommodated within this general context. On the other hand, and rather unexpectedly, the Acmeists shared common ground with certain members of the avant-garde, not least Malevich and Tatlin, who, in their search for a sparse and unadorned visual language, were also returning to a more measured, more Classical syntax.

Acmeism marked an abrupt return to order after the mystery and density of Symbolism, and the appeal for clarity allied its champions with the quest for Apollonian form and the rediscovery of "beauty." To some extent, the position of the Acmeists also coincided with the Neo-Classical or, rather "Neo-Neo-Classical" movement in Russian architecture and the applied arts developing in the 1910s—being as it was indebted to Russia's Neo-Classical and Empire movements of the 1810s–20s [ills. 539–543]. Here was an architectural style, manifest especially in St. Petersburg, which emphasized rational purpose, clear symmetry, and economy of material in contrast to the extravagance of Art Nouveau, and a number of the new commercial and administrative buildings were subject to its laws. Architects such as Fomin, Shchusev, the Vesnin brothers, and even Shekhtel himself supported the new style, designing banks, office buildings, and private residences, some of which, in their simplicity and functionality, prefigured the basic principles of Constructivist architecture in the 1920s.

Often using granite as their primary material, the new Classical architects emphasized symmetry, clear lines, and minimal ornament in their buildings and, in the case of office facilities, optimum space and light—identifiable, for example, with the Vesnins' structures for the Main Post Office (1911) and the Yunker Bank in Moscow (1913) [ills. 544–546]. The Vesnins, Fomin, Shchusev, and Shekhtel were also guided by the new criterion of simplicity and efficiency in their many projects for private mansions and country houses in the 1910s, often adding, however, Doric and Corinthian columns and references to the Florentine Renaissance.

Opposite:
541. *Fedor Lidval, architect. Azov-Don Commercial Bank, St. Petersburg, 1908–09.*

Left and below:
542 & 543. *Illarion Ivanov-Shitz, architect. Merchant Club, Moscow, 1907–08. Interior.*

Logically, the Acmeists felt more at home with *Apollon* than with the avant-garde Union of Youth (the agency which in 1913 promoted *Victory over the Sun*) and, certainly, preferred Pushkin to Kruchenykh. *Apollon* cultivated an elegant atmosphere of "men in frock coats and ladies very décolletées,"[7] and just as Diaghilev carefully tended the silver streak in his hair and placed the monocle in his eye, so Makovsky, "immersed in his armchair, dangled his long-nailed hand with its gold bracelet."[8] Even so, there was a major artistic difference between Diaghilev and Makovsky: Makovsky was, to a considerable degree, supporting the same artists and the same styles which Diaghilev had supported a decade before. But to many, the Benois scenes of seventeenth- and eighteenth-century France, the Somov recollections of the commedia dell'arte, and Ostroumova-Lebedeva's and Lancéray's evocations of old St. Petersburg

544. Aleksandr, Leonid, and Viktor Vesnin, architects. Main Post Office on Miasnitskaia Street, Moscow, 1911. What used to be Moscow's main post office—and still operative today—is a manifest example of the Revivalist style which affected a number of Russian public buildings in the 1910s, and although the building is eclectic, its columns and roof rotunda, in particular, tell of a strong Neo-Classical influence. The Vesnin brothers sometimes worked together on projects such as this post office, but each is now best remembered for his own talent and vision, especially Aleksandr who, as painter and designer, became a stellar contributor to the Constructivist movement in the early 1920s.

[see ills. 342, 343] were now suddenly anachronistic in a world inhabited by such dissident forces as the Burliuks, Goncharova, Larionov, and Malevich [see ills. 3, 508, 523, 524]. Makovsky condemned the avant-garde almost as forcefully as Benois did, and *Apollon*, to the young revolutionaries, was a citadel of conservatism and a den of iniquity.

Nevertheless, as if to confirm his commitment to the World of Art, which by 1909 had become a secure part of the cultural establishment, Makovsky invited Benois to write the lead article for the first issue of *Apollon*, published in October of that year. In his essay, entitled "In Anticipation of a Hymn to Apollo," Benois pronounced that "we can feel the approach of universal death (whether this will lead to resurrection or just to another metamorphosis is not for us to know)" and that the sense of beauty, the "hymn of life, the dancing rhythm of life," had to be rediscovered.[9] Although Benois did not develop this apocalyptic notion, he was obviously voicing what many of his contemporaries were also thinking, i.e., that rhythm was the expression of a social and moral cohesion so lacking in contemporary urban life. As Blok wrote later: "Humanism lost its style; style is rhythm; having lost its rhythm, humanism lost its wholeness."[10] Bakst also alluded to this state in his concurrent article, "The Paths of Classicism in Art," although his attitude was more optimistic: unlike Benois, he regarded the hostility of the twentieth century toward the Classical ideal of beauty as a necessary purgative, arguing that the new savagery indicated that mankind was "advancing toward the childhood of a new, great art, and not toward degeneration."[11]

With a tasteful cover by Dobuzhinsky, with vignettes and illustrations by Bakst, Bilibin, Mitrokhin, Narbut, Somov, et al., with an editorial board including most of the World of Art members, with a professional interest in many disciplines, and with a regular "Russian Artistic Chronicle," *Apollon* was the legitimate successor to *Mir iskusstva* and quickly became a focal point of artistic and literary life, especially after the closure of the Moscow reviews *Vesy* and *Zolotoe runo*. But if *Apollon* upheld certain of the *Mir iskusstva* traditions such as the emphasis on artistic synthesis, the need to establish a close alliance between Russian and Western cultures, and individual initiative, it also differed from its predecessor. Not only was *Apollon* functioning (until 1917) in a different era,[12] but it also catered to a new generation of Post-Symbolist artists and writers, gave unprecedented attention to the discipline of art history (Pavel Ettinger, Nikolai Punin, and Yakov Tugendkhold were regular contributors), and, for all its sense of measure and reserve, publicized the achievements of the avantgarde—from Exter's designs for the Chamber Theater to the "Jack of Diamonds" exhibitions, from Goncharova's 1913 retrospective to Tatlin's reliefs [see ills. 140, 413, 451]. During 1909 and 1910 Kandinsky also published five "Letters from Munich" in *Apollon*.

Above:
545. Aleksandr, Leonid, and Viktor Vesnin, architects. Yunker Bank, Moscow. 1913.

Below:
546. Aleksei Shchusev, architect. Russian pavilion at the "Esposizione Universale," Turin, Italy, 1911.

In other words, Makovsky witnessed and facilitated a "professionalization" of the arts and letters in Russia, especially in the realm of art history, art criticism, and art appreciation and, in this respect his enterprise, *Apollon*, was very much a child of its time. A flurry of other contemporaneous art-historical journals such as *Baian* (Accordion, Moscow, 1914), *Sofiia* (Sophia, Moscow, 1914), and *Svobodnym khudozhestvam* (To the free arts, St. Petersburg, 1910–13) also bore witness to a new tendency in Russia to regard art history as a valid academic discipline and not as a mere handmaiden to literary appreciation or to the individual taste of the private collector. Although *Apollon* was a magazine, its broad range of cultural interests and serious assessments of art, whether Classical or modern, Western or Russian, fine or applied, served as a model for one of Russia's greatest "art events," i.e., the Second All-Russian Congress of Artists, held in St. Petersburg in December 1911–January 1912.

The Second Congress catered to the need for a sophisticated, cosmpolitan debate on the status, role, and function of art in contemporary Russian society. Following the First Congress, which had been organized in Moscow to mark Tretiakov's donation of his collection to the City of Moscow in 1894, the second was multifaceted, covering art education, aesthetics, museology, folk art, preservation, and even the "avant-garde." Opening under the aegis of Grand Duchess Maria Pavlovna, president of the Academy of Arts, the Second Congress was divided into eight sections with two hundred presentations: 1) "Questions of Aesthetics and Art History," 2) "Art Education in the Family and at School and the Teaching of the Graphic Arts," 3) "Painting and Its Technique," 4) "Architecture and the Artistic Appearance of the City," 5) "Russian Antiquity and Its Preservation," 6) "Industrial Art and Handicrafts," 7) "Art in the Theater," 8) "General Meetings" [ill. 547].

Just as *Apollon* brought together representatives of the right and the left, while giving preference to aesthetic measure and historical

accuracy, so the Second Congress, though wide ranging, paid homage to the Academy, following, in many ways, a conservative and sober approach to the problems of art history. In other words, academicians, including Dmitrii Ainalov, Anatolii Kremlev, and Repin (by then a professor at the Academy) were well represented in the proceedings, but adequate space was also given to the World of Art (e.g., Bilibin and Volkonsky) and to more experimental artists such as Sergei Bobrov, Kandinsky, and Kulbin. The Second Congress surveyed and summarized the attainments of Russian art at the end of the Silver Age, demonstrating that they were full, rich, and complex, ranging from the extreme right to the extreme left. For the historian today the three volumes of the transactions (published in 1914–15)[13] are still a major source for the study and evaluation of modern Russian art.

EVERYTHINGISM AND NOTHINGISM

One highlight of the Second Congress was Kandinsky's paper "On the Spiritual in Art," with its accommodation of the esoteric, the occult, and the divine and its insistence that the path to true illumination lay via the intuitive and the occult as well as the hard sciences. This reference to the Symbolist heritage helps to explain a number of developments in modern Russian art, including the abstract investigations not only of Kandinsky but also of Malevich, for in many respects such artists were developing formulae elaborated by the preceding generation [see ills. 20, 175]. Like the Symbolists, Kandinsky called for an integration of the individual arts into a *Gesamtkunstwerk*, welcomed the synthetic impulse of the new painting, and maintained that music could undermine the cult of objects, their "inner sound" being apprehended at moments of supersensory or deviant perception.[14]

Reasons for this synthetic approach differed from person to person, although Benois, Diaghilev, and Ivanov, as well as Kandinsky, agreed that Richard Wagner was to be admired for the way in which he had combined narrative, musical, and visual forces in the operatic drama so as to produce an expressive whole.[15] Kandinsky also recognized Wagner as a major source of visual inspiration, admired Scriabin's efforts to draw distinct parallels between the seven colors of the spectrum and the seven notes of the diatonic scale, and sympathized with the theosophists' search for a religious unity and organic wholeness [ill. 548]. Scriabin's exploration into the similarities between the color spectrum and the diatonic scale served as a pseudo-scientific basis for his investigation into the possibility of a total art. In this Scriabin was not alone; his endeavor was paralleled by Kandinsky [ill. 549], by the theosophist and

548. *C. W. Leadbetter and Annie Besant. Plate W. Music of Wagner. Reproduced from C. W. Leadbetter and Annie Besant.* Thought-Forms, *Wheaton, Ill.: The Theosophical Publishing-House, first published 1901. Adepts of theosophy, Leadbetter and Besant maintained that thoughts and emotions emanated in auras and shapes and that these could be captured in colors and forms. Similarly, music, the most emotional and emotive of the arts, could also be rendered pictorially.*

music teacher Aleksandra Zakharina-Unkovskaia, and by Čiurlionis, who, in trying to integrate the visual and musical arts, created pictorial symphonies from the natural sounds in earth and sky, trees and wind [ill. 551]. Occasionally, his lyrical evocations such as *Fairy Tale* (1907) bring to mind Kandinsky's abstract compositions.

As he was writing "On the Spiritual in Art," Kandinsky pointed toward other new aesthetic criteria, emphasizing the value of the primitive, the ethnographical, and the popular, thereby establishing a fragile alliance with the new generation of Moscow artists led by Goncharova and Larionov. Praising the vigorous colors and formal simplicity of Gauguin and Matisse on the one hand and the energy of indigenous art forms on the other, the avant-garde rejected Symbolist mystery in favor of the concrete and the material [ill. 552]. Their first major exhibition, the "Jack of Diamonds" of 1910–11, signaled

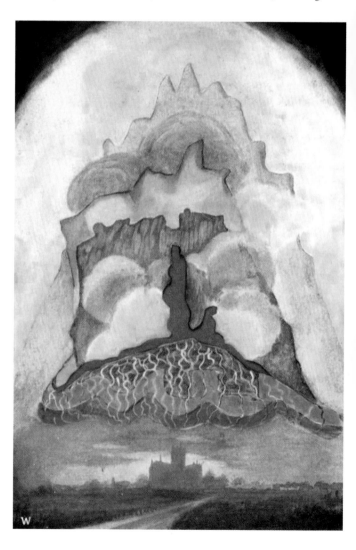

Таблица IV.

Элементарная жизнь простой краски и ея зависимость отъ простѣйшей среды.

549. Vasilii Kandinsky. Tabulation entitled "Elementary Life of a Primary Color and Its Response to a Very Simple Environment." Illustration for Kandinsky's essay "O dukhovnom v iskusstve" (On the Spiritual in Art) published in I. Repin et al. Trudy vtorogo sezda russkikh khudozhnikov (Transactions of the second congress of Russian artists). Petrograd: Golike and Vilborg, 1914, Vol. 1, reproduced between pages 76 and 77.

the tarnishing of the Silver Age, for instead of impalpable visions of the astral plane and religious ecstasy, it showed the vulgar and the ugly, promoting store signboards, graffiti, and children's drawings as genuine works of art [see ill. 88]. The new barbarians even advocated that a pair of boots was a greater work of art than the Venus di Milo.[16]

Reasons for the avant-garde's flaunting of the vulgar are many, although a simple and immediate one lies in the rural derivation and "primitive" energy of many of the stellar writers and artists—from Sergei Esenin to Kazimir Malevich. In turn, the freedom of spirit, panache, and mobility of the avant-garde may owe something to the geographical vastness of the movement, which operated in Moscow and St. Petersburg, Tiflis and Baku, Kazan and Chita, and encompassed many nationalities—Russian, Jewish, Ukrainian, Georgian, Armenian, and Azerbaijani; Kruchenykh even maintained that he knew and could write in all languages. Perhaps a less obvious reason

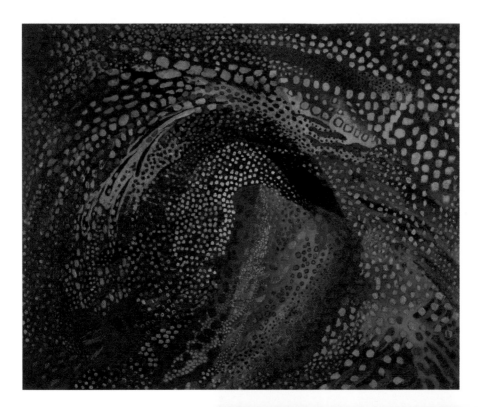

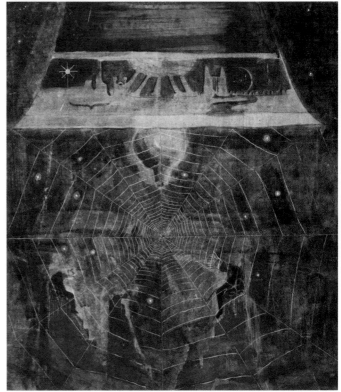

Above:

550. *Mikhail Matiushin.* Painterly Musical Construction, *1918. Oil on board, 51 x 83 cm (20 x 32 ³/₄ in.). State Museum of Contemporary Art, Thessaloniki. Matiushin elaborated a theory of "expanded viewing," according to which he could extend the normal optical radius by judicious ocular exercises which would regenerate lost optical nerves on the back of the head and the soles of the feet.*

Right:

551. *Mikalojus Čiurlionis.* Sonata of the Sun. Finale, *1907. Tempera on paper, 63 x 59.7 cm (24 ⁷/₈ x 23 ¹/₂). Mikalojus Čiurlionis Art Museum, Kaunas (see ill. 399).*

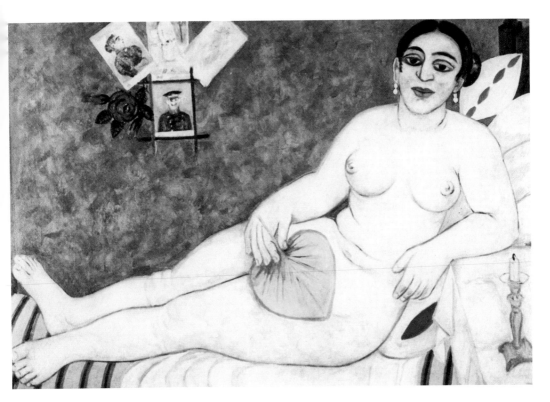

552. *Mikhail Larionov. Jewish Venus, 1912.*
Oil on canvas, 98 x 139 cm (38 ¹/₂ x 54 ³/₄
in.). Ekaterinburg Museum of Visual Art,
Ekaterinburg.

for such catholicity lies in the particular attitude toward the artistic process; of primary importance to the Russian Futurists was not the result but the procedure, not the printed or painted artifact but the spontaneous gesture, and not "knowledge" but "cognition," as the poet and philosopher Belyi might have argued.[17] This is manifest, for example, in the emphasis on the improvisation, the gesture, the manuscript, and the handmade book.

The Russians' concern with instantaneity also extended to a passion for clowning and the impromptu speech at their *disputy* (public debates); for the unfinished production (Kruchenykh invited his readers to finish the story themselves,[18] while Khlebnikov would abort his recitations by interpolating "etc., etc."); and for the ephemeral and facile ("We paint ourselves for an hour," Larionov and Zdanevich announced in one of their manifestoes) [ill. 553].[19] Such extreme modes of comportment bring into relief several characteristics of "Russian Futurism": it was both national and international; it was a single, indigenous movement called *budetlianstvo* (from the future tense of the Russian verb "to be"); and yet also a mix of Cubism, Futurism, Cosmism, Expressionism, Rayonism, Fuism, Eggism, and other outlandish categories,[20] moving between "Nothingism" and "Everythingism."[21] Symptomatic of this apparent arbitrariness of taste and lack of discrimination is the fact that

553. Page from the journal Argus, *St. Petersburg, December 1913, pp. 114–15, showing Mikhail Larionov's and Ilia Zdanevich's face-painting manifesto accompanied by a photograph of a couple dancing the tango, at that time an audacious and provocative dance (see ills. 463, 464).*

the Russian Futurists were certified—by practicing physicians—as both sane and insane.[22]

The very different attitudes toward life and art assumed by the writers and artists of Russia's avant-garde demonstrate not only impetuous temperaments and uncompromising behaviors, but also a strong, organic relationship between the personal and the public or, rather, between physiological function and the body politic. In different terms, the Russian Futurists—or, as they preferred to call themselves, Cubo-Futurists—moved constantly between implosion or self-immolation and explosion or self-promotion, summarized by the names of two of their booklets, Riurik Ivnev's *Samosozhzhenie* (Self-immolation) of 1916 and Kruchenykh's *Vzorval* (Explodity) of 1913 [ill. 555], and the names of their two major publishing houses, EUY (a neologism which Kruchenykh equated with the word "lily") and Centrifuge. Ultimately, as Larionov and Zdanevich indicated in their interview with the editor of the magazine *Teatr v karikaturakh* (Theater in caricatures) on January 1, 1914, Futurism even denoted the denial of itself:

> *"Are you Futurists?"*
> *"Yes, we are."*
> *"Do you deny Futurism?"*
> *"Yes, we do. May it vanish from the face of the earth."*[23]

This all and nothing of Russian Cubo-Futurism makes historical reconstruction and assessment difficult indeed, because Cubo-Futurism was not only an aesthetic exercise in abstract philosophy, but also a way of life with its own innovations in behavior and language [ill. 554]. After 1917 it even assumed a concrete political bias, embodied in the movement called Komfut (Communist Futurism). Like their Italian colleagues, the Russian Futurists cultivated violence, if not military then at least metaphorical, as is clear from their exhortations and titles: *A Slap in the Face of Public Taste* (the Futurists' manifesto), *Victory over the Sun* (its devils, persons of ill intent, muggers, Nero, enemies, strongmen, and a pallbearer witness the crash of the aviator onto the stage in Act III), *Death of a Person Simultaneously in an Airplane and at the Railroad* (the Malevich lithograph which Kruchenykh included in his *Vzorval*), and *Misticheskie obrazy voiny* (Mystical images of the war)—Goncharova's album of lithographs [ill. 556].[24] Violence would seem to be the latent connection between Anton Balashev's slashing of Repin's *Ivan the Terrible and His Son*[25] and Maiakovsky's play *Vladimir Maiakovsky. A Tragedy* (designed by Filonov and Iosif Shkolnik) in which the dramatis personae include the Man without an Ear, the Man without a Head, and the Man without an

Above:

554. Olga Rozanova. Cover of Aleksei Kruchenykh's booklet Te li le, St. Petersburg, 1914. Handpainted lithograph.

Left:

555. Olga Rozanova. Cover of Aleksei Kruchenykh'a booklet Vzorval (Explodity). St Petersburg: EUY, 1913. Lithograph. Like other limited editions produced by Kruchenykh and Rozanova (see ills. 554, 615, 628), Vzorval was an example of verbal and visual zaum, or transrational communication, which drew upon neologisms and pictorial distortions to refurbish and reenergize literary and artistic language.

556. *Natalia Goncharova.* The Maiden on the Beast, *Plate Five from her* Misticheskie obrazy voiny *(Mystical images of the war). Moscow: Kashin, 1914, lithograph, 32.5 x 24.9 cm (12 3/4 x 9 3/4 in.). Goncharova interprets Russia's misfortunes during World War I as a national Calvary, identifying the theater of action with both the Apocalypse and the ultimate triumph of Holy Russia.*

Eye and a Foot. As if taking account of all these phenomena, Burliuk exclaimed: "You have to stupefy the bourgeoisie and the philistine with the cudgel of novelty."[26]

Russian Futurism was also highly chameleonic and sometimes its staunchest opponents were its staunchest supporters, as was the case with Repin, who condemned Futurism in no uncertain terms and yet entertained the Burliuks, Ivan Puni, and many other bohemians at his home. The targets of the Futurists' abuse—the "perfumed lechers" of Symbolism and Acmeism such as Balmont, Briusov, and Kuzmin[27]—often adapted their strategies and devices, while the Futurists themselves found inspiration in shadowy zones of cultural manifestation such as nursery rhymes and folk riddles, in second-rate poetry of the nineteenth century, and even in the "art of animals."[28] Finally, many of the Russian poets who called themselves "Futurist" such as Ivan Ignatiev and Igor Severianin were little more than latter-day Baudelaires, disguising a paucity of linguistic and gestural experiment with erotic and necrological motifs which titillated bourgeois taste but appalled the "real" Futurists such as Kruchenykh and Maiakovsky. On the other hand, most of the avant-gardists began their careers under the strong influence of Symbolism, as is clear from Maiakovsky's early poetry, which bears unabashed reminiscences of the *poètes maudits*—such as "The street caved in like the nose of a syphilitic."[29] In any case, the primary Russian Cubo-Futurists, i.e., the members of the Hylaea society, identified the beginning of their movement with the poetry and painting of Elena Guro [ill. 557], whose late Romantic musings on nature and the cosmos now seem incongruously antiquated when compared with the thematic and formal experiments of Khlebnikov and Kruchenykh.

Perhaps the Russians' creative meddling with the word *Futurism* itself, i.e., their inventions of Cubo-Futurism, Ego-Futurism, Neo-Futurism, Pseudo-Futurism, and then *budetlianstvo*, indicates a fundamental disbelief in the validity of the initial term and a strong resistance to Marinetti's proprietorship (the Russian radicals boycotted his visits to St. Petersburg and Moscow in January–February 1914) [ills. 558, 559].[30] On the other hand, the Russians were well aware of the principles and potentials of Italian Futurism from its birth in 1909. They discussed its manifestoes and artifacts and paraphrased—

Left:
557. Elena Guro. Autumnal Dream, *1911.*
Oil on canvas, 100 x 75 cm
(39 3/8 x 29 1/2 in.).

Below:
558. Evening reception for Filippo Tommaso
Marinetti in St. Petersburg on February 1, 1914.
Marinetti, smoking a cigarette, is seated in the
center of the first row; Nikolai Kulbin and the
art dealer Nadezhda Dobychina are seated to his
left, the composer Artur Lurie (Arthur Lourié),
wearing a bowtie, to his right.

559. *Nikolai Kulbin.* Portrait of Filippo Tommaso Marinetti, *1914. Red ink on paper, 33.2 x 21 cm (13 x 8 1/4 in.). State Russian Museum, St. Petersburg.*

explicitly and implicitly—the concerns with mechanical speed (cf. Olga Rozanova's cityscapes) [see ill. 515], with *parole in libertà* (Kruchenykh's linguistic experiments), and with noise (Matiushin's discordant music for *Victory over the Sun*). In other words, in Russia the germ of Italian Futurism fell on a fertile, if somewhat polluted, soil, yielding a rich harvest of hybrids—a weird and wonderful species which, ultimately, seems to have had little in common with the Italian matrix.

If many of the avant-garde artists emphasized a debt to indigenous sources, they were well aware of Western trends, especially Post-Impressionism and Cubism. Some, such as Mariia Vasileva, moved to Paris permanently; some, including Chagall, worked in Paris for extended periods; others, such as Exter and Lentulov, went for shorter visits; yet others knew the paintings of Braque, Gauguin, Matisse, and Picasso from the Morozov and Shchukin collections in Moscow, saw examples at international exhibitions in Russia, such as the "Salon of the 'Golden Fleece'" (Moscow, 1908), or contented themselves with illustrated articles on modern French art in Russian periodicals. Russian and Western artists often contributed to the same exhibitions both at home and abroad—such as Vladimir Izdebsky's "Salon" in Odessa, 1909–11; the "Jack of Diamonds" in Moscow, 1910–11; the "Blaue Reiter" in Munich, 1911–12; the "Salon des Indépendants" in Paris, 1913; and "Der Sturm" in Berlin, 1913. That Larionov scrutinized Gauguin's Polynesian images is clear, for example, from his *Gypsy in Tiraspol* [see ill. 527], while Malevich's cityscapes bring to mind both Cézanne and Seurat. In any case, Tatlin would hardly have arrived at his assemblages—his reliefs—without visiting Picasso in 1914 [see ill. 451]; Popova's paintings, too, such as *Traveling Woman* [see ill. 186], carry literal borrowings from the "bible of Cubism"[31] of Braque, Léger, Le Fauconnier, Metzinger, and Picasso.

David Burliuk, "fieldmarshal of Russian Futurism,"[32] liked to brag that "all women were attractive up to ninety years of age,"[33] while the painter and "apostle"[34] Filonov was a jealous custodian of

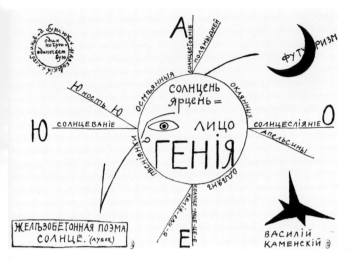

his own private space, even sleeping and eating separately from his wife. Mikhail Le-Dantiu, advocate of "Everythingism,"[35] declared that the artist had the right to draw upon any source for inspiration, while the "Nothingists" exclaimed "Write nothing! Read nothing! Say nothing! Print nothing!"[36] The poet Zdanevich found Marinetti to be "very likeable," but thought his arrival in Moscow was "pathetic and repulsive."[37] Responding to the question "What charges you up today?" in 1922 the Futurist poet, painter, and aviator Kamensky listed a potpourri of "Revolution. Life. Sun. Love. Sea. Poetry. Friends. Dogs. Fruit. Cigars. Perfection. Aviation. Circus. Books [ill. 560]."[38] Here were loud extensions of "Everythingism" into the public domain. On the one hand, these appeared to be casual and arbitrary, yet on the other, they were collocated by the poetics of performance and were still compatible with the dramatic contrasts distinguishing the later phase of Russian Modernism. Such extremism was no more apparent than in the cultural density of the banquet year of Russian Modernism: 1913.

Above left:
560. Vasilii Kamensky. "Ferro-Concrete Poem 'The Sun'" from Vasili Kamensky's collection of poems and drawings called 1918, Tiflis, 1917. Kamensky was drawing on pagan rituals of sun worship and on Old Church Slavonic to produce his composite image of a ferro-concrete sun.

Above right:
561. Vladimir Maiakovsky about to embark on one of his Futurist promenades, 1914.

13.

THE YEAR 1913
CROSSROADS OF PAST AND FUTURE

THE SAMOVAR AND THE ABYSS

In 1907, from the heights of the Symbolist Parnassus, Belyi surveyed the tensions between the canonical old and the wayward new which Tolstoi and Repin had highlighted, integrating them in a curious but effective rondo of samovar and abyss. Evoking the traditional associations of the samovar with coziness, family, and tradition, Belyi contended that "In Petersburg the Modernists are used to walking above an abyss. The abyss is a must for the Petersburg writer. They go and fall in love above the abyss, they visit each other above the abyss, make their careers above the abyss, and place the samovar above the abyss."[1] This interplay of two phenomena linked inextricably with the Russian way of life brings us to the penultimate chapter in this survey of the Silver Age, for, embedded in this counterpoint is a broader resonance of fateful cognates: the traditional, solid corporality and complacency of the samovar is now challenged by the dynamic act of drinking *chai* (tea) with its automatic evocations of *sluchai* (chance), *chaianie* (hope), and *otchaianie* (despair). This contrast between static past and dynamic future is epitomized in the coincidence of two major events which took place in St. Petersburg in 1913—the celebration of the Romanov Tercentenary and the production of *Victory over the Sun*. Their concourse provides a fitting commentary on this history of the Russian Silver Age.

1913: A CASE STUDY

In a very real sense, 1913, not 1900, was Russia's fin de siècle. The year 1913 marked the "twilight of the Tsars"[2] and of a vast political, social, and cultural enterprise, but it was also the moment of a transnational rebirth, when progressive Russian scientists, artists, writers, and businesspeople were racing to borrow from, and contribute to, global progress. In 1913 Kandinsky, Larionov, and Malevich, taking ideas from Munich, Milan, and Paris, were developing original systems of abstract painting [see ills. 20, 233]; poets such as Belyi, Kruchenykh, and Maiakovsky, aware of both Slavonic etymology and Italian Futurism, were reinventing language; Akhmatova and Kuzmin were building their new literary movement of Acmeism;[3] while Russia's capitalists such as Morozov, Riabushinsky, Shchukin, and Zheverzheev were ruling over financial empires. These individuals, never denying their organic link with the Motherland, looked not backward to the "dark kingdom" of patriarchal Russia,[4] but forward to a radiant, international future. In contrast to the aged

Opposite:
562. Kazimir Malevich. Costume design (1920s) for a Strongman in the opera Victory over the Sun, *produced first in St. Petersburg, December 1913. Watercolor and pencil on paper, 53.3 x 36.1 cm (21 x 14 ¼ in.). State Russian Museum, St. Petersburg.*

Above:
563. Nicholas Roerich. Costume for Le Sacre du printemps, *1913. Tempera, watercolor, ceruse, pencil, bronze, and silver on paper mounted on cardboard. 24.3 x 15.3 cm (9 ½ x 6 in.). Bakhrushin State Central Theater Museum, Moscow.*

Above:

564. Nicholas Roerich. Costume for Le Sacre
du printemps, *1913. Tempera, watercolor,
ceruse, pencil, bronze, and silver on paper
mounted on cardboard. 24.3 x 15.3 cm
(9 ¹/₂ x 6 in.). Bakhrushin State Central
Theater Museum, Moscow.*

Below:

565. Six dancers in Le Sacre du printemps,
1913.

and ailing Romanovs, they represented both a rebirth of reason and a
renaissance of beauty.

To assert that a particular moment in time marks the end or
beginning of a historical era or cultural movement is a hazardous
proposition, inasmuch as any such moment is only one link in a chain
of preceding and subsequent conditions which inform, influence,
and define. However, while precedents to, and consequences of, a
fateful moment (e.g., 1917) can always be found, there is sometimes a
constellation of events and circumstances which hastens or highlights what may have been a latent action, giving rise to its manifestation as a strong cultural expression (e.g., Constructivism after the
October Revolution). The year 1913 is such a moment, for it marked
an important juncture in the evolution of the Russian state and, in
retrospect, it supplies a strategic date for establishing a division
between the Silver Age and the brave new world of revolutionary culture which followed. Of indisputable consequence is the fact that
1913 was the last year of peace and prosperity, for in August 1914 Germany and the Austro-Hungarian Empire declared war upon Russia.[5]

The emblematic double-headed eagle of Russia in 1913 was faced
with a quandary, hesitating between tradition and the unknown, just
like the medieval knight in Viktor Vasnetsov's celebrated painting
Warrior at the Crossroads (1882) [see ill. 117]. Although it is clear that the
hero will make the right choice and press forward, the temptation to
return and tread the beaten path is strong. Just such a set of choices
can be identified with many of Russia's cultural manifestations in
1913, not least the celebrations for the Tercentenary of the Romanov
dynasty and the Cubo-Futurist opera or, rather, anti-opera *Victory over
the Sun*. Of course, the verdict was preordained, because however
strong its outward signs of vitality, by 1913 the appeal to indigenous
tradition and the Style Russe—the Neo-Russian style which vested
the festivities of the Tercentenary—was being ousted by the dynamic

566. *The composer Mikhail Matiushin (standing), the designer Kazimir Malevich (seated right), and the playwright Aleksei Kruchenykh (seated left) during their preparations for* Victory over the Sun, *St. Petersburg, 1913.*

tendencies not only of Cubism and Futurism, but also of a new vogue for Ancient Slavdom.

After all, 1913 was also the year of *Le Sacre du Printemps* with its barbaric, shamanistic roots, expressed in Stravinsky's bold discordance and Nijinsky's wild stomping. Here was a savage and fastidious ritual enhanced by the "archaeology" of Roerich's sets and costumes (effective, if contrived) [ills. 563–565; see also 344]; and here was yet another double conflagration at the dusk of the ancien régime and the dawn of the new age, i.e., a pagan ritual of the "natives" cast within the philological and historicist reconstructions which Roerich had elaborated after his early ethnographical expeditions (cf. *Idols*, 1901 [see ill. 324]). *Le Sacre du printemps* was seen in Paris, not St. Petersburg, but it nevertheless contained the paradoxes and contradictions of the Silver Age, owing much to the remote past and yet remarkably predictive of things to come.

A similar reliance on archaic tradition and supreme modernity can also be associated with the avant-garde spectacle *Victory over the Sun*. Produced on December 3 and 5, 1913, by the society of artists and writers known as the Union of Youth at the Luna Park Theater in St. Petersburg, this radical burlesque poked fun at grand opera, promoting audacious experiments in libretto (Khlebnikov's and Kruchenykh's neologistic language), décor (Malevich's Cubist and proto-Suprematist backdrops and costumes), and sound (Matiushin's experimental music). Everything signaled "dislocation . . . and how much the media of expression change over time,"[6] and, as if to symbolize this dislocation, Kruchenykh, Malevich, and Matiushin had themselves photographed against the background of an upside down grand piano.[7]

A challenge to literary, musical, and pictorial conventions, this bold composition integrated a number of different linguistic, artistic, and musical ideas of the time. The language, often transrational and recondite, tells the story of a band of Futurist strongmen [ills. 562, 567–574] bent upon disrupting all norms by challenging and conquering the sun; the music advances by parallel fifths and octaves and semichromatic dissonance; and central images in the opera such as bayonets, fish, a saw, and piano keys recur in Malevich's paintings of the time, as do the strutted wheels of the ill-fated airplane which crashes to the stage during the course of the action.

Naturally, the opera caused a scandal and evoked vociferous and conflicting responses, as the following description would indicate:

> *Since the Futurists did not wish to be like "everyone else," instead of pulling up the curtain, they tore it in half. That was when the "opera," if I may call it that, began. . . . At the end it became tedious, so the public itself tipped in to help the exhausted \Futurists. After almost every cue, you could hear some witty remark, so that very shortly, instead of one spectacle in the theater, we had two: one on stage, the other in the audience. The occasional "music" was replaced by catcalls which, incidentally, harmonized very well with the crazy décor and with the gibberish that resounded from the stage.*[8]

As far as Malevich's "abstract" design of two triangles for Act II, Scene 5, is concerned, he later on regarded its geometry as an important junction in his own artistic development [ill. 575]. Whether the image was abstract or a rendering of the sun's surface against the night sky, in preparing a second collection of designs for a new edition of the libretto *Pobeda nad solntsem* (Victory over the Sun) in May 1915 (not published), Malevich actually drew a black square. As he wrote to Kruchenykh at that time, "This sketch is going to have great significance in painting; what had been done unconsciously is now yielding remarkable fruit."[9] Malevich also returned to *Victory over the Sun* in 1920 in Vitebsk, when, with the Unovis group, he contributed designs to a new production, but what his new response to the square within a square was for that production is not known. In any case, Malevich's backdrop of the two black and white triangles was

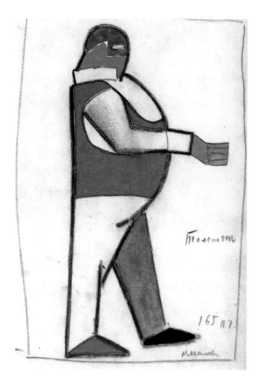

destined to revolutionize the course of contemporary art. Later on, as he reflected upon the theory of Suprematism, Malevich referred to 1913 and specifically *Victory over the Sun* as the departure point of his intellectual and artistic quest for Suprematism, the "new painterly Realism,"[10] and in dressing his egocentricity in universal terms ("By 'I' I mean mankind"), he reached the existential conclusion that "I am the beginning of everything, because worlds are created within my consciousness. I seek God. I seek myself within myself."[11]

Metaphorically speaking, while the left head of the Russian eagle was contemplating *Victory over the Sun*, the right was observing a very different ceremony—the celebrations of the Romanov Tercentenary, of Mother Russia, and of the Neo-Russian style with its mandate to recapture a pristine Slavic culture which, allegedly, had flourished in Russia before the accession of Peter the Great. Peter's military, institutional, legal, and cultural reforms, his "Westernization," had, in the eyes of

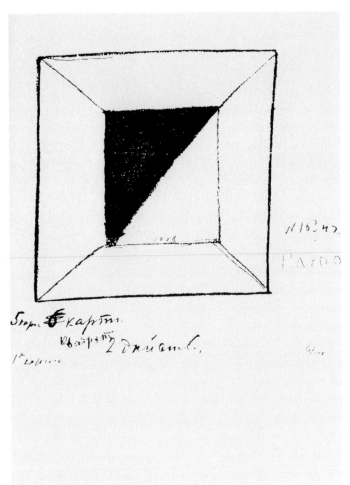

many Russians, damaged, if not destroyed, an entire national heritage of ritual, deportment, and artifact—from Boyar costumes to Old Believer icons, from church rites to the wearing of beards—which now needed to be rediscovered and preserved.

This Russophile or Slavophile trend had gained increasing support in the later nineteenth century, culminating, for example, in the establishment of the two Neo-Russian or Neo-Nationalist art colonies at Abramtsevo and Talashkino. Sponsored by Mamontov and Princess Tenisheva, respectively, these two retreats did much to foster a Neo-Russian style in the applied arts, studio painting, and architecture. Artists such as Bilibin, Polenova, V. Vasnetsov, Vrubel, and Yakunchikova were invited to study the indigenous artistic heritage, including folklore, fairy tales, embroideries, furniture, pottery, toys, and household utensils [see ills. 268, 316, 380, 483].

These artists borrowed themes, motifs, and compositions from domestic culture, applying them to often fabulous ceramics (e.g.,

576. *Boris Zvorykin. Cover of program for the celebration of the Tercentenary of the House of Romanovs at the Alexandrinsky Theater, St. Petersburg, 1913. Color lithograph, 35.5 x 22 cm (14 x 8 3/4 in.).*

Vrubel's *Mikula Selianinovich and Volga*, book illustrations (e.g., Bilibin's for Pushkin's *Tale of Tsar Saltan* and Boris Zvorykin's for the Imperial Alexandrinsky Theater commemorative program [ill. 576, see also 289]), stage designs (e.g., Golovin's for *Boris Godunov* [ill. 577]), and architecture—as in the case of Ropet (pseudonym of Ivan Petrov) [ill. 578] and Viktor Gartman (whose pictures at an exhibition inspired Modest Mussorgsky's brilliant music). Nesterov alluded to the faith of Holy Russia by evoking the vision of the child Bartholemew and by portraying Prince Dmitrii, murdered allegedly by Tsar Boris, against the landscape of Zagorsk (center of Russian Orthodoxy) and Abramtsevo [ills. 579, 580]. Such courtly retrospectivism was not so very distant from the

Above:
577. *Aleksandr Golovin.*
Plebiscitary Meeting in the
Pskov Kremlin. *Set design for the
prologue of Nikolai Rimsky-
Korsakov's opera* The Maid of
Pskov *at the Bolshoi Theater,
Moscow, 1901. Gouache and water-
color on cardboard, 54 x 93.4 cm
(21 1/4 x 36 3/4 in.). State Tretiakov
Gallery, Moscow.*

Left:
578. *Ivan Ropet (pseudonym of
Ivan Petrov). Design for a pavilion
promoting Russian tobacco for a
French trade exhibition, 1879.*

Right:
579. Mikhail Nesterov. Dmitrii, the Slain Tsarevich, *1899. Oil on canvas, 197 x 175 cm (77 ¹/₂ x 68 ⁷/₈ in.). State Russian Museum, St. Petersburg.*

Below:
580. Mikhail Nesterov. The Holy Trinity Appearing as Three Angels, *1895. Oil on canvas, 61 x 88 cm (24 x 34 ⁵/₈ in.). Kostroma Art Museum, Kostroma.*

Opposite left:
581. Mikhail Vrubel. Tsarevna Volkhova (Nadezhda Zabela-Vrubel as Volkhova in Nikolai Rimsky-Korsakov's opera "Sadko"), *1897–98. Watercolor on paper, 160.1 x 61.5 cm (63 x 24 ¹/₄ in.). State Russian Museum, St. Petersburg.*

Opposite top right:
582. Boris Anisfeld. Costume for the Sea Princess in Nikolai Rimsky-Korsakov's opera Sadko, *1911.*

Opposite bottom right:
583. Mikhail Vrubel. Volkhova (from a series of sculptures based on Nikolai Rimsky-Korsakov's opera Sadko), *1897–1900. Majolica, luster glaze, height 39 cm (15 ³/₈ in.).*

mythical Russia of tinseled snow and magical reincarnations in the operas *Snegurochka* and *Sadko*, a condition evoked by Vrubel's costume for his wife, Zabela-Vrubel, as Tsarevna Volkhova [ills. 581–583].

Even if by 1913 the Neo-Russian style was passé, its appeal to national tradition was eminently appropriate to the purpose and function of the Tercentenary commemoration and was applied ad nauseam to the memorabilia, from menus for official banquets to special calendars, from utensils of everyday use to music programs.

Fabergé & Co. even produced precious bagatelles in the Neo-Byzantine and Neo-Russian styles, and as late as the émigré cabarets in Berlin and Paris and the Russian Tea Room in New York, the Neo-Russian style was still continuing to attract supporters [ills. 584–586].

The imprint of this vogue was especially strong on architecture—Shchusev's Kazan Railroad Station in Moscow (1910s), for example, stands to this day as a monument to the Neo-Russian style enhanced by a fabulous

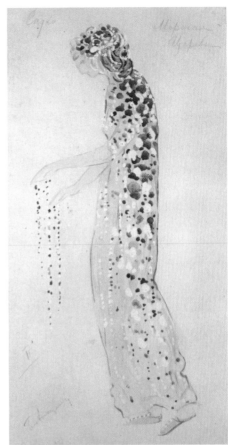

Opposite:
584. Ivan Bilibin. Cover of a program for the Beliaev Symphonic Concerts and Quartet Evenings, St. Petersburg, 1905. Color lithograph. Before his death in 1903 the musician, publisher, and impresario Mitrofan Beliaev had been known in particular for the "Musical Fridays" which he organized at his St. Petersburg home. At these musical events, leading composers and performers of the time, including Aleksandr Glazunov and Nikolai Rimsky-Korsakov, played and discussed their works. Beliaev also directed a publishing company—in Leipzig and St. Petersburg—which specialized in contemporary Russian music.

Above:
585. Nicholas Remisoff (Nikolai Remizov; pseudonym: Re-mi). Costume designs for Alexandre Transman's Tragedy of the Cello, *1927. Pencil and watercolor on paper, 27.9 x 37.9 cm (11 x 15 in.). Produced by Adolph Bolm at the Eighth Street Theater, Chicago.*

Right:
586. Nicholas Remisoff (Nikolai Remizov; pseudonym: Re-mi). Poster advertising the Chauve- Souris (Bat) cabaret in New York, 1922.

mix of Art Nouveau, Moscow Empire, and even Italian Baroque reminiscences [ill. 588]. With its quaint frills and pilasters recalling the folklore of pre-Petrine Russia, the Kazan Station was decorated on the inside by the St. Petersburg painters Benois, Lancéray, and Serebriakova between 1913 and 1917. As we look at the Kazan Station in Moscow or, for that matter, the Cathedral on the Blood in St. Petersburg [ill. 587], monumental and eclectic pâtisseries, we can appreciate Bakst's sentiment of 1914:

> There are two dominant movements in art at the moment. One is slavishly retrospective and the other, hostile to the former, is futuristic, with its sights set far ahead. . . . The former movement pulls us back to our predecessors, to the art of the deceased, to their illumined canons, while the latter destroys everything old and builds the foundation for the art of the future that will be judged by our great-grandchildren. But where is our own art, where is the new art, where are the contemporary joy and delight in an art that really expresses our life and not that of our grandfathers or our great-grandchildren?[12]

Opposite:
587. Alfred Parland, architect. Church of the Resurrection (the Church of the Savior on the Blood), St. Petersburg, 1903–07. The Church of the Resurrection is known more commonly as the Church of the Spilled Blood, because it was erected as a memorial on the place where Tsar Alexander II was assassinated in 1881.

Above:
588. Aleksei Shchusev, architect. Kazan Railroad Station, Moscow, 1913.

POMP AND CIRCUMSTANCE

The spectacle of the Romanov Tercentenary drew upon illustrious precedents, including the coronation of Nicholas in 1896 [see ill. 348] and the Grand Costume Ball of 1903 [see ill. 70], which had coincided with the Bicentenary of the founding of St. Petersburg: here was Tsar Nicholas dressed in the red velvet brocade costume of his ancestor Aleksei Mikhailovich, borrowed from the Historical Museum of Moscow; and here was his sister-in-law Grand Duchess Elizaveta Fedorovna sporting the traditional *kokoshnik*, a tiara-shaped headdress [ills. 589, 590].[13]

Opposite:
589. Tsar Nicholas II and Tsarina Alexandra wearing seventeenth-century royal costumes at the Grand Costume Ball in the Winter Palace on the occasion of the bicentenary of St. Petersburg in 1903. The Tsar is wearing the red velvet brocade costume of his ancestor Aleksei Mikhailovich, borrowed expressly from the Historical Museum of Moscow.

Left:
590. Grand Duke Sergei Alexandrovich and Grand Duchess Elizaveta Fedorovna at the Grand Costume Ball, 1903.

The official eulogy of the Romanov dynasty inspired a "Russian-ization" of everyday life, both visually and practically. The Russian theater was also quick to acknowledge the royal presumption; Diaghilev staged *Boris Godunov* (with designs by Bakst, Bilibin, and Konstantin Yuon, and the title role filled by Fedor Chaliapin) as well as *Khovanshchina* (with designs by Fedor Fedorovsky), both in Paris, while Korovin designed the Bolshoi Theater production of *The Tale of Tsar Saltan.* Even the young avant-gardist Tatlin was drawn to this dramatic appeal to pre-Petrine Russia, accepting a commission to design sets and costumes for Mikhail Glinka's *A Life for the Tsar (Ivan Susanin)* for Moscow in 1913 (not produced) [ill. 592].[14] In some sense, Lentulov's large paintings *Moscow* (1913) and *St. Basil's Cathedral* (1913) also pay homage to the Tercentenary with their bright colors from old Russian tiles and vestments and their central images of the Bell Tower of Ivan the Great and St. Basil's Cathedral—even if these trenchant symbols of Old Russia, in Simultanist red, yellow, and blue, can also be read as a Russian paraphrase of one of Robert Delaunay's Eiffel Towers [ills. 591, 593].

593. *Aristarkh Lentulov.* St. Basil's
Cathedral, *1913. Oil and paper collage on
canvas, 170.5 x 163.5 cm (67 ¹/₈ x 64 ³/₈ in.).
State Tretiakov Gallery, Moscow.*

594. Fedor Riukert (Rückert), designer. Enamel box, Moscow, 1908–17. Silver-gilt and cloisonné enamel, length 12.4 cm (5 ¹/₄ in.). The lid carries a reproduction of Konstantin Makovsky's painting The New Dress.

SACRED AND SECULAR

The Orthodox Church, as the designated agent of Holy Russia, was a willing receptacle of the Neo-Russian style, and the decorative revival which informed so much of Russian visual and material culture during the Silver Age also left a profound imprint upon icons and icon frames, as well as upon ecclesiastical architecture, furnishings, textiles, and utensils. Artists such as Fedor Riukert (Rückert), Sergei Vashkov, and V. Vasnetsov and ateliers such as the Khlebnikov Manufactory and the Ovchinnikov Workshops fulfilled major commissions for the Orthodox Church, designing candelabra, icon and incense lamps, frames, and vessels in the Neo-Russian style, often adding motifs from Art Nouveau[15] [ills. 594–597]. Although Vashkov and his colleagues seemed often to treat their commission

Top left:
595. Icon of the Mother of God of the Sign, Moscow, 1908–17. Silver gilt and enameled frame, 11.5 x 8.75 cm (4 ¹/₂ x 3 ¹/₂ in.).

Above:
596. Anonymous designer. Silver and enamel liturgical items, 1910. Orest Kurliukov Company, Moscow.

Bottom left:
597. Dmitrii Smirnov, designer. A Russian icon pendant of the Guardian Angel with champlevé enamel silver frame, Moscow, ca. 1910.

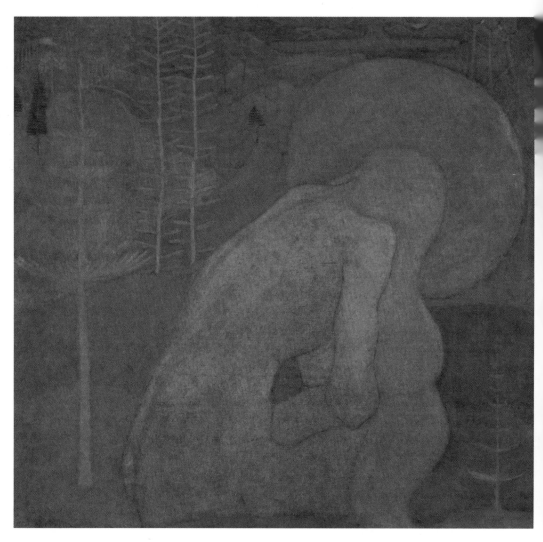

more as subsidized explorations of formal and aesthetic combinations than as paeans to Christendom and Tsardom, the fact that during the Silver Age the Russian Church was one of the strongest supporters of the Neo-Russian style—and then of the Style Moderne—indicates an eagerness to reinforce the ancient legacy of a patriarchal axis shared by the Orthodox faith and the Imperial household.

As was to be expected, the avant-garde was not privy to this partnership of power, although Malevich designed church murals [ill. 598], Filonov painted icons [ill. 599], and Tatlin may have derived his fascination with the spiral from his study of the late-fourteenth-century icon of the Virgin of the Don by Feofan the Greek [ill. 600; see also 451].[16] Occasionally, however, the relationship came full circle both metaphorically and practically: Malevich referred to his *Black*

Square as both a regal infant and a new icon [see ill. 215][17] and *Victory over the Sun*, perhaps the most extreme expression of the avant-garde endeavor, was subsidized by Levkii Zheverzheev, a St. Petersburg businessman who made his money from the sale of church utensils in the Neo-Russian style, while assembling a major collection of modern Russian stage designs and financing the St. Petersburg Union of Youth group (which, inter alia, sponsored *Victory over the Sun* and major exhibitions of the avant-garde) [ill. 601].[18]

These particular junctures between feudal history (imagined or not) and cultural prescience (the avant-garde), between nationalist culmination and artistic rebirth, relate directly to the "official" rediscovery of Russian icons in 1913. As part of the Tercentenary celebrations, the Moscow Archaeological Institute organized the historic "Exhibition of Ancient Russian Art" early in the year under the curatorial tutelage of Pavel Muratov, the first major display of such objects outside of their cultic environment. Divided into four sections (icons, manuscripts, embroideries and fabrics, and silver and

Above:
600. *Feofan the Greek. Holy Virgin of the Don, 1380–90s. Tempera on wood,*
86 x 67 cm (33 7/8 x 26 3/8 in.). State Tretiakov Gallery, Moscow.

Below:
601. *Iosif Shkolnik, designer. Poster advertising the "Exhibition of the Russian Theater,"*
Petrograd, 1915. Lithograph, 105 x 77.5 cm (41 3/8 x 30 1/2 in.).

602. *Dmitrii Stelletsky.* Exalted Boiarynia
Marfa, the Governess, *1910. Painted wood,
height 69 cm (27 ¹/₈ in.). State Russian
Museum, St. Petersburg.*

bronze of the fourteenth to seventeenth centuries), the exhibition acquainted the public at large with a neglected artistic (rather than ecclesiastical) legacy, especially with the original colors and forms of the schools of Dionysius and Rublev.[19] The effect of the illumination was instantaneous, stimulating painters such as Goncharova and Lentulov to reinforce their interest in bright color, inverted perspective, and anatomical deformation and even to turn to the Bible as an

iconographic source. Dmitrii Stelletsky, for example, imparted saintly attributes to his female personification of the night, while his *Exalted Boiarynia Marfa the Governess*, with her earnest attendants, brocaded investiture, and seriousness of mien, reminds us of some Orthodox dignitary [ills. 602, 604].[20] Goncharova's audacious figures for the unrealized ballet *Liturgie* (1915) [ill. 603] were clear reminiscences of the "Exhibition of Ancient Russian Art."[21]

The "Exhibition of Ancient Russian Art" was not totally without precedent. The historian Dmitrii Nikiforov had organized a similar exhibition of ecclesiastical items in Moscow in 1901 under the title "Treasures in Moscow," publishing a handsome catalogue [ill. 605].[22] Diaghilev, too, had ensured that antique icons were included in his Russian section for the "Salon d'Automne" in Paris of 1906 [ill. 607]. Still, Muratov's project was the most scholarly and most ambitious of

605. *View of the collections of antiquities belonging to Aleksei and Mikhail Morozov and Olga Budygina. Items from the collections were included in the exhibition "Treasures in Moscow" organized in Moscow in 1901.*

its kind and provided an essential platform upon which subsequent intellectual, philosophical, and aesthetic investigations into Russia's ecclesiastical art drew substantially. St. Petersburg never matched the "Exhibition of Ancient Russian Art"; indeed, the northern capital could not draw upon the wealth of the private and public collections which Moscow boasted in this area such as those of Ilia Ostroukhov [ill. 606] and the Riabushinsky family. True, some important, but more recent, pieces were included in the Russian Popular Art section at the "Second Handicraft Exhibition," which opened in St. Petersburg in March 1913 under the aegis of Empress Alexandra Fedorovna,[23] but, next to embroidered lace, handmade furniture, and metal utensils, they emerged as just one more product of the popular national consciousness rather than as masterpieces of painting.

With special sections representing the traditions of the various territories comprising the Russian Empire, the "Second Handicraft Exhibition" was a celebration of abundance and diversity. The visual impact of the exhibition and of its catalogue, along with that of the other Imperial festivals of 1913, was one of wealth and strength. No doubt the aristocracy and the bourgeoisie were pleased to see such optimistic fullness. If, however, that same audience happened to check the latest publications, they might have been drawn to a very different artifact, a thin volume of poetry called *Smert iskusstvu* (Death to art) written by the Futurist Vasilii Gnedov.[24] The collection contained neologisms, ending with a "Poem of the End," i.e., a blank page, as if the author were maintaining that art denoted zero or that true poetry was silence. As in the case of the Tercentenary and *Victory over the Sun*, here were two cultural phenomena, connected in time and yet disconnected in subject and purpose, which summarized the diametric contrasts—the polarization—of Russia in 1913. But there is a tailpiece to this polemic, for in tiny letters at the bottom of the page of the "Poem of the End" is the name of the printshop—"Svet" (Light)—as if to imply that enlightenment would come not from the traditional, the orthodox, and the known, but from the innovative, the radical, and the unpredictable.

Above:
606. *Valentin Serov.* Portrait of the Artist Ilia Ostroukhov, *1902. Oil on canvas, 86 x 76 cm (33 7/8 x 29 7/8 in.). State Tretiakov Gallery, Moscow.*

Left:
607. *Ivan Bilibin. Cover of the catalog for the "Exposition de l'art russe" at the Salon d'automne, Paris, 1906.*

APOCALYPSE NOW
War, Revolution, and Cultural Centrifuge

THE GREAT WAR

In his essay entitled "The Apocalypse in Russian Poetry," Belyi defined the apocalypse as chaos which "appears to us from within as madness, and from without as a fragmentation of life into an innumerable quantity of separate channels."[1] The apocalypse, or the presentiment of a cataclysm of global proportions, served as a primary subject for many Russian artists and writers of the Silver Age, as Bakst demonstrated in his *Terror Antiquus* [see ill. 165]. A different, but still pressing sensibility is offered by Zamirailo in his daunting wilderness of wild dogs, wolves, stampeding horses, and desperate humans, as if the artist were asserting that human initiative and inventiveness were ineffectual in the face of the bestial and the savage [see ill. 366]. Konstantin Yuon identified the October events of 1917 with the apocalypse, imbuing them with a religious and ecstatic illumination as in his *New Planet* (1921) [ill. 609], while Bilinsky, disciple of Bakst, saw the apocalypse as a moment of blinding light, of disintegration—and also of reintegration, which he expressed in his cycle of pictures called *The Apocalypse* (1930s and 1940s) [see ill. 44].

Opposite:
608. *Olga Rozanova. Illustration for Aleksei Kruchenykh's book* Voina *(War), Petrograd, 1916. Linocut and collage.*

Below:
609. *Konstantin Yuon. A New Planet, 1921. Oil on canvas, 71 x 101 cm (28 x 39 3/4 in.). State Tretiakov Gallery, Moscow.*

610. *Vasilii Kandinsky.* Composition VI,
*1913. Oil on canvas, 195 x 300 cm
(76 3/4 x 118 1/8 in.). State Hermitage,
St. Petersburg.*

Viewed in retrospect, this eschatological mood with its intense religious search appears as part of a general desire to take flight—to escape the harsh moments of political and social reality. If the early 1910s witnessed an Imperial euphoria as well as a fascination with the occult, the consolidation of the avant-garde, and what Benois regarded as a suicidal "cult of emptiness,"[2] it also presaged the military apocalypse of World War I, echoing and amplifying the misgivings of the Symbolists. Kandinsky presaged all these conditions in his two compositions *VI* and *VII* (both 1913) [ills. 610, 611].

On July 28, 1914, the Austro-Hungarian Empire declared war on Serbia; on August 1, 1914, Germany declared war on Russia; within a week France and Great Britain had entered the theater of action; by the end of the month Japan had joined the Triple Entente (France, Great Britain, and Russia); and at the end of September Turkey allied with Germany, opening a second military front for Russia. The ensuing months saw the involvement of Rumania, Bulgaria, Italy, and the United States (April 1917), and China and Greece (summer 1917). In other words, within a little over two years, what was at first called the "German" or "Austro-Hungarian" War became the "European" War and then the "Great War," the "War of the Peoples," and "World" War.

The Great War was characterized not by a single advance or retreat, but by many interactions, and the Russia of August 1914 was a very different nation from the Russia that signed the Treaty of Brest-Litovsk on March 3, 1918. In any case, for Russia the violence of the Great War did not stop with the Treaty of Brest-Litovsk, but continued into the Civil War and, some would argue, into a dictatorial aggression for many decades to come. Russian public response to the Great War changed dramatically over the course of the war—from naïve patriotism with its attendant faith in Church and Tsar, through increasing disenchantment with the military capacity, to an abrupt dislocation between the soldiers at the front and the civilians at home. Suffice it to recall that in February 1915, just as the Russian army was retreating to the east bank of the Vistula, the Stray Dog cabaret in Petrograd was celebrating its most lavish party, or *kapustnik*, and in retrospect, the loss of seven million Russian soldiers during the forty months of the war seems incompatible with the carefree lifestyle of the beau monde and the intelligentsia at home [ills. 612, 613, 616–621].

Only a small percentage of Russia's practicing artists saw action, but many contributed paintings, drawings, and sculptures to special exhibitions such as "The War and the Press" (1914), "Artists for

611. Vasilii Kandinsky. Composition VII, 1913. Oil on canvas, 200 x 300 cm (78 3/4 x 118 1/8 in.). State Tretiakov Gallery, Moscow.

Above:
612. *World War I. Russian Soldiers in the trenches, 1915.*

Right:
613. *Tsarina Alexandra with her daughters Olga and Tatiana at a field hospital for the wounded, 1915.*

Left:
614. Aleksandr Lozhkin.
Cover of Ivan Lazarevsky's
survey Velikaia voina v
obrazakh i kartinakh (The
Great War in images and
pictures). Moscow: Mamontov,
1915, Vol. 1.

Below:
615. Olga Rozanova and
Aleksei Kruchenykh. Heavy
Artillery. Collage for their
book Vselenskaia voina
(Universal war), Petrograd,
1916 (see ills. 554, 555, 628).

Overleaf:
616. World War I. Austro-
Hungarian soldiers in
gas masks during a gas alarm
in their trenches. Zlota Gora
(East Galicia), August 1916.

Top:
617. World War I.
Russian infantry. 1916.

Center:
618. World War I.
Russian artillery, 1916.

Bottom:
619. World War I.
Russian Cossack cavalry
with lances, 1916.

Opposite top:
620. World War I.
Russian soldiers on their
way to a prisoner's camp in
East Galicia, 1917.

Opposite bottom:
621. World War I. Dead
Russian soldiers on the
battlefield of Baranovichi
(White Russia), 1916.

Their Comrade Warriors," and "Artists of Moscow for the Victims of War"; and popular magazines such as *Lukomore* (Cove), *Sinii zhurnal* (Blue journal), *Novyi Satirikon*, and *Solntse Rossii* reproduced their interpretations. In addition, the war inspired the publication of many surveys, picture books, and albums compiled by artists and writers, conservative and radical (from Ivan Lazarevsky's *The Great War in Images and Pictures*[3] [ill. 614] to Rozanova's and Kruchenykh's *Vselenskaia voina* (Universal War) of 1916 [ill. 615].[4] Serious intellectual and critical studies of war and the visual arts were also published, including Yakov Tugendkhold's *The Problem of War in World Art* and, much later, Valentine Gross's *War in Art*.[5]

The military conscription or exemption of artists, the censorship of visual data, and the activities of the Class of Battle Painting at the Academy of Arts in Petrograd—these and many other elements are vital to an adequate understanding of the position of artists vis-à-vis the Great War. Rudolf Frents, Lebedev, Miturich, and the architect Leonid Sologub, for example, trained in the class before going off to the war as frontline artists [ill. 622]. Serving on the Prussian front, Vasilii Rozhdestvensky (a member of the Jack of Diamonds group)

Above:
622. Rudolf Frents. Partisan, 1915. Oil on canvas, 130 x 94 cm (51 1/8 x 37 in.). State Russian Museum, St. Petersburg.

Opposite:
623. Kazimir Malevich. "Just Look at This, Near the Vistula the Germans Got All Screwed Up—Which Is Sour Luck for Them!" Patriotic broadsheet with verse by Vladimir Maiakovsky, 1914. Color lithograph, 56 x 38 cm (22 x 15 in.).

likened the effect to a "day of eclipse,"[6] while Nikolai Ulianov remarked on the coincidence of the unusual heat wave and forest fires in August 1914, and the "shadows of Veronese" which prefigured the impending catastrophe.[7]

Not surprisingly, presentiment, if not prediction, of cosmic collision and transformation was one of the manifest characteristics of the fin de siècle. The radical deportment of the avant-garde, in particular, in constant battle with its public, is symptomatic of the aggression, real or implied, which characterized certain aspects of the Russian Silver Age. The general response of Russian artists and writers to the outbreak of World War I was ambivalent. Given the heavy apocalyptic mood of the time, the war seemed to be, on one level, a physical fulfillment of the Symbolists' vision of dawns and twilights intensified by the First Revolution and the Russo-Japanese War. In this sense, the Great War was not unexpected— Kandinsky, for example, interpreting the image of cannons in his *Improvisation No. 30 (Cannons)* (1913) as a gesture to the "constant war talk that had been going on throughout the year."[8] Early in 1914 one writer even

Глядь, поглядь, ужъ близко Вислы
Нѣмцевъ пучитъ, значитъ кисло!

Шелъ австріецъ въ Радзивилы,
Да попалъ на бабьи вилы.

624. *Kazimir Malevich. "An Austrian Was Marching to Radzivil, but Fell onto a Peasant Woman's Pitchfork." Patriotic broadsheet with verse by Vladimir Maiakovsky, 1914. Color lithograph, 32.8 x 49.5 cm (13 x 19 ¹/₂ in.).*

published a novel called *The War of the "Ring" and the "Union,"* subtitled *A Tale of Coming Events*, in which he predicted a military conflict between Great Britain, France, and Russia on the one hand, and Germany, Austria, and Italy on the other.[9]

Naturally, the shift in national mood was reflected in pictorial interpretations. At first, the buoyant and colorful posters, postcards,[10] and broadsides (including the fifty that the Modern Broadside Corporation produced in Moscow between August and November 1914) expressed the manifest strength and valor of the Russian troops and the alleged stupidity of the Germans [ills. 623. 624]; but in 1915–16, as Russian fallibility became all too apparent, a new wave of images came to emphasize the atrocities of the German army. As pessimism replaced optimism, artists and writers evoked the pain and remorse of the Russian people, alluding to a Russian Calvary that was to be suffered for the sins of mankind.

True, many artists seemed completely detached from the events—for example, Benois, Kliun, Puni, and Somov avoided overt reference to the war in their paintings and drawings. Certain administrative prerequisites, such as ill health and primogeniture, disqualified eligible artists from recruitment (e.g., David Burliuk and Kamensky), and the Ministry of Defense was besieged by petitions from artists claiming exemption. On the other hand, a number of artists volunteered or were recruited as soldiers, sailors, or airmen, among them Vladimir Burliuk, Vasilii Chekrygin, Konchalovsky, Larionov, Lebedev, Le-Dantiu, Rozhdestvensky, and Aleksandr Shevchenko; in 1916 Malevich was called to serve in the 56th Reserve Infantry in Viazma, Smolensk, and Moscow; Rodchenko was mobilized to serve as quartermaster for a hospital train; Filonov fought on the Rumanian front and then with the Baltic Marine Division.

Curiously enough, however, "eye-witness" accounts of the war by Russian artists are few and far between. Mention might be made of Miturich's drawings of barracks and fields, Lebedev's cycle of sketches called *War of 1917*, Malevich's painting *Warrior of the First Division* (1914) [ill. 626] and drawings such as *Death of a Cavalry Officer*, and Chagall's harrowing images of the wounded passing through Vitebsk [ills. 625, 627]. Many renderings of the war tended to be metaphorical such as David Burliuk's *In Battles of Yore Fathers Perished and Now It Is the Turn of the Sons* and Rozanova's album *Voina* (War) of 1916 [ills. 608, 628]. Some works were inspired by military strategies and experiments rather than by actual events—such as the counterreliefs which Tatlin named by analogy with "counterattack" and Pavel

Above:
625. Marc Chagall. Wounded Soldier. 1914. Ink on paper. 22.6 x 13.3 cm (8 7/8 x 5 1/4 in.) oval. State Tretiakov Gallery, Moscow.

Left:
626. Kazimir Malevich. Warrior of the First Division (also known as Private of the First Division), 1914. Oil on canvas with collage of postage stamp, thermometer, and other items, 53.7 x 44.8 cm (21 1/8 x 17 5/8 in.). The Museum of Modern Art, New York.

Right:
627. *Marc Chagall.* Off to War, *1914. Ink on paper, 21.7 x 17.8 cm (8 ¹/₂ x 7 in.). Back in Vitebsk from Paris after the outbreak of World War I, Chagall witnessed the hardships and misfortunes of local conscripts detached forcibly from their families. He also saw the maimed and the crippled who returned from the front.*

Below:
628. *Olga Rozanova.* Battle in Three Spheres (Land, Sea, and Air). *Illustration for Aleksei Kruchenykh's book* Voina (War), *Petrograd, 1916. Color lithograph. (See ills. 554, 555, 615).*

Mansurov's first "painterly formulae," which were intended to illustrate the trajectories of projectiles.

Dismemberment, death, and destruction were rendered by the new and diabolical apparatuses of big guns, gas, submarines, and by what Tatlin described as the "iron wings" of airplanes,[11] their novel images and miraculous dimensions bursting into the rarefied imagination of artists and writers. Radio and aerial photography recorded these deadly devices. Long-range guns and radio, for example, conquered space, confounding there and here and East and West within a theater-in-the-round where distance and perspective now seemed redundant. Here was an elliptical sense wherein observation and vanishing point become the same— a totality of military space inherent in Filonov's *German War* [ill. 629] and Petrov-Vodkin's *In the Line of Fire* [ill. 630].

629. *Pavel Filonov.* German War, *1915. Oil on canvas, 176 x 156.3 cm (69 ¹/₄ x 61 ¹/₂ in.). State Russian Museum, St. Petersburg.*

Even so, for many artists of the Modernist generation war in general—and the Great War in particular—was an abstraction. True, the Russo-Japanese War was fresh in memory, but it had been a brief and distant adventure.[12] Similarly, the centennial festivities for Russia's defeat of Napoleon in 1912 elicited the impression of a gallant game of cards or of a hunt or ball rather than of the massacre of thousands, and much of the Silver Age commentary, reflected, for example, on the pages of *Starye gody* or in Georgii Narbut's silhouettes for *The Year of 1812 in the Fables of Krylov* [see ills. 363, 364],[13] tells us more about the filigree on a cannon or the niceties of a coat of arms than about Napoleon's tragic campaign. For many artists of the Silver Age, then, war often meant little more than the Tolstoyan philosophy of *War and Peace* or at worst a fanciful *War of the Mushrooms* or *War of the Mice and the Frogs.*[14]

The initial optimism and lightheartedness which accompanied the first months of the war, when few realized how arduous the encounter would be, can be identified with several major pictorial evocations of military action. Painted as the storm clouds of war approached, Lentulov's *Allegorical Depiction of the Patriotic War of 1812* (1914) [ill. 631], strongly tinged with Italian Futurism, tells of the chaos and confusion which awaits the trespasser on Russian soil.

The fanciful *Battle of Two Ships* [ill. 632], however, turns military confrontation into a highly stylized and colorful romance with guns ablaze, a sinking battleship, and an Imperial Russian flag confirming who is friend and who is foe. The composition might entertain as a candy wrapper or frame in a comic strip, but hardly functions as a record of the ferocious combat between Imperial Germany and Imperial Russia.

But such specificity of military identity is rare among the artists concerned, for "victory" tended to mean more than a local conquest. For Filonov, for example, "victory" denoted a transcendental victory, and by 1915 he was interpreting the Great War as an instrument of human regeneration which would witness the birth of a "victor of the city," of a cosmic "bearer of victory," and a "victory over eternity" [ills. 633, 634]. As a soldier, Filonov saw the corpses of his fallen comrades, mutilated, dismembered, and piled high upon the battlefield—which is the tragic subject of *German War* with its bloody strata of heads and limbs pressing downward as if in some medieval descent into hell.

Filonov's *German War* bears comparison with a parallel painting by his avowed enemy, Petrov-Vodkin, i.e., *In the Line of Fire*. Painted in

633. *Pavel Filonov. Victory over Eternity,*
1920–21. Oil on wood, 41 x 37.5 cm
(16 1/8 x 14 3/4 in.). State Russian Museum, St.
Petersburg.

October 1915, *In the Line of Fire* identifies the Russian contribution to the war effort as one of human sacrifice. Here is a rural Russia fighting at dawn and entrapped in an endless war within an elliptical and, therefore, endless space. Yet if the ensign has received a mortal wound, his gaze is one of inspiration and revelation—and the firing becomes the fire of spiritual illumination. The Russian soldiers, as in Goncharova's portfolio *Mystical Images of the War*, are presented as the bearers of salvation and emissaries of the spirit who will conquer all enemies, whether the Kaiser or the profane viewer.

Cast within the environment of World War I , Malevich's *Black Square* also takes on a new meaning. Shown in December 1915–January 1916 at the "0.10" exhibition in Petrograd, the "line of fire" which demarcated the first phase of the avant-garde, the *Black Square*, or *Black Quadrilateral*, as it was called in the catalogue [see ill. 215], must have aroused associations—and not only with death, the funerary shroud, and the blackness of the tomb. Here also were the forces of good (white) and evil (black) in close confrontation, the armies of light pressing in upon the hosts of the darkness, a strategic encasement reflecting the popular sentiment that Holy Russia would vanquish the German Antichrist. Of course, the military symbology of the *Black Square* is yet another fragment in an intricate mosaic of interpretations, but its very position in time (at a desperate turning point in the Russo-German conflict) and its absolute reduction to positive and negative must have elicited associations with the fatal collision of powers on the Western front. The same is true of the enigmatic collection of illustrations produced in Petrograd ca. 1915 (undated) under the title *O voine* (About the war), in which neither compiler, editor, nor artist is indicated, but which contains the caricature captioned "'Great,' said Malevich" [ill. 635].

The attitude of Russian artists toward World War I was fragmentary and inconsistent, and the energy of the battlefield does not form a major component of their visual lexicon. In contrast to the Italian Futurists and the English Vorticists, the Russian Cubo-Futurists

634. *Pavel Filonov.* Victor of the City, *1914–15. Watercolor, ink, Indian ink, brush, and pencil on cardboard, 42.1 x 34.2 cm (16 1/2 x 13 1/2 in.). State Russian Museum, St. Petersburg.*

635. *Anonymous artist. "'Great,' said Malevich."*
Illustration for the anonymous book O voine
(About the war), Petrograd, ca. 1915.

chose not to paint exploding shells, trenches, and cascading air-planes. For them the true battle was being waged on other planes—against time, three-dimensional space, and the appearance of things. In this sense, the new artists of Russia were far in advance of the mil-itary avant-garde and, ultimately, they conquered, while others lost.

DIASPORA

Generally speaking, the Silver Age was an apolitical movement and, except for a brief involvement in the revolutionary journals of 1905–06, the artists and writers of Russian Symbolism felt more easily aligned with "there" than with "here." Inevitably, their reaction to the October Revolution of 1917 and the far-reaching ideological impositions which it brought was negative or cantankerous, to say the least, in large part because the uprisings, marauding masses, and Civil War brought further economic chaos, material deprivation, and cultural disorientation. While in some quarters political optimism replaced economic viability, it is easy to forget just how dislocated Russian society was during the chaotic years of 1917–21. Already ravaged by the misfortunes of World War I and now torn by mass emigration and universal unrest, the Russian population experi-enced extreme hardships and deficits on all levels. It was a case of bare survival, not least for the artists and writers; a principal reason why many, leftist and rightist, responded with such alacrity to the call for politicized art forms (Lenin's Plan of Monumental Propaganda, agit-art, mass actions) was perhaps more a material than an ideological one.

The political culture generated by the October Revolution—the mass action, the flying banners, the statues—disguised a dearth of solid, durable creations during the first years of the new Republic; and the history of the visual arts then is as much the history of what was not produced as of what was. It was a time of elaborate theory and meager practice, of visionary projects for a utopian future, of models and prototypes which could never be manufactured, and of theatrical spectacles and architectural visions which were never realized. Even though Lenin's Plan of Monumental Propaganda of April 1918 (whereby statues to the heroes of Socialism were to be erected in the streets and squares) and the program of agit-art (redesigning and redecorating buildings with posters, banners, and billboards celebrating the Revolution) attracted many progressive artists, everyday reality did not seem to change much:

> You go into a Soviet restaurant, or any institution, a railroad
> station, a club, or a new theater. Do you see the hand of an artist?
> Everywhere is filth, disorder, and a lack of even the most primitive
> cultivation of beauty. For the most part they're just pigsties,
> repulsive sewers. Why aren't artists indignant? Why don't they
> hang their paintings, their posters, their panels here? Why don't
> they paint the walls of these rooms?[15]

As far as culture is concerned, it is now very difficult to dispense with the accumulated mythology surrounding the October Revolution and assess the real predicament of the artist, the writer, and the musician. But perhaps at least one common perception may and should be questioned, i.e., that October 1917 represented a clear dividing line between the old culture and the new. The more we examine the process of Russian culture during the Modernist period, the more we find that the apparent innovations of the early 1920s (e.g., Constructivism) derived directly from artistic concepts elaborated well before the Revolution. Of course, the social and political ramifications of the Bolshevik coup could not fail to affect the thematic orientation of the arts, and by the late 1920s there was increasing pressure to create an art form which once again was narrative, illustrative, and accessible. But the historic, experimental productions such as Meierkhold's *Magnanimous Cuckold* and *The Death of Tarelkin* at his Theater of the Revolution in 1922 could not have been implemented without the precedents of the Silver Age.

Nurtured beneath the banner proclaiming "Life is Bound, Art is Free," the Modernists were hard put to accept an artistic code demanding political adjustment, reportorial purpose, and social relevance. To preserve individual freedom, many chose to emigrate. True, some fortunate individuals, Bakst and Diaghilev among them, were already living in the West, but the majority was caught in the domestic mesh of revolution and civil war. There were many practical reasons why artists and writers, musicians and dancers fled Russia after the Bolshevik coup, which brought social and material chaos and destroyed the traditional components of cultural practice. The very way of life and livelihood of artists, leftist and rightist, was endangered, and monetary, as well as ideological, reasons often compelled many to seek security in Europe and the United States. For the more moderate artists, such as the World of Art members, there was also the perverse pressure of artistic and personal rivalry from the left. Radical artists and critics sympathetic to the revolutionary ideals, such as Rodchenko and Tatlin, formed a momentary dictatorship of the left which led to the widespread exclusion of more conservative elements from the restructured art schools, exhibition facilities, and purchasing committees.

There is no question that straitened circumstances, fear of Bolshevik reprisal, and experience of the licentious behavior of ignorant plenipotentiaries resolved many artists and writers to leave Russia, driving them to the Baltic States, Germany, France, Italy, the Americas, and even China and Australia. This was particularly true of those who had been a part of the Moscow and St. Petersburg cultural bohemia, who had hobnobbed with patrons, dandies, and merchants' wives at nightspots such as the Stray Dog and the Comedians' Halt, who had achieved fame for their tangos and foxtrots, if not for their art, and who had passed nights of pleasure at weekend dachas. These artists included Anisfeld, Annenkov, Benois, Grigoriev, Mak, Re-mi, Somov, and Sudeikin, to mention just a few, and their emigration was also motivated by the sudden disappearance of the very class—the bourgeoisie—which had guaranteed patronage, recognition, and welfare.

For many representatives of the Silver Age, Berlin was the primary destination, and by 1922 the Russian émigré community there comprised a colony of over half a million artists, writers, actors, and businesspeople. One consequence of this arrival was an extraordinary mosaic of Russian artistic, literary, and theatrical enterprises which, to some degree, maintained the momentum of the Silver Age. Belyi, Chagall, Korovin, and Simon Lissim, among many others, contributed to a cosmopolitan mix of vivid personalities, supporting the most disparate ideas, events, venues, and pub-

636. *Sergei Chekhonin. Cover for the journal* Zhar-ptitsa *(Firebird), Berlin, 1921, August, no. 1.*

lications, including the last journal of the Silver Age, *Zhar-ptitsa* (Firebird, 1921–26) [ill. 636].[16]

Directed by Georgii Lukomsky, *Zhar-ptitsa* invited many World of Art artists to collaborate, including Bakst, Benois, Dobuzhinsky, Jacovleff, Shukhaev, Somov, and Sudeikin; writers such as Balmont, Ivan Bunin, and Aleksei Remizov were also represented; and the journal gave considerable attention to the ballet and dramatic theater. In appearance, *Zhar-ptitsa* cultivated elegance and measure, reproducing vignettes by Chekhonin, Dobuzhinsky, Vladimir Levitsky, and Narbut, and it supported an aesthetic position which may have promoted, for example, the bold distortions of Boris Grigoriev, but certainly not the experiments of the "Soviet avant-garde." Perhaps the greatest service rendered by *Zhar-ptitsa* was its promotion of a younger generation of artists such as Nicola Benois (son of Alexandre), Dmitri Bouchène, and Lissim who, captivated by the traditions of the Silver Age, made their reputations as stage, film, and book designers [ill. 637]. *Zhar-ptitsa* also gave attention to modern sculpture,

often neglected in previous Russian periodicals, providing commentary on, and reproductions of, works by Naum Aronson, Gleb Derujinsky, Chana Orloff, and Serafim Sudbinin, in particular, the latter represented at the 1921 "World of Art" exhibition in Paris.

But it was Paris which became the real center of the Russian emigration. For many Russians, setting up house in Paris was easier than in most other Western cities because there was already a long tradition of Russian residence there with Russian publications, exhibitions, clubs, and stores. Many of the World of Art artists, especially those involved with the Ballets Russes, had been living in Paris for shorter or longer periods since at least 1909, and their society, Le Monde Artiste, active from 1921 until 1927, continued the exhibition activity of the old World of Art. Similarly, building on the precedent of the Ballets Russes, several other Russian ballet, theater, and opera companies opened in Paris such as the Théâtre

Opposite:
*637. Dmitri Bouchène (Dmitrii Bushen).
Trophée pour une danseuse (Trophy for a
Dancer). Gouache illustration for Léandre
Vaillat: Olga Spessivtseva: Ballerine en
marge des Ballets Russes et des Ballets de
l'Opéra de Paris, 1944.*

Left:
*638. Sergei Sudeikin. Poster for the Chauve-
Souris (Bat) cabaret in Paris, 1922.*

Right:

639. Sergei Chekhonin. Design for a program cover advertising Vera Nemtchinova's Ballets Russes, Paris, 1930. Watercolor on paper, 32 x 24.5 cm (12 ¼ x 9 ½ in.). The driving force behind this poster was the dancer Vera Nemtchinova, some of whose productions Chekhonin designed in 1930, including the ballet Islamey at the Théâtre des Champs-Elysées. Nemtchinova also commissioned Chekhonin to design evening gowns for her.

Below:

640. Sergei Sudeikin. Poster advertising the production of Nikolai Evreinov's play The Chief Thing at the Theatre Guild, New York, 1926. Color lithograph, 66.5 x 35.7 cm (25 ½ x 14 in.).

de la Chauve-Souris, the Ballets Russes Vera Nemtchinova, and the Opéra Privé de Paris, attracting Bilibin, Chekhonin, Korovin, Lissim and many other champions of the Silver Age [ills. 638, 639].

Not unexpectedly, the Russian colony in Paris had little enthusiasm for the extreme gestures of the avant-garde, which, to many, was "Soviet" and "Communist," and the émigré intelligentsia continued to support the art of the past, such as icons and eighteenth-century portraits or the stylized evocations of the fin de siècle. In the 1920s and 1930s this taste was promoted by the flourishing Russian art market in Paris and by the leading Russian art critics there—Benois, Lukomsky, Makovsky, and Muratov—whose first aesthetic criterion continued to be the Parnassus of the Silver Age.

Finally, if Berlin and Paris were the European centers of the Russian emigration, New York was the American one and haven to the last shades of the Silver Age. But even if New York was already aware of Russian Modernism, thanks to the debut of the Ballets Russes in 1916 and to Anisfeld's retrospective at the Brooklyn Museum in 1918, the city was, in many respects, a cultural satellite of Paris—and the constant points of reference there were the Ballets Russes, the music of Stravinsky, and the Chauve-Souris. Many of the World of Art artists came to the United States in those years, including Anisfeld, Bakst, Roerich, Somov, and Sudeikin, and some of the more memorable cultural activities of Russian New York were associated with their talents—Anisfeld's and Sudeikin's sets for the Metropolitan Opera, Roerich's construction of the Nicholas Roerich Museum, Nicholas Remisoff's designs for the Russian Tea Room, and so on [ills. 640, 641, see also 585, 586]. The visual and intellectual results of these exploits may have been impressive, but devoid of a single axis—national, philosophical, or patronal—they were centrifugal forces receding into the last rays of a dying sun.

641. *Nicholas Roerich at the Master Institute of United Arts, which he founded in 1921, New York, 1929.*

The destiny of the Russian Silver Age was both full and empty. On the one hand, the poets and painters, philosophers and musicians, actors and dancers offered a positive and potential construct, because many of their ideas and artifacts prefigured the linguistic and visual experiments of later years; perhaps even the notion of a single, cohesive style joining architecture and the applied arts, which the Constructivists promoted in the wake of the October Revolution can be viewed as an outgrowth of the Symbolists' concern with the total, organic work of art. On the other hand, if the Russian Symbolists glimpsed beyond the veil, they rarely completed the voyage to the other shore. In their search for a spiritual equilibrium they explored synesthesia, delirium, transubstantiation, and the occult, but as they journeyed they often erred, and if occasionally their fine antennae did apprehend the astral signal, the resonance was often so powerful that, both metaphorically and physically, it caused a deregulation of all the senses.

On the other hand, it was this deregulation or emancipation of the senses which acted as such a strong inspiration to the cultural, intellectual, and commercial prosperity of late Imperial Russia. As they tested new frontiers, artists, writers, musicians, and businesspeople questioned convention and broke the mold, ascending to azure heights or descending to sapphire depths. Bakst, Belyi, Diaghilev, Fabergé, Kandinsky, Riabushinsky, Scriabin may have cultivated elements of the past, from primordial, collective consciousness and Classical antiquity to Russian Orthodoxy and folklore, but, guided by their vision—now scintillating, now clouded—they advanced toward the new horizon, exploring umbrageous territories and precarious waters.

Born between the dusk of the nineteenth century and the dawn of the twentieth, the Russian Silver Age inevitably drew heavily upon cultural tradition, recognizing the artistic and literary accomplishments of many epochs and many countries. From the nineteenth century, in particular, the Silver Age inherited the Romantic notion of the majesty and selectivity of artistic inspiration and the special, alchemical power of the work of art. However disparate the painters, poets, and composers of that moment, they all shared a strong belief in the noble, if not divine, mission of the artist, provocative and iconoclastic behavior notwithstanding.

At the same time, however, the Silver Age carried the seeds of theories, practices, deportments, and rituals which can be readily associated with the culture and civilization of our own time—abstract painting, religious plurality, alternative lifestyles, social utopianism, body art, and so on. The Russian Modernists, inhabitants of their own Machine Age, also recognized the innovations of science and technology—from the phonograph to the airplane—and turned to this brave new world for images, sounds, and movements. Consequently, if many aesthetic concepts of our own leading edge can be identified in embryo with the Silver Age, we can also recognize material phenomena which distinguish our social practices today, especially in the new Russia.

Early twenty-first-century Russia, chronologically, is post-Modernist, but its brash, new social and cultural codes are curiously reminiscent of the mercurial societies of Moscow and St. Petersburg at the time of Symbolism and the avant-garde. In the new Russia, with her cultural vibrancy, commercial drive, patriotic confidence, and political momentum, the culture of the Silver Age has assumed a new resonance and potentiality, a rediscovery culminating in numerous publications, exhibitions, performances, and debates. True, a century has passed since Vrubel created his tormented paintings, Blok his ecstatic verse, Stravinsky his bold dissonances, and Riabushinsky his financial empire, but today their legacy has never been more vital and more insistent—clear testimony to the permanence and prescience of the Russian Silver Age.

642. *Anna Pavlova performing* The Dying Swan *in New York, 1918. Pavlova had first danced* The Dying Swan, *choreographed by Michel Fokine to the music of Camille Saint-Saëns, in St. Petersburg in 1905. It remained her signature piece, symbolizing perhaps the passing of time and the ephmerality of life more than the physical demise of a single creature.*

The following abbreviations have been used in the bibliographical references below:
L = Leningrad, M = Moscow, P = Petrograd, SP = St. Petersburg, RGALI= Russian State Archive of Literature and Art, Moscow

Introduction

1 See S. Makovsky: *Na parnase Serebrianogo veka*, Munich: ZOPE, 1962.
2 M. Matiushin: preface to *Troe* (1913). Quoted in I. Muravieva: *Byloi Peterburg. Vek moderna*, SP: Izdatelstvo "Pushkinskogo fonda," 2004, Book 2, p. 174.
3 Much has been written about "Modernism" as an international trend. For useful discussions of the position of Russia within the movement see O. Kuznetsova, ed.: *Russkii modernizm. Problemy tekstologii*, SP: Aletei, 2001; *N. Pavlova et al., eds.: Modern. Modernizm. Modernizatsiia*, M: RGGU, 2004.
4 For information on Ukrainian Modernism see J. Bowlt, ed.: *Ukrainskii modernizm/Ukrainian Modernism, 1910–1930*. Catalogue of exhibition circulated by the Foundation for International Arts and Education, Bethesda, 2006. On Modernism in Japan, China, and Siberia see A. Panov et al.: *Modernism in the Russian Far East and Japan 1918–1928*. Catalogue of exhibition at the Machida City Museum of Graphic Arts, Japan, and other venues, 2002.
5 For information on the Russian sciences during the time of Modernism see A. Vucinich: *Science in Russian Culture 1861–1917*, Stanford: Stanford University Press, 1970; K. Bailes: *Science and Russian Culture in an Age of Revolutions. V. I. Vernadsky and His Scientific School, 1863–1945*, Bloomington: Indiana University Press, 1990.
6 A. Benois: *Istoriia russkoi zhivopisi v XIX veka*, SP: Evdokimov, 1901–1902, pp. 271–72.
7 F. Tiutchev: "Silentium" (1850s).
8 For commentary on the relationship of the Russian avant-garde to the Symbolist movement see G. Kovalenko, ed.: *Simvolizm v avangarde*, M: Nauka, 2002.
9 On the synthesis of the arts during the Russian Silver Age see A. Mazaev: *Problema sinteza iskusstv v estetike russkogo simvolizma*, M: Nauka, 1992.
10 See Further Reading. A useful bibliography of recent publications on Symbolist art is provided by Oksema Petrova in her book *Simvolizm v russkom izobrazitelnom iskusstve*, SP: SbGPU, 2000.
11 See V. Kruglov et al.: *Simvolizm v Rossii*. Catalogue of the exhibition at the State Russian Museum, St. Petersburg, 1996. For other important exhibitions pertaining to the Russian Silver Age see Further Reading.

A Double-Headed Eagle: Russia, Land of Paradox

1 Muravieva: *Byloi Peterburg. Vek moderna*, Book 1, p. 91.
2 For information on the publishing business and readership in Russia during this time see Jeffrey Brooks: *When Russia Learned to Read. Literacy and Popular Literature, 1861–1917*, Evanston: Northwestern University Press, 2003; and N. Patrusheva, ed.: *Knizhnoe delo v XIX-nachale XX veka*, SP: RNB, 2004.
3 Statistical information from A. Anfimov et al.: *Rossiia 1913 god. Statistiko-dokumentalnyi spravochnik*, SP: Blits, 1993.
4 For information on Moscow's material, economic, and technological boom during the Silver Age see V. Ruga and A. Kokorev: *Moskva povsednevnaia. Ocherki gorodskoi zhizni nachala XX veka*, M: Olma-Press, 2006.
5 The idea of an electric railroad running under Moscow was discussed as early as 1897. See N. Smurova: "Mosca del futuro" in *Ricerche di Storia dell'Arte*, Rome, 1990, no. 39, p. 54.
6 M. Kuzmin: "Vospominaniia o N.N. Sapunove" in V. Briusov et al.: *N. Sapunov. Stikhi. Vospominaniia. Kharakteristiki*, M: Karashev, 1916.
7 Thomas Edison recorded Tolstoi's voice at Yasnaia Poliana in 1908. For information on the recording industry in Russia see V. Yanin and P. Griunberg: *Istoriia nachala gramplastinki v Rossii*, M: Yazyki slavianskoi kultury, 2002.
8 Aleksandr Drankov filmed Tolstoi at Yasnaia Poliana in 1908.
9 E. Kuzmina-Karavaeva: "Vstrechi s Blokom (k piatnatsatiletiu so dnia smerti)" in *Sovremennye zapiski*, Paris, 1936, no. 62. Quoted in G. Sternin: *Khudozhestvennaia zhizn Rossii 1900–1910-kh godov*, M: Iskusstvo, 1988, p. 148.
10 Letter from Valentin Serov to Ilia Repin dated January 20, 1905. Quoted in Muravieva, *Byloi Peterburg. Vek moderna*, Book 1, p. 258.
11 N. Vrangel: *Venok mertvym (khudozhestvenno-istoricheskie stati)*, SP: Sirius, 1913, p. 87.
12 From Gorky's speech at the First All-Union Congress of Soviet Writers in I. Luppol et al., eds.: *Pervyi Vsesoiuznyi sezd sovetskikh pisatelei, 1934. Stenograficheskii otchet*, M: Khudozhestvennaia literatura, 1934, p. 12.

Azure Heights, Sapphire Depths: Philosophical Concepts of the Russian Silver Age

1 V. Ivanov: *Po zvezdam*, SP; Ory, 1909, p. 52.
2 Viacheslav Ivanov was especially drawn to this Jungian condition. See his *Po zvezdam*, especially the chapter "Krizis individualizma."
3 Anon. "Svedeniia" in *Mir iskusstva*, 1899, Vol. I, no. 5 (Art Chronicle), p. 39.
4 A. Benois: "K. Somov" in *Mir iskusstva*, 1899, Vol. 2, no. 7 (Chronicle), pp. 127–40.
5 From Blok's poem "Neznakomka" (The Stranger, 1906).
6 A. Benois: "Khudozhestvennye eresi" in *Zolotoe runo*, M, 1906, no. 2, pp. 80–88.
7 S. Yaremich: "Peredvizhnicheskoe nachalo v russkom iskusstve" in *Mir iskusstva*, 1902, Vol. 7, Section III (Chronicle), p. 24.
8 S. Przybyszewski: "Na putiakh dushi" in *Mir iskusstva*, 1902, Vol. 7, Secion III (Chronicle), p. 102.

9 S. Diaghilev: "Slozhnye voprosy, Nash mnimyi upadok" in *Mir iskusstva*, 1898, Vol. I, no. 1 (Chronicle), p. 15.

10 N. Berdiaev: (1904). Quoted in Muravieva, *Byloi Peterburg. Vek moderna*, Book 1, p. 196.

11 See E. Ivanova, comp.: *Florensky i simvolisty*, M: Yazyki slavianskoi kultury, 2003.

12 A. Blok: "Vkhozhu ya v temnye khramy" (1902).

13 A. Kruchenykh: "Vysoty. Vselenskii yazyk" (1913).

14 See A. Rusakova, ed.: *K. Petrov-Vodkin. Khlynovsk. Prostranstvo Evklida. Samarkhandiia*, L: Iskusstvo, 1970, pp. 422–35.

15 After the dress rehearsal of the play at Komissarzhevskaia's theater in St. Petersburg, the Holy Synod refused to let the production go ahead on the grounds of allegedly sacrilegious content.

16 For further information on censorship during the Russian Silver Age see N. Patrusheva, ed.: *Tsenzura v Rossii v kontse XIX-nachale XX veka. Sbornik vospominanii*, SP: Bulanin, 2003.

17 For information on Abramtsevo and Princess Mariia Tenisheva's retreat called Talashkino see E. Paston: *Abramtsevo. Iskusstvo i zhizn*, M: Iskusstvo, 1993; L. Zhuravleva: *Talashkino*, M: Izobrazitelnoe iskusstvo, 1989. For a general discussion of the development of the Neo-Russian style see P. Aksenov et al.: *"Natsionalnyi stil" v russkom iskusstve XIX–nachala XX vekov*. Catalogue of exhibition at the All-Russian Museum of Decorative and Applied Art, Moscow, 1990; V. Egorov et al.: *Russkii stil*. Catalogue of exhibition at the State Historical Museum, Moscow, 1998; E. Kirichenko and M. Anikst: *Russian Design and the Fine Arts 1750–1917*, New York: Abrams, 1991; W. Salmond: *Arts and Crafts in Late Imperial Russia. Reviving the Kustar Art Industries*, Cambridge: Cambridge University Press, 1996; E. Paston et al.: *Stil zhizni—stil iskusstva*, M: State Tretiakov Gallery, 2000.

18 For information on Zagorsk, i.e., the monastery of Sergiev Posad, and the activities of Florensky there just before and after 1917 see N. Misler, ed.: *Pavel Florensky. Beyond Vision. Essays on the Perception of Art*, London: Reaktion, 2002.

19 See P. Florensky: "The Church Ritual as a Synthesis of the Arts" in Misler: *Pavel Florensky. Beyond Vision*, pp. 95–112.

20 S. Shcherbatov: "Russkie khudozhniki" in *Vozrozhdenie*, Paris, 1951, no. 18, p. 117.

21 B. Livshits: *Polutoraglazyi strelets* (1933). English translation by J. Bowlt: Benedikt Livshits: *The One and a Half-Eyed Archer*, Newtonville. Mass.: ORP, 1977, p. 81.

22 "Brattsy estety" in *Golos Moskvy*, M, 1910, March 25, no. 69. For details on Goncharova's clerical and legal battles see J. Sharp: "Redrawing the Margins of Russian Vanguard Art. N. Goncharova's Trial for Pornography in 1910" in J. Sharp et al.: *Sexuality and the Body in Russian Culture*, Stanford: Stanford University Press, 1993, pp. 97–123.

23 On the development of theosophy in Russia see M. Carlson: *"No Religion Higher Than the Truth." A History of the Theosophical Movement in Russia, 1875–1922*, Princeton: Princeton University Press, 1993.

24 On the presence of the *khlysty* in Russian Modernist culture, for example, see A. Etkind: *Khlyst*, M: NLO, 1998. Also see B. Rosenthal, ed.: *The Occult in Russian and Soviet Culture*, Ithaca: Cornell University Press, 1997.

25 N. Kulbin: "Svobodnoe iskusstvo kak osnova zhizni" [Free art as the basis of life] (1908). English translation in J. Bowlt: *Russian Art of the Avant-Garde. Theory and Criticism, 1902–1934*, London: Thames and Hudson, 1988, p. 13.

26 A. Belyi: *Serebrianyi golub*, M: Skorpion, 1910.

27 A. Blok: "Vechera 'iskusstv'" (1908) in V. Orlov, ed.: *Aleksandr Blok. Sochineniia v dvukh tomakh*, M: Khudozhestvennaia literatura, 1955, Vol. 2, p. 74–79.

28 On Scriabin and the Silver Age see O. Tompakova: *Scriabin v khudozhestvennom mire Moskvy kontsa XIX–nachala XX veka. Novye techeniia*, M: Muzyka, 1997.

29 See D[iaghilev]: "K postanovke, 'Tristan i Izolde,'" *Mir iskusstva*, 1899, Vol. 1, Art Chronicle, pp. 135–37; A. Benois: "Postanovka Valkirii," ibid., 1900, Vol. 4, Literary Section, pp. 241–243; S. Diaghilev: "Gibel bogov." ibid., 1903, no. 4, pp. 35–38.

30 F. Nitche [Nietzsche]: "R. Vagner v Bairete," ibid., 1900, Vol. 3, Literary Chronicle, pp. 59–63, 99–102.

31 Letter from Alexandre Benois to Walter Nouvel dated late November 1896, in RGALI, f. 938, op. 1, ed. khr. 46, I. 45.

32 S. Diaghilev: "V teatre. 1. Balety Deliba" in *Mir iskusstva*, 1902, Vol. 8, Section III (Chronicle), p. 32.

33 V. Rozanov: "Balet ruk" in his *Sredi khudozhnikov*, P: 1914, p. 41.

34 For detailed information on Modernist music in Russia see D. Gojowy: *Neue sowjetische Musik der 20er Jahre*, Regensburg: Laaber, 1980; L. Sitsky: *Music of the Repressed Russian Avant-Garde, 1900–1929*, Westport, Conn.: Greenwood, 1994.

35 Bowlt: Benedikt Livshits: *The One and a Half-Eyed Archer*, p. 173.

36 N. Kulbin: "Svobodnoe iskusstvo kak osnova zhizni" in Bowlt: *Russian Art of the Avant-Garde. Theory and Criticism, 1902–1934*, p. 13.

37 A. Lourié et al: Poster proclaiming "Nash otvet Marinetti" (Our response to Marinetti, 1914). Reprinted in Bowlt: Benedikt Livshits: *The One and a Half-Eyed Archer*, p. 206.

38 On Gastev and the new industrial body see K. Johansson: *Aleksej Gastev. Proletarian Bard of the Machine Age*, Stockholm: Almqvist and Wiksell, 1983.

39 A. Alexandre and J. Cocteau: *The Decorative Art of Léon Bakst*, New York: Dover, 1972, p. 6 (first published in 1915).

40 B. Bugaev (=A. Belyi): "Formy iskusstva" in *Mir iskusstva*, 1902, Vol. 8, Section III (Literature Chronicle), p. 347.

41 V. Ivanov (1912). Quoted in E. Ermilova: *Teoriia i obraznoi mir russkogo simvolizma*, M: Nauka, 1989, p. 16.

42 Quoted in A. Grishchenko: *"Krizis iskusstva" i sovremennaia zhivopis*, M: Gorodskaia tipografiia, 1917, p. 16. Grishchenko was responding to the lecture "On the Crisis of Art," which Berdiaev gave in Moscow on November 1, 1916.

43 A, Belyi: "Budushchee iskusstva" (1907) in his *Simvolizm*, M: Musaget, 1910, p. 452.

The Shock of the New: Technology, Science, Engineering

1 L. Tolstoi: *Anna Karenina*, M: Pravda, 1962, Vol. 2, p. 376. The novel was first published in 1877.

2 A. Blok: "Novaia Amerika" (1913).

3 D. Merezhkovsky: "O prichinakh upadka i o novykh techeniiakh sovremennoi russkoi literatury" (1892) in D. Merezhkovsky: *Polnoe sobranie sochinenii*, St. Petersburg: Sytin, 1914, Vol. 18, p. 180.

4 Quoted in S. Lifar: *Serge Diaghilev. His Life, His Work, His Legend*, London: Putnam, 1940, p. 99.

5 For useful commentary on Russia's technological progress in the late 19th and early 20th centuries see N. Gulianitsky et al., eds.: *Konstruktsii i arkhitekturnaia forma v russkom zodchestve XIX–nachala XX vv.*, M: Stroiizdat, 1977; M. Gize: *Ocherki istorii khudozhestvennogo konstruirovaniia v Rossii. XVIII–nachala XX veka*, L: LGU, 1978; N. Rivosh: *Vremia i veshch*, M: Iskusstvo, 1990; and N. Misler and L. Tonini, eds.: *Tradizione artigianale e rivoluzione industriale in Russia tra '800 e '900*. Special issue of *Ricerche di Storia dell'arte*, Rome, 1989, no. 39.

6 A. Benois: "Posledniaia futuristicheskaia vystavka" (1916). English translation: "'The Last Futurist Exhibition'" in J. Bowlt, ed.:

Theater of Reason / Theater of Desire. The Art of Alexandre Benois and Léon Bakst. Catalogue of exhibition at the Thyssen-Bornemisza Foundation, Lugano. 1998, p. 151.

7 A. Chekhov: "Novaia dacha" (1899). Quoted in N. Smurova: "Inzhernernye sooruzhennia i ikh vliianie na razvitie russkoi khudozhestvennoi kultury" in Gulianitsky, *Konstruktsii i arkhitekturnaia forma v russkom zodchestve XIX–nachala XX vv.*, p. 68.

8 From a speech delivered by the architect Nikolai Dmitriev in 1840. Quoted in E. Kirichenko: "Teoreticheskie vozzreniia na vziamosviaz formy i konstruktsii v russkoi arkhitekture XIX-nachala XX vv." in Gulianitsky: *Konstruktsii i arkhitekturnaia forma v russkom zodchestve XIX–nachala XX vv.*, p. 44.

9 Mamontov then acquired the two works, built a special pavilion in Nizhnii-Novgorod and exhibited them. Works by the Neo-Nationalists Sergei Maliutin, Elena Polenova, and Andrei Riabushkin were also rejected by the jury.

10 N. Sultanov: "Odna iz zadach stroitelnogo uchilischa" in *Zodchii*, SP, 1882, no. 5, p. 54.

11 N. Sultanov: "Vozrozhdenie russkogo iskusstva" in *Zodchii*, 1881, no. 2, p. 11.

12 The incident is described by Irina Muravieva in her *Byloi Peterburg. Vek moderna*, Book 1, pp. 205–06.

13 From El Lissitzky's foreword to the portfolio *Die Plastische Gestaltung der Elektro-mechanischen Schau "Sieg über die Sonne,"* Hanover: Leunis and Chapman, 1923, unpaginated.

14 Words ascribed to Vladimir Maiakovsky by V. Nezhdanov in *Trudovaia gazeta*, Nikolaev. January 26, 1914. Quoted in J. Bowlt and M. Konecny, eds.: *Nikolai Khardzhiev. A Legacy Regained*, SP: Palace, 2002, p. 112.

15 V. Briusov: "M. A. Vrubeliu" (1906).

16 A. Blok: "Aviator" (1912) in Orlov: *Aleksandr Blok*, Vol. 1, p. 367. Blok wrote the poem after witnessing the fatal crash of the pilot Vladimir Smit at the Komendantskii Aerodrome, St. Petersburg.

17 D. Burliuk et al.: *Poshchechina obshchestvennomu vkusu*, M: Kuzmin, 1912.

18 Fedorov expounded his theory of resurrection in his magnum opus, *Filosofiia obshchego dela* (The Philosophy of the Common Cause), published in Moscow in 1906. See A. Gulyga, ed.: *Nikolai Fedorovich Fedorov. Sochineniia*, M: Akademiia nauk SSSR, 1982.

19 Muravieva: *Byloi Peterburg. Vek moderna*, Book 2, p. 20. For useful information on gadgets see Yu. Leving: *Vokzal-garazh-angar (Vladimir Nabokov i poetika russkogo urbanizma)*, SP: Limbakh, 2004.

The Style Moderne: Russian Refractions of Art Nouveau

1 For a comprehensive discussion of the Style Moderne in Russia see W. Brumfield: *The Origins of Modernism in Russian Architecture*, Berkeley: University of California Press, 1991; W. Salmond, ed.: *The New Style. Russian Perceptions of Art Nouveau*. Special issue of *Experiment*, Los Angeles, 2001, Vol. 7.

2 V. Dudakov: "Vmesto predisloviia" in his *Simvolizm Rossii 1890–1930 gg. Iz chastnykh kollektsii*, M: Sovetskii fond kul'tury, 1982, p. 3.

3 P. Vaulin: "K voprosu ob iskusstve v promyshlennosti" in *Iskusstvo kommuny*, P, 1919, 2 March, no. 13, p. 2.

4 F. Shekhtel: "Skazka o trekh sestrakh, zhivopisi, arkhitekture, skulpture" (1919) in M. Barkhin et al., eds.: *Mastera sovetskoi arkhitektury ob arkhitekture*, M: Iskusstvo, 1975, Vol. 1, p. 21.

5 S. Shcherbatov: *Khudozhnik v ushedshei Rossii*, New York: Chekhov. 1955, p. 161.

6 I. Grabar: *Moia zhizn. Avtomonografiia*, M-L: Iskusstvo, 1937, pp. 184–85.

7 S. Diaghilev: "Sovremennoe iskusstvo" in *Mir iskusstva*, 1903, Vol. 10, no. 3 (Chronicle), pp. 23, 24.

8 F. Batiushkov: "Na khudozhestvennykh vystavkakh. Zametki i vpechatleniia" in *Mir Bozhii*, SP. 1903, no. 3, Section II, p. 11.

9 A. Benois: "Russkoe sovremennoe iskusstvo" in *Rech*, SP, 1912, 9 March, no. 67.

10 "Pismo kn. S.A. Shcherbatova" in *Mir iskusstva*, 1904, Vol. 12, no. 4 (Chronicle), p. 80.

11 G. Sternin: *Khudozhestvennaia zhizn Rossii na rubezhe XIX–XX vekov*, M: Iskusstvo, 1970, p. 204.

12 A. Blok. Quoted in *Teoriia i obraznyi mir russkogo simvolizma*, p. 122.

13 For useful commentary on Russian buildings in the Style Moderne see, for example, E. Borisova: *Arkhitektura Serebrianogo veka*, M: GII, 1999; E. Borisova and G. Sternin: *Russian Art Nouveau*, New York: Rizzoli, 1988; and M. Nashchokina: *Sto arkhitektorov moskovskogo moderna. Tvorcheskie portrety*. M: Zhiraf, 2000.

14 Quoted in Muravieva: *Byloi Peterburg. Veka moderna*, Book 2, p. 55 (original source not provided).

15 A. Belyi: "Lirika i eksperiment" (1909) in *Simvolizm*, p. 254.

16 Also see Feofilaktov's collection of drawings, i.e., *66 risunkov*, M: Skorpion, 1909.

17 For information on the relationship of Russian and Scandinavian Art Novueau see O. Cherkasova, ed.: *Severnyi modern. Dialog kultur*, SP: Evropeiskii Dom, 2005.

The World of Art: Sergei Diaghilev and His Circle

1 A. Belyi: "Emblematika smysla" (1909) in Belyi, *Simvolizm*, p. 143.

2 For information on writers' visual experiments during the Silver Age see N. Shakhalova, ed.: *Poeta pingens / Pisatel risuiushchii*. Catalogue of exhibition at the State Literary Museum, Moscow, 2004.

3 The primary sources on the World of Art group are V. Petrov: *"Mir iskusstva"*, M: Izobrazitelnoe iskusstvo, 1975; J. Kennedy: *The "Mir iskusstva" Group and Russian Art, 1898–1912*, New York: Garland, 1977; J. Bowlt: *The Silver Age. Russian Art of the Early Twentieth Century and the "World of Art" Group*, Newtonville: ORP, 1979; V. Petrov and A. Kamensky: *The World of Art Movement*, L: Aurora, 1991; E. Petrova et al.: *Mir iskusstva*, SP: Palace, 1998; and G. Guroff et al.: *Mir iskusstva. Russia's Age of Elegance*. Catalogue of exhibition circulated by the Foundation for International Arts and Education, Bethesda, MD, 2005–06.

4 For information on the Union of Russian Artists see I. Antonova et al., *Mastera Soiuza russkikh khudozhnikov*. Catalogue of exhibition at the Pushkin Museum of Fine Arts, Moscow, 2003; on the Moscow Salon see Yu. Loev: *Obshchestvo khudozhnikov "Moskovskii Salon."* Catalogue of exhibition at the Elizium Gallery, Moscow, 2001.

5 The Wanderers, i.e., the members of the Society of Wandering (or Traveling) Exhibitions, supported a narrative, Realist style exemplified by Repin's didactic paintings. For further information on the group see E. Valkenier: *The Wanderers. Masters of 19th Century Russian Painting*, Austin: University of Texas, 1991; D. Jackson: *The Art of Ilya Repin*, Schoten, Belgium: BAI, 2006.

6 A. Benois: *"Vozniknovenie 'Mira iskusstva,'"* L: Komitet populiarizatsii khudozhestvennykh izdanii, 1928, p. 6.

7 D. Filosofov: "Tozhe tendentsiia" in *Zolotoe runo*, M, 1908, no. 1, p. 73.

8 S. Diaghilev: "Osnovy khudozhestvennoi otsenki" in *Mir iskusstva*, 1899, Vol. I, no. 3–4, pp. 51, 57.

9 For useful information on the connections between the Modernist stage and the Orient in Russia see S. Serova: *Teatralnaia kultura Serebrianogo veka v Rossii i khudozhestvennye traditsii vostoka*, M: Iv

Ran, 1999.

10 S. Diaghilev and V. Gorlenko: *Russkaia zhivopis v XVIII veke. Tom 1-yi. D.G. Levitsky, 1735–1822*, SP: Evdokimov, 1902.

11 S. Diaghilev: "V chas itogov" in *Vesy*, M, 1905, no. 4, pp. 45–46. Diaghilev delivered his speech at a dinner held in his honor at the Metropol Hotel, Moscow.

12 Makovsky: *Na parnase Serebrianogo veka*, p. 306.

13 Grabar: *Moia zhizn. Avtomonografiia*, p. 215.

14 Statement in *Zritel*, SP, 1905, no. 1. Quoted in V. Botsianovsky and E. Gollerbakh: *Russkaia satira pervoi revoliutsii 1905–1906*, L: Gosizdat, 1925, pp. 44–45.

15 See, for example, A. Benois: "Materialy dlia istorii vandalizma v Rossii: razrushenie Mikhailovskogo dvortsa" in *Mir iskusstva*, 1903, Vol. 9, no. 12 (Chronicle), pp. 117–20.

16 A. Benois: unsigned preface to *Khudozhestvennye sokrovishcha Rossii*, SP, 1901, no. 1, p. 11.

17 A. Benois: "Zhivopisnyi Peterburg" in *Mir iskusstva*, 1902, Vol. 7, Secion III (Chronicle), pp. 1–5.

18 Moskvich: "Moskovskaia vystavka khudozhestvennykh proizvedenii stariny" in *Mir iskusstva*, 1901, Vol. 5 (Art Chronicle), p. 325.

19 Many of the World of Art artists, including Bakst and Benois, contributed illustrations to Nikolai Kutepov's monumental record of the traditional Imperial hunt, i.e., *Tsarskaia i imperatorskaia okhota na Rusi. Konets XVII i XVIII vek*, SP: Ekspeditsiia zagotovleniia gosudarstvennykh bumag, 1902.

20 A. Benois: "Kitaiskii dvorets v Oranienbaume" in *Khudozhestvennye sokrovishcha Rossii*, 1901, Vol. 1, pp. 196–201.

21 S. Diaghilev: "Slozhnye voprosy. Nash mnimyi upadok", p. 2

22 Serge Lifar attributed these words to Diaghilev. See S. Lifar: *Serge Diaghilev*, London: Putnam, 1940, p. 180.

23 S. Diaghilev: Letter to Elena Panaeva-Diaghileva (October, 1895). Quoted in N. Lapshina: *Mir iskusstva*, M: Iskusstvo, 1977, p. 23.

24 Benois: *Vozniknovenie*, p. 52.

25 See, for example, *Pechatnoe delo* (Printing), SP, 1902, *Iskusstvo i pechatnoe delo* (Art and Printing), K, 1909. For information on Russian graphics of the fin de siècle see A. Sidorov: *Russkaia grafika nachala XX veka*, M: Iskusstvo, 1969.

26 Particular mention should be made of the critic and collector Vasilii A. Vereshchagin, who published a number of studies on the history of Russian book design and ex-libris designs. See, for example, his *Russkie illiustrirovannye izdaniia 1729–1870*, SP: Kirshbaum, 1898; *Russkii knizhnyi znak*, SP: Golike, 1902; *Pamiati proshlogo*, SP: Sirius, 1914; *Kruzhok liubitelei russkikh iziashchnykh izdanii*, Paris: Obshchestvo druzei russkoi knigi, 1928 (three volumes).

27 F. Blei: *Le Livre de la marquise*, St. Petersburg: Golike and Vilborg, 1918. This was the St. Petersburg edition of the original 1908 German edition, i.e., *Das Lesebuch der Marquise*, of which there were several other editions (e.g., Berlin: Hyperionverlag, 1917).

28 Miss, much influenced by Beardsley and Julius Dietz, published a collection of her naughty drawings entitled *Kupidony prokazy. Les aventures galantes*, SP: Kornfeld, 1913 [see ill. 112].

29 For commentary on the role of the World of Art artists in the satirical press of ca. 1905 see V. Shleev: *Revoliutsiia 1905–07 godov i izobrazitelnoe iskusstvo* (four volumes), M: Izobrazitelnoe iskusstvo, 1977–89. Vol. 1 (1977) on St. Petersburg; Vol. 2 (1978) on Moscow and the Russian provinces; Vol. 3 (1981) on Ukraine and Moldavia; Vol. 4 (1989) on Latvia and Estonia. Also see E. Gomberg-Verzhbinskaia: *Russkoe iskusstvo i revoliutsiia 1905-go goda. Grafika. Zhivopis*, L: Gos. Leningradskii universitet, 1960; D. King and C. Porter: *Graphic Art from 1905 Russia*, New York: Pantheon, 1983.

30 M. Gorky. Quoted in Gomberg-Verzhbinskaia: *Russkoe iskusstvo i revoliutsiia 1905-go goda. Grafika. Zhivopis*, p. 55.

31 S. Diaghilev. Quoted in ibid, pp. 138–39.

32 M. Dobuzhinsky et al.: "Golos khudozhnikov" (12 November 1905). The statement was published simultaneously in several newspapers. See Gomberg-Verzhbinskaia, *Russkoe iskusstvo i revoliutsiia 1905-go goda. Grafika. Zhivopis*, p. 128.

33 A. Vasnetsov: *Khudozhestvo*, M: Knebel, 1908, p. 122.

34 N. Sokolova: "'Mir iskusstva' i ego epigony" in *Brigada khudozhnikov*, M, 1932, no. 3, p. 46.

35 P. Florensky: "Poiasnenie k oblozhke" in P. Florensky: *Mnimosti geometrii*, M: Pomore, 1922, pp. 58–65. For contextual commentary see Misler: *Pavel Florensky. Beyond Vision*, pp. 183–96.

36 On RAKhN see the special issue of *Experiment*, 1997, no. 3.

37 A. Blok: "Kraski i slova" (1905) in L. Dolgopolov, comp.: *Aleksandr Blok ob iskusstve*, M: Iskusstvo, 1980, p. 213.

Flowers, Flowers to Cover the Tomb! Blooms of Decadence

1 That is how Viacheslav Ivanov referred to the embarrassment of artistic riches of his time. See his *Borozdy i mezhi. Opyty esteticheskie i kriticheskie*, M: Musaget, 1916, p. 177.

2 Nikolai Kulbin referred to Vrubel as a "Cubist" in his article "Kubizm" in *Strelets*, P, 1915, no. 1, p. 104; also see Sergei Makovsky: *Siluety russkikh khudozhnikov*, Prague: Nasha rech, 1922, pp. 120–21.

3 See O. Kovaleva: *O. Uaild i stil modern*, M: URSS, 2002.

4 For information on Borisov-Musatov, especially on his use of color, see O. Kochik: *Zhivopisnaia sistema V.E. Borisova-Musatova*, Moscow: Iskusstvo, 1980.

5 V. Soloviev: "Milyi drug, il ty ne vidish" (1892).

6 The critic was a certain A. S. (Aleksandr Skalon?) reviewing the exhibition of works by students of the Moscow Institute of Painting, Sculpture, and Architecture for *Moskovskii listok*, M, 1895, no. 7. Quoted in A. Rusakova: *V.E. Borisov-Musatov*, L-M: Iskusstvo, 1966, p. 30.

7 A. Benois: *Istoriia russkoi zhivopisi v XIX veke*, p. 205.

8 N. Chernyshevsky: *Esteticheskie otnosheniia iskusstva k deistvitelnosti* (1855) in his *Ob iskusstve. Stati, retsenzii, vyskazyvaniia*, M: Akademiia khudozhestv SSSR, 1950, p. 10.

9 M. Nevedomsky and I. Repin: *Kuindzhi*, SP: Obshchestvo im. A.I. Kuindzhi, 1913, p. 164.

10 V. Borisov-Musatov: Letter to Alexandre Benois (1905). Quoted in Rusakova: *V.E. Borisov-Musatov*, p. 95.

11 For further information on the Blue Rose group see J. Bowlt: "The Blue Rose: Russian Symbolism in Art" in *The Burlington Magazine*, London, 1976, August, pp. 566–76; I. Gofman: *Golubaia roza*, M: Pinakoteka, 2000.

12 For information on the artists and writers connected with *Zolotoe runo* see W. Richardson: *"Zolotoe runo" and Russian Modernism*, Ann Arbor: Ardis, 1986.

13 A. Belyi: "Simvolizm kak ponimanie" in *Simvolizm*, p. 176.

14 Bugaev: "Formy iskusstva," p. 351.

15 V. Kandinsky: "O dukhovnom v iskusstve" in I. Repin et al.: *Trudy Vserossiiskogo sezda khudozhnikov v Petrograde*, P: Golike i Vilborg, 1914, Vol. 1, pp. 60–61.

16 S. Makovsky: "Dematerializatsiia prirody" in his *Stranitsy khudozhestvennoi kritiki*, SP: Panteon, 1909, Vol. 2, pp. 142–46.

17 S. Makovsky: "Golubaia roza" in *Zolotoe runo*, M, 1907, no. 5, p. 25.

18 On the gay scene in St. Petersburg see K. Rotikov: *Drugoi Peterburg*, SP: Liga-Plius, 1998; also see Kuzmin's diaries, i.e., N. Bogomolov and S. Shumikhin, eds.: *M. Kuzmin, Dnevnik 1908–1915*, SP: Limbakh, 2005.

19 See O. Matich: *Erotic Utopia. The Decadent Imagination in Russia's Fin de siècle*, Madison: University of Wisconsin Press, 2005, epecially Chapter 5.

20 For information on Bogdanova-Belskaia and Vrangel see A. Murashev and A. Skakov, comps.: *Baron i muza*, SP: Kolo, 2001.

21 D. Merezhkovsky: "O prichinakh upadka i o novykh techeniiakh sovremennoi russkoi literatury" (1892) in Merezhkovsky, *Polnoe sobranie sochinenii*, p. 180.

22 Only one frame of the movie, directed by Vladimir Kasianov, seems to have survived. For a detailed discussion see J. Heil: "Russian Futurism and the Cinema. Mayakovsky's Film Work of 1913" in *Russian Literature*, Amsterdam, 1986, no. 19, pp. 175–92.

23 A. Belyi: *Na rubezhe dvukh stoletii*, M: Zemlia i fabrika, 1931, p. 170.

24 V. Kandinsky: *Tekst khudozhnika*, M: IZO NKP, 1918, p. 113.

25 N. Evreinov: *Rops. Kriticheskii ocherk*, SP: Butkovskaia, 1910; *Obri Berdslei. Kriticheskii ocherk*, SP: Butkovskaia, 1912; A. Sidorov: *Obri Berdslei. Izbrannye risunki*, M: Venok, 1917.

26 The exhibition "Contemporary French Graphics" opened in the editorial offices of *Apollon*, St. Petersburg, in February 1910.

27 S. Diaghilev: "Slozhnye voprosy. Nash mnimyi upadok," p. 10.

Body Art: Ballet, Theater, Cabaret, Nudism

1 R. Buckle, ed.: *The Diaghilev Exhibition*. Catalogue of the exhibition at the Edinburgh Festival, Edinburgh, and Forbes House; London, 1954.

2 See, for example, L. Garafola: *Diaghilev's Ballets Russes*, New York: Oxford University Press, 1989; L. Garafola and N. van Norman Baer: *The Ballets Russes and Its World*, New Haven: Yale University Press, 1999; A. Schouvaloff: *The Art of Ballets Russes. The Serge Lifar Collection of Theatre Designs, Costumes and Paintings*, New Haven: Yale University Press, 1998.

3 V. Polunin: *The Continental Method of Scene Painting*, London: Beaumont, 1927.

4 C. Beaumont: *The Diaghilev Ballet in London*, London: Maclehose, 1940, p. 58.

5 Although Bakst was aware of particular ethnographic legacies, e.g., of Hellas and Siam, he indulged his fantasy at moments when scientific knowledge failed him. An example of such sweet laxity is the beautiful Negro Dancer in *Le Dieu Bleu* (1912), reproduced in color, for example, in N. Vam Norman Baer, ed., *The Art of Enchantment*. Catalogue of exhibition at the Fine Arts Museums of San Francisco, 1988, p. 61.

6 For some information on Bakst's activities in the St. Petersburg beau monde see J. Bowlt: *Theater of Reason / Theater of Desire. The Art of Alexandre Benois and Léon Bakst*. Catalogue of exhibition at the Thyssen-Bornemisza Foundation, Lugano, 1998, pp. 59–60, 154–59.

7 N. Evreinov: "Ektsessivnyi teatr dlia sebia" in his *Teatr dlia sebia*, P: Butkovskaia, 1911, pp. 139–208.

8 A. Golovin: "Kak my rabotali" in *Rabochii i teatr*, L, 1926, no. 15, p. 10. Quoted in E. Lansere, ed.: *"Maskarad" Lermontova v teatralnykh eskizakh A.Ya. Golovina*, L: VTO, 1941, p. 32.

9 Letter from Leila Mechin to Christian Brinton dated 25 September 1918. Published in the *New York Times*, New York, 1918, 19 October, p. 5.

10 N. Evreinov: "Khudozhniki v teatre V. F. Komissarzhevskoi" in *Alkonost*, SP, 1911, pp. 133–34.

11 L. Bakst: "O sovremennom teatre. Nikto v teatre bolshe ne khochet slushat, a khochet videt" in *Petersburgskaia gazeta*, SP, 1914, 21 January, p. 5.

12 See L. Zheverzheev, intro.: *Opis vystavlennykh v polzu lazarety shkoly narodnogo iskusstva ee Velichestva Gosudaryni Imperatritsy Aleksandry Fedorovny pamiatnikov Russkogo teatra iz sobraniia L.I. Zheverzheeva*. P: Shmidt, 1915, item no. 1146.

13 On Gastev and the new man see Johansson: *Aleksej Gastev. Proletarian Bard of the Machine Age*; and N. Misler; "Le corps Tayloriste, biomécanique et jazz à Moscou dans les années 1920" in C. Rousier, ed.: *Être ensemble. Figures de la communauté en danse depuis le XX\e siècle*, Paris: Centre National de la danse, 2003, pp. 103–22.

14 L. Vaillat: *Olga Spessivtseva: Ballerina en marge des Ballets Russes et des Ballets de l'Opéra de Paris*, Paris: Compagnie française des arts graphiques, 1944. This fine-arts edition carries six gouaches by Dmitri Bouchène.

15 For information on the experiments in free dance in the 1910s and 1920s see the special issue of *Experiment*, 1996, no. 2.

16 Ellin: "Tanets budushchego" in *Vesy*. 1904, no. 3, p. 39.

17 M. Larionov and I. Zdanevich: "Pochemu my raskrashivaemsia" in *Argus*, SP, 1913, December, p. 115.

18 V. Kandinsky: "Program of the Institute of Artistic Culture" (1920) in *Experiment*, no. 8, p. 148.

19 Ibid., p. 224.

20 F. Komissarzhevsky: "'Dekoratsiia' v sovremennom teatre" in *Maski*, M, 1913–14, no. 6, p. 10.

21 Ibid., p. 12.

22 Ibid., p. 13.

23 For commentary on Appia and the Russian theater see M. Babenchikov: "Ot Appia i Krega k budushchemu teatra" in *Novaia studiia*, SP, 1912, 9 November, no. 10, pp. 10–12; E. Znosko-Borovsky: "Tvorchestvo aktera i Gordon Kreg," ibid., pp. 14–15; and 17 November, no. 11, pp. 7–10; also see S. Volkonsky: "Adolf Appia" in *Apollon*, SP, 1912, no. 6, pp. 25–31; and his *Khudozhestvennye otkliki*, SP: Apollon, 1912. For information on Craig in Russia see L. Senelick: *Gordon Craig's Moscow Hamlet: A Reconstruction*, Westport: Greenwood Press, 1982.

24 F. Komissarzhevsky: "Nemtsi i russkii teatr" in *Maski*, 1912–13, no. 7–8, p. 10.

25 N. Alexandrova, ed.: *Aleksandr Benua. Moi vospominaniia*, M: Iskusstvo, 1979. This quotation from Vol. 1, pp. 289, 298.

26 V. Shklovsky: "Narodnaia komediia i '1-yi vinokur'" in *Zhizn iskusstva*, P, 1920, 17-18-19 April, no. 425-426-427, p. 1.

27 Savva Mamontov: [Autobiography], 1869 in RGALI, f. 799, op. 2, ed. khr. 2, l. 2 (verso).

28 Anon.: "Na khudozhestvennykh vystavkakh" in *Kulisy*, M, 1917, January, no. 1, p. 11.

29 Letter from Walter Nouvel to Sergei Diaghilev dated 22 November 1906. Inserted as note 5 to a letter from Benois to Nouvel dated 14 (1) December 1906 in RGALI, f. 938, op. 1, ed. khr. 46, ll. 224–26.

30 F. Komissarzhevsky: "Sapunov-dekorator" in *Apollon*, SP, 1914, no. 4, p. 16.

31 For further information on Russian stage design of the Modernist period see Dzh. Boult [J. Bowlt]: *Khudozhniki russkogo teatra 1880–1930. Sobranie Nikity i Niny Lobanovykh-Rostovskikh*. M: Iskusstvo, 1990 (Vol. 1); 1994 (Vol. 2).

32 On the influence of the Ballets Russes on Western fashion see N. Kalashnikova: *Narodnyi kostium*, M: Svarog, 2002, pp. 47–56.

33 For a discussion of *zhiznetvorchestvo* and the Modernist theater see L. Borisova: *Na izlomakh traditsii. Dramaturgiia russkogo simvolizma i simvolistskaia teoriia zhiznetvorchestva*, Simferopol: Tavricheskii natsionalnyi universitet, 2000.

34 Belyi: *Na rubezhe dvukh stoletii*, p. 219.

35 A. Belyi: *Mezhdu dvukh revoliutsii*, L: Izdatelstvo pisatelei, 1934, p.

219.

36 Belyi: *Na rubezhe dvukh stoletii*, pp. 224–25.

37 N. Shinsky: *Stikhi*, M: 1907 (publishing house not indicated).

38 Quoted in Shcherbatov: *Khudozhnik v ushedshei Rossii*, p. 41.

39 As reported in "Iz zhizni" in *Pereval*, M, 1906, no. 1, p. 17.

40 For more information on the activities at Ivanov's Tower see Muravieva, *Byloi Peterburg. Vek moderna*, Book 1, pp. 244–49; A. Shishkin, ed.: *Bashnia Viacheslava Ivanova i kultura Serebrianogo veka*, SP: SPbGU, 2006.

41 Yu. Slonimskaia: "Marionetka" in *Apollon*, P, 1916, no. 3, p. 30. For information on Slonimskaia's and other puppet theaters of the time see K. Tribble, ed.: *Marionette Theater of the Symbolist Era*, Lewiston, NY: Mellen, 2002.

42 Kandinsky: "Program of the Institute of Artistic Culture," p. 151.

43 J. Moore: *Gurdjieff and Mansfield*, London: Routledge and Kegan Paul, 1980, pp. 54–55.

44 For information see L. Engelstein: *The Keys to Happiness. Sex and the Search for Modernity in Fin-de-siècle Russia*, Ithaca: Cornell University Press, 1992.

45 For information on the martial arts in early twentieth-century Russia see A. Mazur: *Sem ivanov*, M: Stolitsa, 1995.

46 See Yu. Tsivian: *Early Cinema in Russia and Its Cultural Reception*, London and New York: Routledge, 1994; I. Grashchenkova: *Kino Serebrianogo veka*, M: Mozhaev, 2005.

47 For a discussion of these genres see L. Roshal: *Nachalo vsekh nachal. Fakt na ekrane i kinomysl "Serebrianogo veka,"* M: Materik, 2002.

48 I. Miasoedov: "Manifest o nagote" in N. Evreinov: *Nagota na stsene. Sbornik statei*, SP: Novoe vremia, 1911, pp. 126–27. For reproductions and commentary see J. Bowlt: "Gefährliche Querungen. Ivan Mjassoedoff und die Kultur der Grenzenverletzungen" in A. Willi et al.: *Ivan Mjassoedoff/Eugen Zotow 1881–1953. Spuren eines Exils*, Bern: Benteli, 1997, pp. 102–13; also see A. Kovalenko: *Ivan Miasoedov—khudozhnik serebrianogo veka*, Sevastopol: Mir, 1998.

Aesthetes and Barbarians: Apollo and the Suicide of Art

1 A. Ostroumova-Lebedeva: *Avtobiograficheskie zapiski*, M: Iskusstvo, 1945, Vol. 2, p. 108.

2 Ibid.

3 Ibid.

4 I. Repin: "Kritikam iskusstva" in *Apollon*, 1909–10, no. 6, p. 51.

5 S. Makovsky: Untitled statement in S. Makovsky et al.: *Kuda my idem. Sbornik statei i otvetov*, M: Zaria, 1910, p. 103.

6 D. Burliuk: "Die 'Wilden' Russlands" in W. Kandinsky and F. Marc, eds.: *Der Blaue Reiter*, Munich: Piper, 1912, pp. 13–19.

7 G. Chulkov: *Gody stranstvii*, M: Federatsiia, 1930, p. 188.

8 K. Petrov-Vodkin: notebook. Quoted in L. Diakonitsyn: *Ideinye protivorechiia v estetike russkoi zhivopisi kontsa 19–nachala 20 vv.*, Perm: Permskoe Knizhnoe Izdatelstvo, 1966, p. 144.

9 A. Benois: "V ozhidanii gimna Apollonu" in *Apollon*, 1909, no. 1, p. 10.

10 A. Blok: "Krushenie gumanizma" in Orlov, *Aleksandr Blok*, Vol. 2, p. 313.

11 L. Bakst: "Puti klassitsizma v iskusstve" in *Apollon*, 1909–10, no. 3, p. 46.

12 The last issues of *Apollon*, dated 1917, appeared in early 1918.

13 I. Repin et al.: *Trudy Vserossiiskogo sezda khudozhnikov v Petrograde*, P: Golike i Vilborg, 1914–15, Vols. 1–3.

14 Kandinsky maintained that the successful work of art could evoke the "inner sound." See, for example, his essay "Soderzhanie i forma" in V. Izdebsky, ed.: *Salon 2.* Catalogue of exhibition at the Salon, Odessa, 1910–11, pp. 14–16.

15 For commentary on music and Russian Symbolism see S. Morrison: *Russian Opera and the Symbolist Movement*, Berkeley: University of California Press, 2002.

16 Letter from Ilia Zdanevich to Valentina Zdanevich dated March 26, 1913. Archive of Ilia Zdanevich, Department of Manuscripts, State Russian Museum, Call no. f. 177, ed. khr. 50, ll. 18–20 and verso. Zdanevich elaborated his argument in a separate lecture entitled "Adoration of the Shoe" that he gave at the Stray Dog cabaret in St. Petersburg on April 17, 1914.

17 Belyi affirmed in his essay on the "Problem of Culture" (1909) that "culture cannot be identified with knowledge . . . whereas cognition is the knowledge of knowledge." Belyi: *Simvolizm*, p. 5.

18 A. Kruchenykh: *Sobstvennye rasskazy i risunki detei*, SP: EUY, 1914, p. 47.

19 M. Larionov and I. Zdanevich: "Pochemu my raskrashivaemsia" (1913). English translation in Bowlt: *Russian Art of the Avant-garde*, p. 82.

20 A certain Stepan Dimant wrote to the editor of *Sinii zhurnal* (SP, 1914, April, no. 13, p. 9): "You write a lot about Cubists, Circlists, Arcists, etc. Write about me, too. I'm an Eggist. I'm sending you my picture *Holiday* painted with eggs and a Cubist picture *Mother and Child* for comparison. Long live Bubizm! Long live Eggism!"

21 The Nothingists (*nichevoki*), established in 1919, were a group of writers and artists that identified strongly with the Western Dada movement. Their main publication was the miscellany by Boris Zemenkov et al.: *Sobachii yashchik ili Trudy tvorcheskogo biuro nichevokov v tech. 1920–1921 gg.*, M: Khobo, 1921. For some information on the Nothingists see J. Bowlt: "H2SO4: Dada in Russia" in S. Foster, ed.: *Dada Dimensions*, Ann Arbor: UMI, 1985, pp. 221–48.

22 For example, in his book *Futurizm i bezumie* (SP, 1914), a certain Dr. E. Radin drew what he saw as strong parallels between the art of the mentally impaired and that of the Futurists. In 1922, however, a certain Dr. A. Ostrovsky proclaimed that "after carefully studying examples of Futurist poetry for many years, I have not found anything characteristic of the creativity of the insane; furthermore, psychologically, after medical testimony, the poet Aleksei Kruchenykh proves to be completely healthy" (handwritten note signed by "Doctor A. Ostrovsky" in the Archive of Aleksei Kruchenykh), Russian State Archive of Literature and Art, Moscow. Call no.: f. 1334, op. 1, ed. khr. 132, l. 108 and verso.

23 Anon.: "Nashe prazdnichnoe interviu s futuristami" in *Teatr v karikaturakh*, M, 1914, 1 January, no. 1–2, p. 19.

24 See N. Gurianova: "Voennye graficheskie tsikly N. Goncharovoi i O. Rozanovoi" in *Panorama iskusstv*, M, 1989, no. 12, pp. 63–88.

25 Anton Balashev, a mental patient, "attacked" and slashed Repin's famous painting in the Tretiakov Gallery in January 1913. Repin declared that those really responsible for the deed were the "Modernist artists disrespectful of the old artists" (*Apollon*, 1913, no. 2, p. 61). David Burliuk found the episode entertaining, interpolating references to it in his booklet *Galdiashchie "benua" i novoe russkoe natsional'noe iskusstvo*, SP: Soiuz molodezhi. 1913. Also see K. Platt: 'On Blood, Scandal, Renunciation and History: Repin's *Ivan the Terrible and His Son*' in M. Levitt and T. Novikov, eds.: *Times of Trouble. Violence in Russian Literature and Culture*, Madison: University of Wisconsin Press, 2007, pp. 112–122.

26 According to Boris Lavrenev: "V kanun prazdnika" in *Color and Rhyme*, Hampton Bays, New York, 1964, no. 57, p. 49.

27 D. Burliuk, A. Kruchenykh, V. Khlebnikov, V. Maiakovsky referred to the poetry of the Symbolist Konstantin Balmont as "perfumed lechery" in their manifesto *Poshchechina obshchestvennomu*

vkusu (A Slap in the Face of Public Taste, 1912). Translation in V. Markov: *Russian Futurism*, Berkeley: University of California Press, 1968, p. 46.

28 See N. Kulbin: "Garmoniia, i dissonans i tesnye sochetaniia v iskusstve i zhizni" in Repin et al.: *Trudy Vserossiskogo sezda russkikh khudozhnikov v Petrograde*, Vol. 1, p. 36. Also see N. Evreinov: *Teatr u zhivotnykh*, M: Kniga, 1924.

29 V. Maiakovsky: "Ulitsa provalilas, kak nos sifilitika," i.e., the first line of his poem entitled "A vse-taki" (But nevertheless, 1914).

30 For information on Marinetti's visit to Russia in 1914 see N. Khardjiev: "La tournée de Marinetti en Russie en 1914" in J.-C. Marcadé, ed.: *Présence de Marinetti*, Lausanne: L'Age d'Homme, 1982, pp. 198–233.

31 B. Ternovets: *Pisma. Dnevniki. Stati*, M: Sovetskii khudozhnik, 1977, p. 99.

32 V. Kamensky: "Stati o D.D. Burliuke" (1915–17). Archive of Vasilii Kamensky, RGALI. Call no. f. 1497, op. 1, ed khr. 144, l. 10.

33 Livshits: *Polutoraglazyi strelets* (1933). English translation in Bowlt: Benedikt Livshits: *The One and a Half-Eyed Archer*, p. 243.

34 The critic Abram Efros referred to Filonov as an "apostle" in his article "Ob Aristarkhe Lentulove" (1933) in M. Tolmachev, comp.: *A. M. Efros. Mastera raznykh epokh*, M: Sovetskii khudozhnik, 1979, p. 249.

35 Le-Dantiu founded the Everythingist movement (*vsechestvo*) in St. Petersburg in 1913. For information see E. Yudina: "Mikhail Le-Dantiu. The Painting of Everythingness" in *Experiment*, 1995, no. 1, pp. 201–08.

36 Boris Zemenkov et al.: *Sobachii yashchik ili Trudy tvorcheskogo biuro nichevokov v tech. 1920–1921 gg*, M: Khobo, 1921, p. 8. The Nothingists (*nichevoki*), established in 1919, identified strongly with the Western Dada movement.

37 Letter from Ilia Zdanevich to Natalia Goncharova (undated) in Archive of Ilia Zdanevich, Department of Manuscripts, State Russian Museum. Call no., f. 177, ed. khr. 57, l. 3.

38 V. Kamensky et al.: "Chto uvlekaet Vas segodnia?" in *Moi zhurnal—Vasiliia Kamenskogo*, M, 1922, no. 1, p. 2.

The Year 1913: Crossroads of Past and Future

1 B. Bugaev (=A. Belyi): "Shtempelevannaia kalosha" in *Vesy*, 1907, no. 5, p. 50. For an extended discussion of the symbol of the samovar in this context see Ermilova: *Teoriia i obraznyi mir russkogo simvolizma*, pp. 86–100.

2 The reference is to the exhibition of that name. See D. Elliott et al., eds.: *Twilight of the Tsars. Russian Art at the Turn of the Century*. Catalogue of exhibition at the Hayward Gallery, London, 1991.

3 See T. Civ'jan et al.: *La Pietroburgo di Anna Achmatova*. Catalogue of exhibition at the Museo Civico Archeologico, Bologna, 1996; A. Bogomolov: *Mikhail Kuzmin*, M: NLO, 1995; O. Chervinskaia: *Akmeism v kontekste Serebrianogo veka i traditsii*, Chernovtsy: Ruti, 1997; M. Rubins: *Plasticheskaia radost krasoty. Akmeizm i Parnas*, SP: Akademicheskii proket, 2003.

4 The reference is to Nikolai Dobroliubov's two articles, "Temnoe tsarstvo" (Dark kingdom, 1859) and "Luch sveta v temnom tsarstve" (Ray of light in the dark kingdom, 1860), in which he praised the playwright Aleksandr Ostrovsky for presenting his dramas, especially *The Storm*, as civic documents, exposing the ills of Russian society.

5 The theme of Russia and the year 1913 has inspired a number of publications, not least Anfimov et al.: *Rossiia 1913 god. Statistiko-dokumental'nyi spravochnik* and F. Ph. Ingold: *Der grosse Bruch. Russland*

im Epochenjahr 1913, Munich: Beck, 2000.

6 M. Matiushin: "The Russian Cubo-Futurists" in Bowlt and Konecny: *A Legacy Regained. Nikolai Khardzhiev and the Russian Avant-Garde*, pp. 179–80.

7 The photograph exists in several versions. See, for example, J. D'Andrea, ed.: *Malevich*. Catalogue of exhibition at the National Gallery of Art, Washington, D.C., 1990, p. 179.

8 Anon.: "Peterburg" in *Muzy*, Kiev, 1913, 25 December, no. 1, p. 20.

9 N. Khardzhiev: *K istorii russkogo avangarda*, Stockholm: Almqvist and Wiksell, 1976, p. 95.

10 "New painterly realism" is part of the title of Malevich's primary Suprematist declaration, i.e., *Ot kubizma i futurizma k suprematizmu. Novyi zhivopisnyi realizm*, M, 1916.

11 K. Malevich: "Ya nachalo vsego" (dated 1913, but probably later) in Malevich Archives, Stedelijk Museum, Amsterdam. Call no.: Inv. no. 6, p. 1. The document carries two dates, 1913 and 1921. According to Aleksandra Shatskikh, Malevich added the retrospective "1913" since he identified that year as the central date in his artistic evolution.

12 L. Bakst: "Ob iskusstve segodnishnego dnia" in *Stolitsa i usadba*, 1914, no. 8, p. 18.

13 B. Olmetev and J. Stuart: *St. Petersburg. Portrait of an Imperial City*, New York: Vendome Press, 1990, p. 116.

14 For reproductions see A. Strigalev and J. Harten, eds.: *Vladimir Tatlin. Retrospektive*. Catalogue of exhibition at the Städtische Kunsthalle, Dusseldorf, and other venues, 1993–94, especially plates 66–72.

15 For information on such artifacts see Kirichenko and Anikst: *Russian Design and the Fine Arts 1750–1917*, passim.

16 See L. Zhadova, ed.: *Tatlin*, New York: Rizzoli, 1988, plates 97, 98, 103.

17 See K. Malevich: *Ot kubizma i futurizma k suprematizmu* (1916). Translated as "From Cubism and Futurism to Suprematism" in Bowlt: *Russian Art of the Avant-Garde. Theory and Criticism, 1902–34*, p. 133. The fact that Malevich hung his *Black Square* in the "beautiful corner" of the "0.10" exhibition in Petrograd in December, 1915, a space reserved traditionally for the icon, symbolized his strong identification of Suprematism with a new religion.

18 On the St. Petersburg Union of Youth group see J. Howard: *The Union of Youth*, Manchester: Manchester University Press, 1992.

19 See Anon. (=Pavel Muratov): *Vystavka drevne-russkogo iskusstva*. Catalogue of the exhibition at the Imperial Moscow Archaeological Institute, Moscow, 1913. Pavel Riabushinsky also published a collection of photographs of the exhibition under the same title with a preface by Muratov and identification of the curators for the four sections.

20 Stelletsky often evoked Orthodox associations in his portraits. See, for example, his portrait of the young Prince Mikhail Olsufiev wearing medieval vestments against a background of icons. For a color reproduction of this 1913 portrait see Kirichenko and Anikst: *Russian Design and the Fine Arts 1750–1917*, plate 173.

21 Goncharova's set of *pochoirs* for *Liturgie* is illustrated in color, for example, in Dzh. Boult [Bowlt]: *Khudozhniki russkogo teatra. Sobranie Nikity i Niny Lobanovykh-Rostovskikh*, M: Iskusstvo, 1991, Vol. 1, plates 30–43.

22 D. Nikiforov: *Sokrovishcha v Moskve*, M: Universitetskaia tipografiia, 1901.

23 The religious and popular works, many bearing traces of the Neo-Russian style, were discussed and illustrated in the handsome catalogue. See Anon.: *Russkoe narodnoe iskusstvo na vtoroi Vserossiiskoi kustarnoi vystavke v Petrograde v 1913*, P: Glavnoe upravlenie zemleustroistva i zemledeliia, 1914.

24 I. Ignatiev, ed.: *Vasilisk Gnedov: Smert iskusstvu*, SP: Peterburgskii glashatai, 1913.

Apocalypse Now:
War, Revolution, and Cultural Centrifuge

 1 A. Belyi: "Apokalipsis v russkoi poezii" in *Vesy*, 1905, no. 5, p. 14.
 2 A. Benois: "Posledniaia futuristicheskaia vystavka" in *Rech*, P: 1916, 9 January, no. 8.
 3 I. Lazarevsky: *Velikaia voina v obrazakh i kartinakh*, M: Mamontov, 1915 (three books)
 4 O. Rozanova and A. Kruchenykh: *Vselenskaia voina*, P, 1916.
 5 Ya. Tugendkhold: *Problema voiny v mirovom iskusstve*, M: Sytin, 1916; V. Gross: *Voina v iskusstve*, L: Krasnaia gazeta, 1930. The classic Russian study of battle painting, i.e., V. Sadoven: *Russkie khudozh-niki-batalisty XVIII–XIX vv.*, M: Iskusstvo, 1955, excludes the twentieth century.
 6 V. Rozhdestvensky: *Zapisi khudozhnika*, M: Sovetskii khudozhnik, 1963, p. 43.
 7 N. Ulianov: *Moi vstrechi*, M: Akademiia khudozhestv, 1959, p. 128.
 8 Statement by Kandinsky to Arthur Eddy in H. Roethel and J. Benjamin: *Vasilii Kandinsky. Catalogue Raisonné of the Oil-Paintings 1900–1915*, Ithaca: Cornell University Press, 1983, Vol. 1, p. 445.
 9 Petr R....tsky (undeciphered pseudonym): *Voina "koltsa" s "soiuzom,"* M, 1913
10 On the history of the postcard in early-twentieth-century Russia, including the time of World War I, see V. Terentiev: *Otkrytye pisma Serebrianogo veka*, SP: Slaviia, 2000.
11 V. Tatlin: "Chugunnye krylia" (Lecture on Futurism, 1916). For a reproduction of the poster announcing the lecture see Strigalev and Harten: *Vladimir Tatlin, Retrospektive*, p. 258.
12 An exception was Pavel Muratov, who saw action in the Russo-Japanese War and who maintained a particular interest in military strategy throughout his life, even coauthoring a book on the Soviet battles in World War II, i.e., W. Allen and P. Muratoff: *The Russian Campaign of 1944–1945*, Harmondsworth, 1946. See B. Grashchenkov, ed.: *P. P. Muaratov. Obrazy Italii*, M: Galart, 1993, Vol. 1, pp. 290–92.
13 G. Narbut, ill.: *God 1812 v basniakh Krylova*, SP: Obshchestvo Sv. Evgeniia, 1912.
14 The fairy story *War of the Mushrooms* was illustrated by a number of artists of the Silver Age, including Elena Polenova and Georgii Narbut in 1889 and 1909, respectively. An especially interesting set of illustrations for the *War of the Mice and Frogs* was made by Alisa Poret, i.e., *Voina myshei i liagushek*, M: Akademiia, 1936.
15 P. Kerschenzew: *Das schöpferische Theater*, Hamburg: Nachf, 1922, p. 150.
16 That *Zhar-ptitsa* was the "last" journal of the Silver Age might be contested inasmuch as the Russian colonies in Lithuania and China, for example, also produced magazines such as *Perezvony* (Chimes, Riga, 1925–27) and *Feniks* (Phoenix, Shanghai, 1935–36) which drew upon the Symbolist heritage. However, in artistic spirit and intellectual composition, *Zhar-ptitsa* would seem to be closest to *Mir iskusstva*, *Zolotoe runo*, and *Apollon*.

Academy of Arts: St. Petersburg/Petrograd/Leningrad, founded in 1757; first president was Catherine the Great. In 1918 the Academy was replaced by Svomas (q.v.) and then reinstated in 1921. In the 1920s it was also referred to as Vkhutemas (q.v.)

Apollo: Title of an art and literary journal *(Apollon)* published by S. Makovsky in St. Petersburg 1909–17 (last issues appeared in 1918). Supportive of the Acmeist movement in particular, *Apollo* published articles and exhibition reviews dealing with the new art and also organized exhibitions in its editorial offices.

Blue Rose: Group of Moscow and Saratov Symbolist artists consisting of P. Kuznetsov, Sapunov, Sudeikin, et al. Held one exhibition in Moscow in 1907.

Contemporary Trends: Exhibition organized by Kulbin in St. Petersburg in 1908. D. Burliuk, Lentulov, et al. took part.

Donkey's Tail: Group organized by Larionov in 1911. Held one exhibition in Moscow in 1912 with contributions by Goncharova, Larionov, Malevich, Shevchenko, et al.

Exposition Internationale des Arts Décoratifs et Industriels Modernes: International exhibition of industrial design and applied art in Paris in 1925. Many of the Soviet Suprematists and Constructivists such as Chashnik, Popova, Rodchenko, Stepanova, and A. Vesnin contributed to the Soviet Pavilion designed by Melnikov.

Firebird. title of an art and literary journal *(Zhar-ptitsa)* published in Berlin and Paris 1921–26. *Firebird* promoted the more traditional values of the World of Art artists, including Bakst, A. Benois, Jacovleff, Shukhaev, and Somov, and paid particular attention to stage and graphic design.

GAKhN: See RAKhN

Golden fleece: title of an art and literary journal *(Zolotoe runo)* published by N. Riabushinsky in Moscow 1906–09 (last issues appeared in 1910). *Golden fleece* also organized three exhibitions which did much to propagate the cause of Goncharova and Larionov: "Salon of the *Golden Fleece*" (Moscow, 1908; contributions by Russian and W. European artists); "Golden Fleece" (Moscow, 1909; contributions by Russian and W. European artists); "Golden Fleece" (Moscow, 1909–10; contributions by Russian artists only).

Izdebsky salons: Izdebsky organized two important exhibitions or salons of the new Russian art: the "International Exhibition of Paintings, Sculpture, Engravings and Drawings" (Odessa and other cities, 1909–10; contributions by Russian and W. European artists); and "Salon-2" (catalogue dated "Odessa 1910," but opened in early 1911; contributions by Russian artists only).

Jack of Diamonds: Group organized by Larionov in Moscow in 1910 and supported at first by many radical artists, including Goncharova and Malevich. After the first exhibition in Moscow in 1910–11, the group split into two factions, one led by Larionov, giving rise to the Donkey's Tail (q.v.), the other by Falk, Konchalovsky, Lentulov, Mashkov, et al. The Jack of Diamonds organized regular exhibitions

in Moscow and St. Petersburg between 1910 and 1917, some of them international in scope.

Link: Exhibition organized by D. Burliuk, Bogomazov, Exter, and other artists in Kiev in 1908. Accompanied by a manifesto, this was one of the first avant-garde exhibitions of Russian and Ukrainian art.

Lubok: A cheap, hand-colored print or broadsheet often depicting allegorical and satirical scenes from Russian life. The bright colors and crude outlines of the *lubok* attracted many twentieth-century Russian artists.

Mir iskusstva. See World of Art

Morozov Gallery: The Moscow collection of Impressionist and Post-Impressionist paintings belonging to the businessman Ivan Morozov. In 1918 the collection was nationalized.

Moscow Institute of Painting, Sculpture, and Architecture: The main Moscow art school (Moskovskoe uchilishche zhivopisi, vaianiia i zodchestva) at which many of Russia's nineteenth- and twentieth-century artists studied, including the avant-garde. After 1917 it merged with the Central Stroganov Institute of Technical Drawing to form Svomas (q.v.)

Moscow Salon: A society which held regular exhibitions in Moscow between 1910 and 1918 at which some of the avant-garde, including Goncharova, Konchalovsky, and Stepanova, were represented.

New Society of Artists: A society that held regular exhibitions in St. Petersburg between 1904 and 1915 at which some of the avant-garde, including Exter, Kandinsky, Konchalovsky, and Mashkov, were represented.

No. 4: Group organized by Larionov in 1914. Held one exhibition in Moscow with contributions by Exter, Goncharova, Larionov, Shevchenko, et al.

0.10: Short title of the "Last Futurist Exhibition of Paintings, 0.10" held in Petrograd in 1915–16 with contributions by Kliun, Popova, Puni, Rozanova, Tatlin, et al. This was also the first public showing of Malevich's Suprematism.

Pushkin Museum of Fine Arts: The principal Moscow collection of Western art, ancient and modern. Founded in 1912, it was called the Alexander III Museum of Fine Arts until 1917.

RAKhN: Russian Academy of Artistic Sciences (Rossiiskaia Akademiia khudozhestvennykh nauk). Founded in Moscow in 1921 under P. Kogan, RAKhN, also known as GAKhN (State Academy of Artistic Sciences—Gosudarstvennaia Akademiia khudozhestvennykh nauk), was a research institution which attracted a number of important artists and critics, including Bakushinsky, Kandinsky, Shmit, and Shpet. It functioned until 1931.

Russian Museum: The principal St. Petersburg collection of Russian art. Founded in St. Petersburg in 1898, it was called the Alexander III Russian Museum until 1917.

Scales: title of an art and literary journal (*Vesy*) published by S. Poliakov in Moscow 1904–09 (last issues appeared in 1910). *Scales* published articles and exhibition reviews dealing with the new literary and visual arts, especially international Symbolism.

Shchukin Gallery: The Moscow collection of Impressionist and Post-Impressionist paintings belonging to the businessman Sergei Shchukin. In 1918 the collection was nationalized.

Socialist Realism. A didactic and narrative style of art which emphasized advocacy of, and allegiance to, the political ideology of the Soviet regime. Established in 1932, Socialist Realism dominated Soviet painting, literature, and music until the 1970s.

State Russian Museum: See Russian Museum

State Tretiakov Gallery: See Tretiakov Gallery

Stieglits Institute: Stiglits (also Stieglitz) Central Institute of Technical Drawing, St. Petersburg. Founded in 1878, the Institute emphasized the applied arts and industrial design. In 1922 it merged with the Petrograd Svomas (q.v.) and later on was renamed the Mukhina Institute.

Stroganov Institute: Central Stroganov Institute of Technical Drawing, Moscow (also known as the Stroganov Art and Industry Institute). After 1917 it merged with the Moscow Institute of Painting, Sculpture, and Architecture to form Svomas (q.v.).

Svomas: Free State Art Studios (Svobodnye gosudarstvennye khudozhestvennye masterskie). In 1918 the Moscow Institute of Painting, Sculpture, and Architecture and the Stroganov Institute were integrated to form Svomas, and leading art schools in other major cities, including the Academy of Arts, Petrograd, were closed down. In 1920, however, Svomas, Moscow, was renamed Vkhutemas (q.v.) and the Academy in Petrograd was reinstated. Many avant-garde artists, including Kliun, Popova, Rodchenko, and Tatlin, contributed to the radical pedagogical and administrative developments which accompanied these name changes.

Target: Group organized by Larionov in 1913. Held one exhibition in Moscow in 1913 with contributions by Chagall, Goncharova, Larionov, Malevich, Shevchenko, et al.

Tramway V: Short title of "Tramway V, the First Futurist Exhibition of Paintings" held in Petrograd in 1915 with contributions by Kliun, Malevich, Popova, Rozanova, Tatlin, et al.

Tretiakov Gallery: The principal Moscow collection of Russian art. Founded in 1892 on the basis of the collection of Pavel Tretiakov, a Moscow businessman.

Triangle: Exhibition organized by Kulbin in St. Petersburg in 1910 and supported by some of the avant-garde artists, including the Burliuks.

Union of Russian Artists: A society which held regular exhibitions in Moscow and St. Petersburg between 1910 and 1924 with contributions by predominantly moderate artists such as S. Ivanov, Vinogradov, and Yuon.

Union of Youth: Group of artists, critics, and esthetes initiated by Markov, Rozanova, Shkolnik, et al. in St. Petersburg in 1910. Published an art journal under the same name, 1912–13, and sponsored a series of exhibitions, 1910–1914, to which many of the avant-garde contributed, including D. Burliuk, Filonov, Larionov, and Puni.

Unovis: Affirmers of the New Art/Affirmation of the New Art (Utverditeli novogo iskusstva/Utverzhdenie novogo iskusstva). Group of Suprematists founded by Malevich in Vitebsk in 1920. The group, including Chashnik, Ermolaeva, Lissitzky, and Suetin, was especially interested in architecture and design. Unovis had affiliations in Smolensk, Samara, and other cities, and held exhibitions in Vitebsk and Moscow.

Vesy. See Scales.

Victory over the Sun: The Cubo-Futurist opera produced in St. Petersburg in 1913 with libretto by Kruchenykh and Khlebnikov, music by Matiushin, and designs by Malevich.

Vkhutein: Higher State Art-Technical Institute (Vysshii gosudarstvennyi khudozhestvenno-tekhnicheskii institut). Vkhutein replaced Vkhutemas (q.v.) in 1926 and was replaced by the Moscow Institute of Visual Arts in 1930.

Vkhutemas: Higher State Art-Technical Studios (Vysshie gosudarstvennye khudozhestvenno-tekhnicheskie masterskie). Vkhutemas replaced Svomas (q.v.) in 1920 and was replaced by Vkhutein (q.v.) in 1926. Although the Moscow Vkhutemas is the most famous, the name was also applied to other art schools such as the reinstated Academy of Arts in Petrograd/Leningrad.

Wanderers: Short title of the Association of Wandering Exhibitions founded in 1870. Held regular exhibitions in St. Petersburg, Moscow, and other cities between 1871 and 1923 with contributions by Levitan, Repin, Surikov, and other Realist artists.

World of Art (Mir iskusstva): Group of St. Petersburg artists, critics, and esthetes founded by Benois, Diaghilev, et al. in the late 1890s. Published an art magazine under the same name 1898–1904 and sponsored a series of exhibitions 1899–1906 so as to propagate contemporary art. Revived as an exhibition society in 1910 (through 1924).

Wreath: Exhibition organized in St. Petersburg in 1908 with contributions by the Burliuks, Exter, Lentulov, et al.

Wreath-Stephanos: Exhibition organized in Moscow in 1907–08 with contributions by the Burliuks, Larionov, Lentulov, Yakulov, et al; also opened in St. Petersburg and other cities with a similar contingent.

Year 1915: Short title of "Exhibition. The Year 1915" organized by Kandaurov in Moscow in 1915 with contributions by Kamensky, Larionov, Lentulov, Malevich, Rozanova, and other avant-garde artists.

Zhar-ptitsa. See **Firebird.**

Zolotoe runo. See **Golden fleece.**

FURTHER READING

BOOKS

In addition to earlier important studies, the past two decades, in particular, have witnessed an intense interest in the Russian Silver Age, especially on the part of Moscow and St. Petersburg historians. The titles below are a representative selection only.

A. Alekseev et al., eds.: *Russkaia khudozhestvennaia kultura kontsa XIX–nachala XX veka*, 4 vols. M: Nauka, 1968–80.

L. Aleshina and G. Sternin: *Obrazy i liudi Serebrianogo veka*. M: Galart, 2002.

M. Anikst and E. Chernevich: *Russian Graphic Design 1880–1917*. New York: Abbeville, 1990.

I. Azizian: *Dialog iskusstv Serebrianogo veka*. M: Progress-Traditsiia, 2001.

T. Bachelis: *Zametki o simvolizme*. M: GII, 1998.

Yu. Balashova: *Shkolnaia zhurnalistika Serebrianogo veka*. SP: S. Peterburgskii universitet, 2007.

N. Beliaeva et al., eds.: *Sergei Diaghilev i khudozhestvennaia kultura XIX–XX vv.* Perm: Permskoe knizhnoe izdatelstvo, 1989.

L. Beliakova-Kazanskaia: *Ekho Serebrianogo veka*. SP: Kanon, 1998.

A. Belyi: *Simvolizm*. Moscow: Musaget, 1910.

A. Benois: *Vozniknovenie "Mira iskusstva."* L: Komitet populiarizatsii khudozhestvennykh izdanii, 1928.

N. Bogomolov, ed.: *Zolotoe runo. Rospis zhurnala*. Novgorod: NGU, 2002.

E. Borisova: *Arkhitektura Serebrianogo veka*. M: GII, 1999.

E. Borisova and G. Sternin: *Russian Art Nouveau*. New York: Rizzoli, 1988.

J. Bowlt: *The Silver Age. Russian Art of the Early Twentieth Century*. Newtonville: Oriental Research Partners, 1979.

J. Bowlt, ed.: *Journal of Decorative and Propaganda Arts*, Miami, 1987, No. 5; and No. 11, 1989. Special issues devoted to Russian design 1880–1980.

W. Brumfield: *The Origins of Modernism in Russian Architecture*. Berkeley: University of California Press, 1991.

G. Diatleva et al., eds.: *Simvolizm. Entsiklopediia*. M: Olga-Press, 2001.

V. Dudakov: *Simvolizm v Rossii 1890–1930 gg. Iz chastnykh kollektsii*. M: Sovetskii fond kultury, 1982.

L. Engelstein: *The Keys to Happiness. Sex and the Search for Modernity in Fin-de-siècle Russia*. Ithaca, NY: Cornell University Press, 1992.

E. Ermilova: *Teoriia i obraznyi mir russkogo simvolizma*. M: Nauka, 1989.

P. Fokin and S. Sniazeva: *Serebrianyi vek. Portretnaia galereia kulturnykh geroev rubezha XIX–XX vekov*. SP: Amfora, 2007.

I. Gofman: *Golubaia roza*. M: Pinakoteka, 2000.

S. Grechishkin and A. Lavrov: *Simvolisty vblizi. Ocherki i publikatsii*. M: Skifiia, 2006.

R. Hahmann and J. Hermand: *Stilkunst um 1900*. Berlin: Akademie Verlag, 1967.

A. Hansen-Löve: *Der russische Symbolismus*. Vienna: Die österreichischen Akademie der Wissenschaften, 1998.

B. Holl et al., eds.: *The Silver Age. Russian Literature and Culture 1881–1921*. Journal published by Charles Schlacks, Jr., Idyllwild, Ca., 1998–2000 (three issues).

V. Karkarian: *Modern v arkhitekture Samary*. Samara: Agni, 2006.

N. Kazarinova et al., eds.: *Sergei Diaghilev i russkoe iskusstvo XIX–XX vv*. Perm: Permskaia gosudarstvennaia khudohestvennaia galereia, 2005 (three issues).

J. Kennedy: *The "Mir iskusstva" Group and Russian Art, 1898–1912*. New York: Garland, 1977.

V. Khokhlova, ed.: *Serebrianyi vek v fotografiiakh A.P. Botkinoi*. M: Nashe nasledie, 1998.

E. Kirichenko and M. Anikst: *Russian Design and the Fine Arts 1750–1917*. New York: Abrams, 1991.

B. Kirikov: *Arkhitektura peterburgskogo moderna. Osobniaki i dokhodnye doma*. SP: Kolo, 2006.

G. Kovalenko, ed.: *Simvolizm v avangarde*. M: Nauka, 2002.

O. Kuznetsova, ed.: *Russkii modernizm. Problemy tekstologii*. SP: Aletei, 2001.

N. Lapshina: *"Mir iskusstva."* M: Iskusstvo, 1977.

T. Levaia: *Russkaia muzyka nachala XX veka v khudozhestvennom kontekste epokhi*. M: Muzyka, 1991.

T. Llorens, et al.: *Vanguardias Rusas*. Madrid: Museo Thyssen-Bornemisza, 2006.

F. Lur'e: *Starye gody. Khronologicheskaia rospis soderzhaniia, 1907–1916*. SP: Kolo, 2007.

O. Matich: *Erotic Utopia. The Decadent Imagination in Russia's Fin de siècle*. Madison: University of Wisconsin Press, 2005.

N. Misler: *V nachale bylo telo*. M: Iskusstvo XXI vek, 2010.

I. Muravieva: *Byloi Peterburg. Vek moderna*. SP: Izdatelstvo "Pushkinsko-go fonda," 2004.

G. Nivat et al.: *Istoriia russkoi literatury. XX vek. Serebrianyi vek*. M: Progress, 1987.

E. Paston et al.: *Stil zhizni—stil iskusstva*. M: State Tretiakov Gallery, 2000.

N. Pavlova et al., eds.: *Modern. Modernizm. Modernizatsiia*. M: RGGU, 2004.

V. Petrov: *Russian Art Nouveau. The Diaghilev Group of Russian Artists*. Bournemouth: Parkstone, 1997.

V. Petrov and A. Kamensky: *The World of Art Movement*. L: Aurora, 1991.

E. Petrova et al.: *Mir iskusstva*. SP: Palace, 1998.

M. Petrova, ed.: *Letopis literaturnykh sobytii v Rossii kontsa XIX–nachala XX v (1891–oktiabr, 1917)*. M: IMLI RAN, 2002 (Issue No. 1: 1891–1900)

O. Petrova: *Simvolizm v russkom izobrazitelnom iskusstve*. SP: SbGPU, 2000.

G. Pospelov: *Russkoe iskusstvo nachala XX veka. Sudba i oblik Rossii*. M: Nauka, 1999.

C. and E. Proffer, eds.: *The Silver Age of Russian Culture*. Ann Arbor: Ardis, 1975.

A. Pyman: *History of Russian Symbolism*. Cambridge: Cambridge University Press, 1994.

L. Rapatskaia: *Iskusstvo "Serebrianogo veka."* M: Prosveshchenie, 1996.

A. Riumin: *M.V. Dobuzhinsky: Azbuka "Mira iskusstva."* M: Nashe nasledie, 1998.

O. Ronen: *The Fallacy of the Silver Age in Twentieth Century Russian Literature.* Amsterdam: Harwood, 1997.

A. Rosenfeld, ed.: *Defining Russian Graphic Arts: From Diaghilev to Stalin, 1898–1934.* New Brunswick, NJ: Zimmerli Museum, 1999.

L. Roshal: *Nachalo vsekh nachal. Fakt na ekrane i kinomysl "Serebrianogo veka."* M: Materik, 2002.

A. Rusakova: *Simvolizm v russkoi zhivopisi.* M: Iskusstvo, 1995.

G. Rylkova: *The Archaeology of Anxiety. The Russian Silver Age and Its Legacy.* Pittsburgh: University of Pittsburgh Press, 2008.

E. Saiko: *Kultur-dialog filosofii i iskusstva v epokhu Serebrianogo veka.* M: RAGS, 2004.

E. Saiko: *Obraz kultury Serebrianogo veka.* M: Prospekt, 2005.

W. Salmond: *Arts and Crafts in Late Imperial Russia. Reviving the Kustar Art Industries.* Cambridge: Cambridge University Press, 1996.

W. Salmond, ed.: *The New Style. Russian Perceptions of Art Nouveau.* Special issue of *Experiment*, Los Angeles, 2001, Vol. 7.

D. Sarabianov: *Istoriia russkogo iskusstva kontsa XIX–nachala XX vv.* M: Galart, 2001.

D. Sarabianov: *Modern. Istoriia stilia.* M: Galart, 2001.

V. Shestakov: *Iskusstvo i mir v "Mire iskusstva."* M: Slavianskii dialog, 1998.

A. Sobolev: *Vesy. Annotirovannyi ukazatel soderzhaniia.* M: Truten, 2003.

G. Sternin: *Khudozhestvennaia zhizn Rossii na rubezhe XIX–XX vekov.* M: Iskusstvo, 1970.

G. Sternin: *Khudozhestvennaia zhizn Rossii 1900–1910-kh godov.* M: Iskusstvo, 1988.

L. Tananaeva: *Tri lika polskogo moderna.* SP: Aleteiia, 2006.

B. Tukh: *Putevoditel po Serebrianomu veku.* M: Oktopus, 2005.

M. Voskresenskaia: *Simvolizm kak miroponimanie Serebrianogo veka.* Tomsk: Tomskii universitet, 2003.

T. Zhukovskaia et al., eds.: *"Serebrianyi vek" v Krymu. Vzgliad iz XXI stoletiia.* M: Dom-muzei Mariny Tsvetaevoi, 2007.

I. Zilbershtein and V. Samkov, eds.: *Sergei Diaghilev i russkoe iskusstvo* (two vols.). M: Izobrazitelnoe iskusstvo, 1982.

EXHIBITIONS

The catalogues of the exhibitions mentioned below also provide useful information on the arts of the Russian Silver Age.

P. Aksenov et al.: *"Natsionalnyi stil" v russkom iskusstve XIX–nachala XX vekov.* Catalogue of exhibition at the All-Russian Museum of Decorative and Applied Art, Moscow, 1990.

I. Avtonomova et al.: *Ot simvolizma k avangardu. Grafika i skulptura pervoi treti XX veka iz sobraniia Marii Salinoi i Sergeia Krivosheeva.* M: Trilistik, 2006.

J. Bowlt, N. Misler, and M. Tsantsanoglou: *El Cosmos de la vanguardia rusa. Arte y exploración espacial 1900–1930.* Catalogue of exhibition at the Fundación Marcelino Botín, Santander (Spain), and the State Museum of Contemporary Art, Thessaloniki (Greece), 2010–11.

J. Bowlt, N. Giordano-Rosticher, and Z. Tregulova: *Étonne-moi! Serge Diaghilev et Les Ballets Russes / A Feast of Wonders: Serge Diaghilev and the Ballets Russes.* Catalogue of exhibition at the Nouveau Musée National de Monte Carlo, Monaco, and the State Tretiakov Gallery, Moscow, 2009–10.

S. Causey: *Tradition and Revolution in Russian Art.* Catalogue of exhibition at the City Art Gallery, Manchester, and other venues, 1990.

E. de Diego et al.: *El simbolismo ruso.* Catalogue of exhibition at the Fundación "la Caixa," Madrid, 1999.

A. Dodge et al.: *St. Petersburg 1900.* Catalogue of exhibition at the Art Gallery of Western Australia, Perth, 2005.

R. Donnedieu de Vabres et al.: *L'Art Russe dans la seconde moitié du XIXe siècle en quête d'identité.* Catalogue of exhibition at the Musée d'Orsay, Paris, 2005.

V. Dudakov et al.: *Il Simbolismo russo. Sergej Djagilev e l'Età d'argento nell'arte.* Catalogue of exhibition at the Fondazione Giorgio Cini, Venice, 1991.

V. Egorov et al.: *Russkii stil.* Catalogue of exhibition at the State Historical Museum, Moscow, 1998.

D. Elliot et al.: *Twilight of the Tsars. Russian Art at the Turn of the Century.* Catalogue of exhibition at the South Bank Centre, London, 1991.

I. Gofman, ed.: *Zoltoe runo.* Catalogue of exhibition at the State Tretiakov Gallery, Moscow 2008.

G. Guroff et al.: *Mir iskusstva. Russia's Age of Elegance.* Catalogue of exhibition circulated by the Foundation for International Arts and Education, Bethesda, MD, 2005–06.

I. Hoffmann, ed.: *Le Symbolisme Russe. La Rose Bleue.* Catalogue of exhibition at the Musée communal d'Ixelles, Brussels, 2006.

A. Juppé et al.: *Le Symbolisme Russe.* Catalogue of exhibition at the Musée des Beaux-Arts, Bordeaux, 2000.

V. Kruglov et al.: *Simvolizm v Rossii.* Catalogue of exhibition at the State Russian Museum, St. Petersburg, 1996.

A. Lemmens and S-A. Stommels: *Russian Book Art, 1904–2005.* Catalogue of exhibition for Europalia, Brussels, 2005.

E. Petrova et al.: *Sehnsucht und Aufbruch. Der russische Symbolismus als historische und aktuelle Dimension.* Catalogue of exhibition at the Ludwig Museum in Deutschherrenhaus, Koblenz, 2002.

T. Rappe, ed.: *Na rubezhe vekov. Iskusstvo epokhi moderna.* Catalogue of exhibition at the State Hermitage, St. Petersburg, 2006.

A. Rosenfeld et al: *Defining Russian Graphic Arts. From Diaghilev to Stalin 1898–1934.* New Brunswick: Rutgers State University Press, 1999.

A. Savinov et al.: *Golubaia roza.* Catalogue of exhibition at the Pushkin Museum of Fine Arts, Moscow, 1999.

E. Vodonos et al.: *Stanovlenie russkogo zhivopisnogo simvolizma.* Catalogue of exhibition at the Radishchev State Art Museum, Saratov, 1998.

INDEX

Note: *Italicized* references are illustration numbers.

PHOTO CREDITS

Note: *Italicized* references are illustration numbers.

Beinecke Rare Book and Manuscript Library, Yale University: *55, 56, 101*
Collection of Valerii Dudakov and Marina Kashuro, Moscow: *128, 395*
The Research Institute, J. Paul Getty Center, Los Angeles: *317, 554*
Collection of Nina and Nikita Lobanov-Rostovsky, London: *1, 157, 356, 413, 425, 433, 436, 439, 443, 453, 461, 497, 592, 603, 639, 640*
Library of Congress, Washington, D.C.: *2, 46, 48, 50, 52, 53, 62, 63, 65, 66, 91-93, 96, 97, 105, 109, 118, 178, 202*
Courtesy New York Public Library: *24, 76, 77, 160, 315, 441, 442, 455, 467, 474-478*
Private collections (various): *25, 144, 159, 161, 300, 304, 316, 334, 355, 380, 426, 430, 431, 452, 524, 583, 599, 623, 624*
Sotheby's: *30, 299, 308-312, 597*

Endpapers: Art Resource, N.Y.
33. Private collection. Photograph courtesy of Yuliia Volkhonovich
34. David Wilson, Museum of Jurassic Technology, Los Angeles
39. Archive of the Pasternak Family, Moscow
44. Collection Famille Bilinsky, Paris
54. Boston Public Library
110. Teatr v karikaturakh (Theater in caricatures), Moscow, 1913, no. 3, September, p. 9.
114. Collection of Igor Schleiger, Cologne
145. Mikhail Gerzenshon, ed.: Zapísi A. N. Scriabina. Russkie Propilei, Moscow: Sabashnikov, 1919, Vol. 6, p. 157.
174. Present whereabouts unknown
175. Digital Image © The Museum of Modern Art/Licensed by SCALA/Art Resource, N.Y.
176. Private collection, St. Petersburg
177. Courtesy Yuri Tsivian
185. Imagno/Artothek
210. CNAC/MNAM/Dist. Réunion des Musées Nationaux/Art Resource, N.Y.
213. Tate, London/Art Resource, N.Y.
214. Art Resource, N.Y.
218. Scala/Art Resource, N.Y.
219. Snark/Art Resource, N.Y.
237. Anonymous portfolio of Egorov's decors, "Siniaia ptitsa." Skazka M. Meterlinka na stsene Moskovskogo khudozhestvennogo teatra, Part I. Moscow: Iskusstvo i zhizn, 1908.
244. Mir iskusstva (World of Art), St. Petersburg, 1903, Vol. 9, between pp., 220 and 221.
245. Mir iskusstva (World of Art), St. Petersburg, 1903, no. 3, p. 105.
246. Mir iskusstva (World of Art), St. Petersburg, 1903, no. 3, p. 103.

247. Mir iskusstva (World of Art), St. Petersburg, 1903, Vol. 9, p. 235.
248. Mir iskusstva (World of Art), St. Petersburg, 1903, Vol. 9, p. 229.
267. Erich Lessing/Art Resource, N.Y.
276. A. Kalitinsky, intro., in Kn. M. K. Tenisheva: Emal i inkrustatsiia. Prague: Seminarium Kondakoviarum, 1930, between pp. 10 and 11.
282. M. Tenisheva. Khram Sviatogo Dukha v Talashkine, Paris, 1938.
285. Vesy, Moscow, 1905, no. 5, between pp. 16 and 17.
286. Vesy (Scales), Moscow, 1905, no. 6, between pp. 16 and 17.
288. Mir iskusstva (World of art), St. Petersburg, 1900, no. 11-12, p. 122.
303. Anonymous: Postroiki russkogo otdela Mezhdunarodnoi vystavki v Glasgo, 1901. Proekt i postroiki F. Shekhtel (Buildings of the Russian section of the International Exhibition in Glasgow, 1901. Project and buildings: F. Shekhtel), Moscow (publisher and date not indicated), upaginated.
338. Majd Family Collection
341. CNAC/MNAM/Dist. Réunion des Musées Nationaux/Art Resource, N.Y.
349. Imagno/Artothek/© VG-Bild-Kunst Bonn
359. Zhar-ptitsa (Firebird), Berlin, 1921, no. 1, p. 33.
365. Reprinted as a limited, lithographic edition under the title Die sieben Todsünden. Berlin: Privatdruck, 1923; second printing, 2002, where this plate is numbered III/3.
378. Published by the Department for the Preparation of State Papers, St. Petersburg, 1902.
381. Private collection, Berlin
408. M. Calvesi: L'Arte moderna. Il futurismo russo. Milan: Fabbri, 1967, p. 314.
414. Collection of Dmitrii Sarabianov, Moscow
418. Bibliothèque des Arts Décoratifs, Paris. Archives Charmet/The Bridgeman Art Library, N.Y.
419. Photograph by Claude Harris. The Sketch, London, October 14, 1914.
422. Francis de Miomandre, intr.: Designs on the Dances of Vaslav Nijinsky, London: La Belle Edition, 1913.
427. ©Musée National d'Art Moderne, Centre Pompidou, Paris/Lauros/ Giraudon/ The Bridgeman Art Library, N.Y.
429. Private Collection. Erich Lessing/Art Resource, N.Y.
432. Cyril Beaumont: The Art of Lydia Lopokova, London: C. W. Beaumont, 1920. Jane Voorhees Zimmerli Art Museum, Rutgers,

The State University of New Jersey, Gift of Herbert D. and Ruth Schimmel. Photograph by Jack Abraham
434. Imagno/Roger Viollet, Paris
437. Photograph by Auguste Bert. Arthur Applin: The Stories of the Russian Ballet, London: Everett & Co., 1911.
444. Thyssen-Bornemisza Collection, Zurich
454. Collection of the Bibliothèque Nationale, Paris
457. Chaucer Fine Arts, Ltd., London
458. Private collection, Rome
459, 460. Jane Voorhees Zimmerli Art Museum, Rutgers, The State University of New Jersey. Gift of Herbert D. and Ruth Schimmel. Photograph by Jack Abraham
496. Archive of the Russia Abroad Library and Foundation, Moscow
506. The Bridgeman Art Library, N.Y.
507. Private Collection. The Stapleton Collection/The Bridgeman Art Library, N.Y.
526. CNAC/MNAM/Dist. Réunion des Musées Nationaux/Art Resource, N.Y.
527. Private collection, Paris
528. Courtesy Eugen Zotow-Ivan Miassojedoff-Stiftung, Vaduz
539. Private collection, St. Petersburg
540. Ezhegodnik Obshchestva Arkhitektorov-khudozhnikov (Annual of the Society of Architects and Artists), St. Petersburg, 1907, no. 2, p. 43.
557. Private collection, Moscow
565. The Sketch (supplement), London, 23 July 1913.
585. Nicholas Remisoff Archive (Collection 199), Rare Books and Manuscripts, University of Southern California, Los Angeles.
594, 595. Christie's Images, N.Y.
605. D. Nikiforov: Sokrovishcha v Moskve. Moscow: Universitetskaia tipografiia, 1901, p. 36.
626. Acquisition confirmed in 1999 by agreement with the Estate of Kazimir Malevich and made possible with funds from the Mrs. John Hay Whitney Bequest (by exchange). (814.1935). U.S.A. Digital Image © The Museum of Modern Art /Licensed by SCALA/Art Resource, N.Y.
627. Private collection, Berne
631. Private collection, Moscow
635. No publishing house indicated
637. Paris: Compagnie française des arts graphiques, 1944. This deluxe edition carries six gouaches by Dmitri Bouchène. Jane Voorhees Zimmerli Art Museum, Rutgers, The State University of New Jersey. Gift of Herbert D. and Ruth Schimmel. Photograph by Jack Abraham

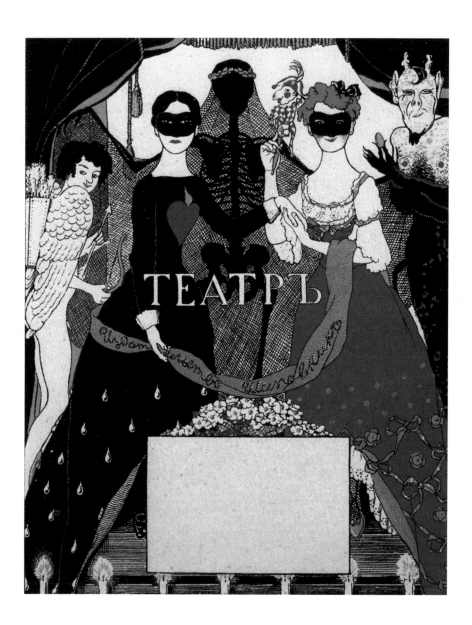

ТЕАТРЪ